The New Suburbanites

The New Suburbanites
Race and Housing in the Suburbs

Robert W. Lake

Center for Urban Policy Research
Rutgers University
New Brunswick, N.J. 08903

© 1981, Rutgers—The State University of New Jersey

Published in the United States of America
by the Center for Urban Policy Research
New Brunswick, New Jersey 08903

Library of Congress Cataloging in Publication Data
Lake, Robert W   1946-
The new suburbanites.

   Bibliography: p.
   Includes index.
   1. Afro-Americans—Housing. 2. Discrimination in
housing—United States. 3. Suburbs—United States.
I. Title.
HD7288.72.U5L35   363.5'9   80-21659
ISBN 0-88285-072-5

Cover design by Francis G. Mullen

Contents

Exhibits .

Chapter 8 HOUSING PRICES, EQUITY, AND RACE

Foreword

The 1970s was the decade in which a large sector of America's black population reached middle-class economic status. Income statistics, the most commonly-used indicator of class attainment, reveal that by the end of the period 30 percent of black households were at or above the median income level for all American households.

But this status is tenuous. Income is merely one component of a household's economic resources, and to look at it in isolation is to fail to consider stored wealth—capital assets. With few exceptions, the current generation of black wage-earners is the first to have obtained jobs with some measure of security of tenure and salary. The principal gap between the black and white middle class may thus be the absence of multigenerational asset formation passed down through inheritance and—particularly in recent years—generated and enhanced through successful home investment.

Homeownership has been the principal vehicle for capital accumulation for most white Americans, especially in the post World War II period. While conventional savings accounts and insurance have withered in recent years in the face of inflation, homeownership has flourished as an investment.

Black homeownership grew from some 35 percent of all black households in 1960 to around 45 percent at the end of the 1970s. The results of this increase, however, viewed not from the perspective of shelter but rather from that of capital accumulation, give reason for pause. The bulk of black homeownership has been concentrated in central cities, areas in which capital gains have not been secured as readily as they had been for European immigrants of a previous era. The black move to the central cities has provided a limited inheritance. There is no substantial successor group to whom blacks can sell their realty holdings. There is no even-more-needy group to inherit the central city.

The very limitations of central city home investment—at least outside the extremely confined areas of true affluence—have contributed to an increasing thrust toward black suburbanization. Though inhibited by a broad array of segregational devices, both de jure and, more strikingly, de facto, this process is taking place at a rate exceeding that for central city whites. But will it be equally successful?

Within American society in the 1980s, successful homeownership is a principal key to the defense of middle class status for blacks. Success must be defined not merely in terms of the quality of life or shelter obtained but rather in terms of fiscal return, i.e., of not merely being able to buy a house, but to sell it as well—and at a profit! This is a matter of concern not only to blacks as the directly impacted group but to all Americans.

The work presented here represents the culmination of more than fifteen years of work at the Center for Urban Policy Research to analyze the relationship between race and housing markets. In earlier efforts we looked at black owners of central city income properties, the inheritors of the slum tenements (*The Tenement Landlord*, 1965), and the beginnings of black suburbanization (*The Zone of Emergence*, 1971).

The study at hand is one of a series dedicated to analyzing the maturing of black suburban migration. The first volume (*Blacks in Suburbs*, 1979) aimed at providing the broad baselines of national trends. A second monograph (*Mortgage Lending and Race*, 1980) pursued the issue of redlining—the availability of mortgage loans to blacks and the scale of financing limitations imposed on black homebuyers as a function of race. In a subsequent publication we shall look at black suburban renters and assess the potential for broadening black homeownership.

This volume has as its target the delineation and definition of black suburban homeownership. Of principal concern are the search for housing, the realities of acquisition, the resale process, and the prospects for equity accumulation.

There have been enormous strides in both the opportunities available and the income levels achieved by black Americans. Significant as they appear, however, these strides were not enough, despite demographic and societal pressures, to ensure black middle class status. How well has this been achieved in the suburban homeownership that is now taking place? What are the rules and what will be the needs of tomorrow?

The New Suburbanites begins to explore these questions.

George Sternlieb

Preface

Homeownership in the United States is a source of security, a sign of status, a means of equity accumulation, and a bond to the community. This book examines the access of black Americans to suburban homeownership.

Housing market access is a two-sided issue. First, how do blacks attain ownership? Is black home purchase geographically restricted to particular areas within suburbia? Are purchase options limited in terms of housing type and quality? Do blacks encounter barriers to housing information? Is housing search more difficult for blacks than for whites? Second, what is the market for black-owned suburban units? The potential for equity accumulation depends on the vitality of demand. What is the effect of white preferences for residential segregation on the resale value of black-owned units? How do the marketing practices of real estate brokers mediate the demand for suburban housing sold by blacks? These questions motivate the analysis reported in the following pages.

The basic premise underlying this study is the preeminence of equal access. I intend no endorsement of either homeownership or suburban living. If such preferences are articulated, however—as they clearly are in American society—then access to these desired goals should be available on equal terms to blacks and whites.

The focus on barriers to suburban homeownership is not meant to imply that racial discrimination is not prevalent in the rental market as well. Survey data collected for this analysis pertain to successful homebuyers—whites and blacks who were able to negotiate safely the treacherous and largely uncharted housing market conditions of the mid-1970s. Those who turned back, decided not to move, or opted for rental housing are of necessity considered only indirectly in the analysis. The research objective is straightforward: among suburban homebuyers, how do the experiences of blacks compare with those of whites? A recurrent refrain in the following chapters is "all other things being equal." In short, do black/white differences in home purchase experiences remain after controlling for socioeconomic, tenure, and mobility characteristics? A subsequent report in this CUPR series of publications on black suburbanization will deal directly with the experiences of black renters in the suburbs.

Further narrowing the research issue, the study primarily addresses problems confronting the black middle class. Past discussions of black access to the suburbs have too often been couched in terms of increasing the supply of low-cost housing. There is little question that suburban exclusionary land use practices have a racial effect but it is equally clear that black access to the suburbs is separate from and broader than the question of low-cost housing.

The term *suburbs* as used in this book refers to the portion of Standard Metropolitan Statistical Areas (SMSAs) outside central cities. *Black suburbanization* refers to a process incorporating several interrelated components: migration of black population to the suburbs, increase in the absolute numbers of blacks in the suburbs, and increase in the proportion of the total black population residing in the suburbs.

The focus on housing places several important issues of black suburbanization beyond the direct purview of this book. I do not deal with the residence/employment nexus highlighted by the suburbanization of jobs, and thus do not directly consider the impact of barriers to suburban residence on access to employment. Similarly, the important issues of school desegregation and educational quality are addressed only indirectly. Questions of redlining and discrimination in financing, though closer to the housing issue, are also considered only indirectly.

Numerous people played a role in the completion of this study, and I gratefully acknowledge their contribution. My greatest debt is owed to the respondents—homebuyers, real estate agents, and local officials—who generously shared with me their insights, experiences, and concerns, and who truly made this study possible. George Sternlieb suggested the initial focus on the inner suburbs as the "zone of emergence" and provided a constant source of both encouragement and critical insight at all phases of research and writing. I owe a special debt to Thomas A. Clark for preparing the careful summary of national trends in black suburbanization presented in Chapter 2 and for his substantive comments on several other chapters. Susan Caris Cutter deserves special thanks for her collaboration on the first part of Chapter 4. I also gratefully acknowledge several individuals who read earlier drafts of selected chapters and offered helpful criticism and suggestions: Brian J.L. Berry, W.A.V. Clark, Donald C. Dahmann, John Goering, David R. Meyer, Peter O. Muller, and Raymond J. Struyk. Thanks are due to the research assistants who contributed to the study over a two-year period: Paula Brackett, Annette Casas, Richard Florida, Kevin Guinaw, Joan Hinck, Carl Horowitz, Kelly K'Meyer, Deborah Love, Hope Melton, Faith Solomon, Pamela Swack, John Swanson, Gillian Thomas, Kathleen Williams, and Jessica Winslow. William Dolphin provided invaluable computer programming assistance in all phases of the project. Linda Life-Gillard drew the maps in Chapters 4 and 5; Jan Limb drew the map in Exhibit 5-1.

Research for this study was supported by Grant No. MH31324 awarded to CUPR by the Center for Studies of Metropolitan Problems, National Institute of Mental Health. Portions of this book appeared in different form in earlier publications and grateful acknowledgment is accorded the publishers for permission to incorporate these materials here. Chapter 3 initially appeared in the *Annals of the American Academy of Political and Social Science*, 441 (January 1979). A portion of Chapter 4 in slightly different form was originally published as Robert W. Lake and Susan C. Cutter, "A Typology of Black Suburbanization in New Jersey Since 1970," *Geographical Review*, 70 (April 1980) and is used here with the permission of the American Geographical Society and Professor Cutter. Portions of Chapter 10 were published in the *Journal of the American Planning Association*, 47 (January 1981).

I am grateful to the CUPR staff who contributed to the tasks of project completion and manuscript preparation. Mary Picarella efficiently handled all aspects of project administration. Joan Frantz, Lydia Lombardi, Anne Hummel, and Diane Martins skillfully, promptly, and patiently typed the manuscript in each of its various drafts. Barbara Tieger ably guided the manuscript through publication.

I owe a final word of sincere appreciation to Carol Lynne Corden, from whose support, encouragement, and substantive insight I have benefitted immeasurably.

All errors of interpretation or analysis remain solely my responsibility.

R. W. L.

The New Suburbanites

PART
I
CONTEXT:

THE PATTERN OF
BLACK SUBURBANIZATION

1

BLACK SUBURBAN HOMEOWNERSHIP

INTRODUCTION

In contrast to the large, highly visible, and occasionally explosive black presence in the central cities, suburban blacks have constituted one of the nation's invisible populations. Blacks comprised less than 5 percent of the suburban population as recently as 1970, while the central cities were 20.5 percent black in that year and several cities had attained black majorities.[1] Suburban blacks historically resided in marginal locations, often in all-black towns or outlying "pockets of poverty" or as "pioneers" in all-white areas, and were socially and economically isolated from the white suburban community.[2] Blacks were *in* the suburbs but not *of* the suburbs. More often than not, blacks were an accidental prior presence in areas that became suburbanized rather than participants in the upward residential mobility that suburbia stereotypically represented for whites.

The 1970s witnessed a break in this pattern. The suburban black population increased by 40 percent over the decade compared to a 10 percent increase for whites. Rising black incomes resulting from social programs as well as from the general economic boom of the 1960s brought suburban housing within reach of a larger share of black households. Civil rights legislation weakened the most overt discriminatory barriers. With respect to older housing in the inner suburbs, falling white demand made such barriers increasingly superfluous.[3] As a result of these factors, the rate of black suburbanization accelerated during the 1970s and the newly visible suburban black population has attracted increasing public attention. Recent accounts in the *New York Times, Newsweek,* and the *Wall Street Journal,* among other periodicals, have noted the black "flight to the suburbs" and observed that "blacks move to the suburbs for the same reasons as whites."[4]

The discovery of black suburbanization by the popular media is explained in part by the perceived novelty of the phenomenon. It is explainable in larger part, however, because suburban black increases have rekindled emotionally charged issues of residential segregation and housing discrimination and because growing numbers of middle-class whites are feeling themselves actually or potentially affected. Yet despite the growing publicity, relatively little is known about the magnitude, direction, and characteristics of suburban black population growth since 1970, and even less is known about the experiences of black homebuyers in the suburban housing market. Does the recent acceleration of black population increase imply that suburban racial barriers are diminishing? Alternatively, is black suburbanization being accompanied by the increasing differentiation of suburbia along racial lines? What are the implications of the answers to these questions for the housing market experiences of suburban black homebuyers?

SUBURBAN STRUCTURE, INSTITUTIONS, AND HOMEBUYER EXPERIENCES

In seeking answers to these questions, we subsume in this research three closely interrelated levels of analysis. These focus on (1) the changing structural organization of the suburbs; (2) the evolving institutional mechanisms governing the residential location decisions of whites and blacks; and (3) the resulting experiences of individual black and white homebuyers. At the structural level, the suburbanization of the black population represents a continuation of the development and maturation of the suburbs, with race now adding a further dimension of territorial differentiation as suburban space continues to become functionally and socially specialized. Such suburban territorial differentiation in turn generates a set of institutional mechanisms with real consequences in constraining individual residential choice to conform to and reinforce the existing structure. As race emerges as a basic dimension of suburban differentiation, the institutionalized constraints mediating residential choice differ for whites and blacks. The result is radically different housing market experiences for blacks and whites in the suburbs.

The suburbs originated largely as a means for residents to ensure social homogeneity and to separate themselves from the problems of the central cities.[5] Political autonomy provided the authority to legislate homogeneity through zoning and land use controls, and the taxing power yielded the revenues necessary to ensure the suburb's fiscal independence from the city.[6] The acceleration of black suburbanization within this context raises several broad hypotheses relevant to both the continuing evolution of suburbia and the nature of the black experience in the suburbs.

The first hypothesis is that *improved black access to the suburbs suggests that the desire for social homogeneity on the part of suburban residents is diminishing.* This hypothesis rests on the argument that social contacts are increasingly extralocal and that who lives next door is increasingly unimportant.[7] Accordingly, the increasing rate of black suburbanization coincides with a progressive reduction in the social and racial differentiation of suburban territory.

An alternative hypothesis suggests that *suburban homogeneity persists as a desired state but increasing black suburbanization is evidence that race is dimishing as a significant status-differentiating mechanism.* According to this argument, ascendancy of large numbers of blacks to the middle class has generated greater cleavages within the black population than between racial groups, and middleclass black homeowners are being assimilated within the suburban fold.[8]

The third hypothesis proposes that *both the desire for homogeneity and the invidiousness of race persist as strong cultural values and that black suburbanization is therefore synonymous with neither social nor spatial integration.* Thus, despite recent increases in magnitude, the suburban black population still inhabits marginal locations and is no less isolated from mainstream white suburbia than it was in the earlier period.

This book examines a range of interrelated issues and attendant policy considerations in testing among these three hypotheses. While by no means allinclusive, the following list summarizes seven principal research issues addressed in subsequent chapters.

ISSUES IN BLACK SUBURBANIZATION

National Trends

The first issue is to define the broad national outlines of black suburbanization since 1970. Are post-1970 trends a true departure from previous patterns? Have black suburban growth trends been consistent throughout the decade or have they fluctuated over time? Do these patterns vary by region? Within this context, is black suburbanization contributing to a convergence of black and white population characteristics? How do blacks moving from cities to suburbs compare with the characteristics of blacks moving from suburbs and nonmetropolitan areas to cities?

Suburban Integration

Is black entry to the suburbs synonymous with residential integration? Insight on this issue requires the disaggregation of summary data on suburban black population growth into its component parts. Is overall black growth dispersed throughout the suburbs or concentrated in particular communities? What types of suburbs account for observed black increases? Does suburbanization represent access to the stereotypical "suburban life" or is black increase concentrated in aging, unattractive areas that have been relegated by whites to black residential space? Similar questions extend the analysis to patterns *within* communities as well. Is suburban resegregation occurring at the neighborhood level, with the block-by-block pattern of racial transition typical of central cities being replicated in the suburbs? At the finest scale, what are the characteristics of suburban housing units transferred from white to black occupancy?

Characteristics of Black Homebuyers

Who are the actors? How do suburban black homebuyers compare with their white counterparts in socioeconomic characteristics, previous tenure, previous residence location, and reason for moving? Convergence in the characteristics of black and white suburbanites depends on the similarity of blacks and whites within respective migration streams (e.g., movers from city to suburb, movers within suburbs) and on proportionate contributions of individual migration streams to total white and black suburban populations. Do black/white socioeconomic differences persist after controlling for city versus suburban origin? What share of all suburban black homebuyers is accounted for by city-to-suburb movers, and how does this proportion compare with that for whites? In addition to objective socioeconomic characteristics, attitudes are also important. How do black and white homebuyers compare in their preferences for integration? Do blacks and whites define the benefits and costs of integration differently?

Housing Search Experiences

The major issue addressed in this book is that of the actual experiences of blacks and whites in the suburban housing market. To what extent—and in what ways—do the housing search experiences of black homebuyers differ from those of whites? Differential access to suburban housing market information would result in disparity in the residential destinations of whites and blacks. Is access to information on housing availability more restricted for black homebuyers? What information sources are used, and how helpful are they? How does the search for housing by blacks and whites compare in length of time and in number of units inspected and communities searched? Are differences in length or extensiveness of search due to background socioeconomic characteristics and previous tenure or do they reflect differential treatment based on race? Do differences in search experience remain after controlling for socioeconomic background and prior experience in the housing market? What is the evidence of racial steering by brokers?

Race and Housing Prices

Racial differences in the search for housing are complemented by the issue of differential housing prices. The question of whether blacks pay more than whites for equivalent housing has generated conflicting conclusions. An adequate answer requires evidence on resale values and equity accumulation as well as on initial purchase price, controlling for housing and neighborhood quality. Are prices paid by blacks reduced due to the weakness of white demand for housing in integrated neighborhoods? Or is there evidence of a "race tax" imposed on blacks by discriminatory white sellers? Conversely, what is the effect of race on the resale value of black-owned suburban units, all other things being equal? A discount in initial purchase price for blacks may be an illusory saving if it is exceeded by a loss in resale value due to the absence of white demand for black-owned units. The three-way *interaction* between the race of the buyer, the seller, and the neighborhood is a crucial but heretofore inadequately examined determinant of both the purchase prices paid by blacks and the resale value of black-owned units.

Real Estate Broker Perspectives

The pattern of white demand for housing in integrated neighborhoods is due to both explicit white preferences and also to the institutional structures mediating the operation of the housing market. The real estate broker has often been identified as the key housing market intermediary responsible for channeling white demand and for discriminating against black homeseekers. What is the broker's perspective? What are the pressures moving the broker from the role of commercial middleman to one of social arbiter of neighborhood compatability? To what extent does the broker's day-to-day *modus operandi* arise from discriminatory pressure inherent in the structure of the industry and in the broker's perceived role in the community? In what ways do these day-to-day operations contribute to differential housing market experiences for blacks and whites, irrespective of discriminatory intent?

Policy Implications

What does all of the foregoing imply for the development of policy? Are existing federal fair housing initiatives adequate in the light of research findings on the black homebuyer's experiences? What do the research results suggest regarding the relative efficacy of policy aimed at reducing the incidence of housing discrimination versus policy aimed at broadening the dissemination of information on housing availability? What further steps are indicated?

THE LOGIC OF ANALYSIS

The discussion of these issues is divided into three parts. Part I, comprised of four chapters, draws on national and regional data to establish the context and pattern of black suburbanization. In Chapter 2, Thomas Clark provides a succinct summary of national data on the pace and magnitude of suburban black population growth in the 1970s.[9] Annual Housing Survey data on a national sample of 15.9 million suburban housing units matched in two successive years are used in Chapter 3 to measure the importance of white-to-black transition as a source of owner-occupied versus renter housing for blacks in the suburbs, and to identify the size, value, and quality of suburban housing units obtained by blacks. The structural organization of suburbia is addressed in Chapter 4 with a narrowing of geographic scale to consider the spatial distribution of black population increase in the New Jersey suburbs. Racial school enrollment data for the universe of 405 suburban school districts in the State of New Jersey are linked to a broad range of land use and community characteristics to identify the types of suburbs with growing black populations.

The five chapters in Part II, representing the heart of the analysis, utilize a range of unique data sources to examine the black experience in the suburban housing market at the end of the 1970s. Chapter 5 introduces the five case study suburban communities that provide the focus for the remainder of the analysis. The remaining chapters in Part II examine data from an extensive survey of 1,004 recent homebuyers—black and white—representing a 100 percent sample of home buyers within the case study communities. The Recent Buyers Survey, conducted between September and November 1978, included 150 questions on all facets of the homebuying experience and yielded upwards of 150,000 data items for analysis.

The actors in the process are identified in Chapter 6, with the Recent Buyers Survey providing data on the characteristics, origins, and reasons for moving of black and white suburban homebuyers. This chapter clarifies the characteristics of the constituent black and white migration streams contributing to suburban population growth, develops profiles of black and white homebuyers locating in black, white, and integrated suburban neighborhoods, and contrasts white and black attitudes toward residential integration.

Chapter 7 focuses on access to housing market information and the housing search experiences of blacks and whites. Data from the Recent Buyers Survey are used to test three models explaining racial differences in the length and extensiveness of housing search, distinguishing between the effects of socioeconomic characteristics and prior tenure and the direct and indirect effects of racial discrimination.

Chapter 8 considers the economics of housing prices, with survey data identifying the race of the buyer and the seller and the racial composition of the neighborhood. The data provide a unique opportunity to consider the race of the seller within a model of demand for housing in neighborhoods defined by racial composition. Sale price data were obtained from 100 percent records of real estate transactions furnished by the New Jersey State Treasury Department. We first compare purchase prices paid by whites and blacks for comparable suburban housing units and then examine resale value and equity accumulation in black-owned units. This question is the complement of the analysis of housing search in Chapter 7. Holding socioeconomic factors constant, black/white differences in housing search represent racial inequalities in access to the housing market. Black/white differences in resale and equity accumulation represent racial inequalities within the housing market.

Chapter 9 turns to the institutional mechanisms contributing to the differential experiences of blacks and whites in the suburban housing market. Detailed interviews with twenty principal real estate brokers in the case study communities yielded over forty hours and two hundred pages of transcripts focusing on the potential for discrimination in the day-to-day operations of the real estate industry.

Finally, Part III (Chapter 10) provides a summary of findings and a consideration of policy implications. The challenge to policy is to define a set of alternative institutional mechanisms that avoid the incentives to discriminate inherent in the racial organization of suburbia.

RACE AND RESIDENCE IN NATIONAL CONTEXT

The context within which this study is set is one in which residential segregation has persisted despite the socioeconomic improvement of the nation's black population. An extensive literature documents the convergence that occurred during the 1960s and 1970s in the educational attainment, occupational distribution, and income of blacks and whites.[10] According to data summarized by James P. Smith, female earnings attained almost complete racial parity by the early 1970s and the black/white income ratio for males rose from just .61 in 1959 to .77 in 1975.[11] Smith ascribes this near-parity in income to convergence in educational attainment and a narrowing of between-region wage scale differences, given the rapid rise of wages in the South. Several authors credit the civil rights legislation of the mid-1960s with a major role in contributing to the growing socioeconomic similarity of blacks and whites. Moreover, this convergence continued despite the economic downturn of the 1970s. Freeman's examination of black income and occupational attainment found "much greater increases after (the Civil Rights Act) of 1964 than before despite . . . the serious recession of the 1970s."[12]

Segregated residential patterns remained relatively undiminished despite the increasing socioeconomic similarity of blacks and whites. The benchmark data on residential segregation exist in segregation indexes computed by Taeuber and Taeuber for 109 central cities for 1940, 1950, and 1960.[13] These indexes updated to 1970 reveal a slight overall decrease in segregation during the 1960s.[14] Van Valey and his associates, however, recalculated the 1960 and 1970 indexes for metropolitan areas rather than central cities and found less evidence of decline in segregation.[15] Declines were most noticeable in the smallest metropolitan areas and those with proportionally small minority populations. They concluded that "recent improvements in the social and economic status of blacks, and in white attitudes toward blacks, do not necessarily herald large-scale advances in racial integration: segregation levels in American SMSAs remained virtually unchanged between 1960 and 1970."[16] Similarly, Schnare measured the exposure of blacks to whites (and vice versa) within census tracts in 130 SMSAs in 1960 and 1970. She found that blacks experienced an increase in segregation over the decade, that more blacks lived in tracts that were over 90 percent black, and that black population growth was accommodated by the outward expansion of predominantly black areas.[17]

The persistence of high levels of metropolitan area residential segregation has been reflected in the severe underrepresentation of blacks in the suburbs. It is abundantly clear that these discrepancies in white and black population distributions cannot be accounted for by income differences alone. As Kain and Quigley pointed out using 1970 data, if the concentration of blacks in central cities resulted from low income, then low-income whites should be similarly distributed. They found, instead, that white and black patterns diverged sharply, and they showed that a larger proportion of low-income whites than high-income blacks lived in the suburban ring: 53.1 percent of whites with incomes below $3,000 but only 25.9 percent of blacks with incomes above $10,000 resided in the suburbs.[18] Calculations show that these proportions had barely shifted by 1977: 47.2 percent of SMSA white households earning less than $3,000 versus 28.5 percent of SMSA black households above $10,000 lived in the suburbs.[19] Using data on the twenty-nine largest urbanized areas for the period 1950 to 1970, Hermalin and Farley found that at all income levels and at all levels of housing value, blacks are overrepresented in the central cities and underrepresented in the suburbs. They found further that increases in black family income were not reflected in proportionate increases in the size of the black suburban population. They concluded that "the increasing income of blacks has done little to reduce their concentration in central cities . . . . Apparently, a low income white family can obtain a suburban home or apartment more readily than a higher income black family."[20]

Similar findings have emerged from analyses of destinations of black and white movers. Focusing on movers in the Philadelphia metropolitan area between 1965 and 1970, Cottingham found that 57 percent of upper-income white movers but only six percent of upper-income black movers left the central city for the suburbs.[21] At all income levels, blacks were less likely than whites to move to the suburbs. Increasing incomes were associated with a higher probability of suburban selection among whites but not among blacks. These findings are supported by Frey's analysis of black movement to the suburbs in twenty-four SMSAs.[22]

Data on the overall rate and magnitude of black suburbanization up to 1970

reflect these racial disparities. Pendleton has argued that the relative consistency in the black proportion of the suburban population during a period of rapid white suburban growth is indicative of comparable black and white growth rates.[23] Schnore and his associates, however, examined suburban black growth rates between 1930 and 1970 in the twelve largest SMSAs, using boundaries as in 1960.[24] Although suburban black growth rates exceeded growth rates for whites in each decade since 1940, Schnore, et al. point out the potentially misleading effect of percentage increases calculated on a small base population. The result was a gradual increase in the absolute number of blacks in the suburbs at the same time that blacks maintained a stable—and low—proportion of the total suburban population.

The process of black suburbanization appears to have entered a new phase in the decade since 1970. A careful and thorough analysis of black suburban migration patterns since 1970 has been provided by Nelson.[25] Comparing the years 1970-73 with 1975-78 in nineteen SMSAs, she found that an increase in the rate of black suburban in-migration combined with a decrease in the rate of black suburban out-migration resulted in a "sharp increase" in net black movement to the suburbs in the late 1970s. While this pattern reflected an increased flow of black movers from the central cities to the suburbs, however, Nelson also found that black suburban selection rates were still lower than the rate for whites. Further, while black migration after 1970 resembled the white pattern in being directed toward the suburbs, Nelson ascribes this more to decreases in black suburb-to-city moves than to increases in black city-to-suburb moves. In short, while the data reveal a "national reversal" in the direction of black migration in the 1970s—from city to suburb rather than in the other direction—Nelson concludes that "the mid-1970s disparities between black and white patterns suggest that black access to the suburbs remains less than [that for] whites."[26] The research reported in the following chapters is aimed at elucidating some of the factors contributing to this persisting inequality in access of blacks and whites to suburban homeownership.

NOTES

1. U.S. Bureau of the Census, *The Social and Economic Status of the Black Population in the United States, 1790 to 1978,* Current Population Reports, Special Studies, Series P-23, no. 80, 1979.
2. Harold Rose, *Black Suburbanization: Access to Improved Quality of Life or Maintenance of the Status Quo* (Cambridge, Mass: Ballinger, 1976); Leonard Blumberg and Michael Lalli, "Little Ghettoes: A Study of Negroes in the Suburbs, *Phylon* 27 (Summer 1966): 117-31; L. K. Northwood and Ernest A.T. Barth, *Urban Desegregation: Negro Pioneers and Their White Neighbors* (Seattle, Wash.: University of Washington Press, 1965).

3. George Sternlieb and Robert W. Lake, "Aging Suburbs and Black Home-ownership," *Annals of the American Academy of Political and Social Science* 422 (November 1975): 105-17.

4. Paul Delaney, "Black Middle Class Joining the Exodus to White Suburbia," *New York Times,* January 4, 1976; "34% Increase in Suburban Blacks Tied to Incomes and New Laws," *New York Times,* December 3, 1978; Neil Maxwell, "Black Flight: Much Like Whites, Many Blacks Move Out to the Suburbs," *Wall Street Journal,* August 20, 1979; "The Black Move to the Suburbs," *Newsweek,* December 31, 1979.

5. Richard A. Walker, "The Transformation of Urban Structure in the Nineteenth Century and the Beginnings of Suburbanization," in *Urbanization and Conflict in Market Societies,* ed. Kevin R. Cox (Chicago: Maaroufa Press, 1978), pp. 165-212.

6. Michael N. Danielson, *The Politics of Exclusion* (New York: Columbia University Press, 1976).

7. Melvin Webber, "Culture, Territoriality, and the Elastic Mile," *Papers and Proceedings of the Regional Science Association* 13 (1964): 59-69.

8. William J. Wilson, *The Declining Significance of Race: Blacks and Changing American Institutions* (Chicago: University of Chicago Press, 1978).

9. For an extended discussion of these data see Thomas A. Clark, *Blacks in Suburbs: A National Perspective* (New Brunswick, N.J.: Center for Urban Policy Research, 1979).

10. Reynolds Farley, "Trends in Racial Inequalities: Have the Gains of the 1960s Disappeared in the 1970s?" *American Sociological Review* 42 (April 1977): 189-208; Reynolds Farley and Albert I. Hermalin, "The 1960s: A Decade of Progress for Blacks?" *Demography* 9 (August 1972): 353-70.

11. James P. Smith, "The Improving Economic Status of Black Americans," *American Economic Review* 68 (May 1978): 171-78; see also Marcus Alexis, "The Economic Status of Blacks and Whites," *American Economic Review* 68 (May 1978): 179-85.

12. Richard Freeman, "Black Economic Progress Since 1964," *The Public Interest* 52 (Summer 1978): 52-69; Stanley H. Masters, *Black-White Income Differentials* (New York: Academic Press, 1975), esp. pp. 143-49.

13. Karl E. Taeuber and Alma F. Taeuber, *Negroes in Cities: Residential Segregation and Neighborhood Change* (New York: Atheneum, 1969).

14. Annemette Sorensen, Karl E. Taeuber, and Leslie J. Hollingsworth, Jr., "Indexes of Racial Residential Segregation for 109 Cities in the United States, 1940 to 1970," *Sociological Focus* 8 (April 1975): 125-42.

15. Thomas L. Van Valey, Wade Clark Roof, and Jerome E. Wilcox, "Trends in Residential Segregation, 1960-1970," *American Journal of Sociology* 82 (January 1977): 826-44.

16. Ibid., p. 842.

17. Ann B. Schnare, "Trends in Residential Segregation by Race: 1960-1970," *Journal of Urban Economics* 7 (May 1980): 293-301; Ann B. Schnare, *The Persistence of Racial Segregation in Housing* (Washington, D.C.: The Urban Institute, 1978).

18. John F. Kain and John M. Quigley, *Housing Markets and Racial Discrimination* (New York: National Bureau of Economic Research, 1975).

19. U.S. Bureau of the Census, *Financial Characteristics of the Housing Inventory for the United States and Regions,* "Current Housing Reports, Series H-150-77, Annual Housing Survey: 1977, Part C." 1979.

20. Albert I. Hermalin and Reynolds Farley, "The Potential for Residential Integration in Cities and Suburbs: Implications for the Busing Controversy," *American Sociological Review* 38 (October 1973): 595-610.

21. Phoebe H. Cottingham, "Black Income and Metropolitan Residential Dispersion," *Urban Affairs Quarterly* 10 (March 1975): 273-96.

22. William H. Frey, "Black Movement to the Suburbs: Potentials and Prospects for Metropolitan-Wide Integration," in *The Demography of Racial and Ethnic Groups,* ed. Frank D. Bean and W. Parker Frisbie (New York: Academic Press, 1978), pp. 79-117.

23. William W. Pendleton, "Blacks in Suburbs," in *The Urbanization of the Suburbs,* ed. Louis H. Masotti and Jeffrey K. Hadden (Beverly Hills, Calif.: Sage Publications, 1973), pp. 171-84.

24. Leo F. Schnore, Carolyn D. Andre, and Harry Sharp, "Black Suburbanization, 1930-1970," in *The Changing Face of the Suburbs,* ed. Barry Schwartz (Chicago: University of Chicago Press, 1976), pp. 69-74; see also Reynolds Farley, "Components of Suburban Population Growth," in *The Changing Face of the Suburbs,* pp. 3-38.

25. Kathryn P. Nelson, *Recent Suburbanization of Blacks: How Much, Who, and Where* (Washington, D.C.: Office of Policy Development and Research, U.S. Department of Housing and Urban Development, 1979).

26. Ibid., p. 13.

2

NATIONAL TRENDS
IN BLACK SUBURBANIZATION

Thomas A. Clark

INTRODUCTION

Recent nationwide data indicate a substantial acceleration in the growth of the black population in American suburbs.[1] Between 1970 and 1977, the black population in the suburban portions of American metropolitan areas increased by 1,163,000, a growth rate of 34 percent.[2] This rate outpaced both the rate of suburban white increase (10.3 percent) and the rate of black increase in central cities (4.2 percent) over the same period. Most important, the growth of the suburban black population during these seven years was larger in both absolute and relative terms than the suburban black increment of 758,000 (a 28.3 percent increase) registered during the entire decade of the 1960s.

The accelerating rate of black suburbanization represents a departure from longstanding trends and may signal a new phase in the continuing redistribution of the black population of the United States. In an earlier phase, between 1910 and 1960, this process involved the concentration and urbanization of a predominantly rural black population.[3] The first several decades of this century saw the nation's black population become at once less southern and more urban as it undertook a massive migration to the urban industrial employment centers of the North.[4] As this trend continued and as significant numbers of prosperous white households fled the urban core in favor of residential neighborhoods on the periphery, the core grew more congested, impoverished, and racially segmented. Present black population patterns are largely a product of the encirclement of the central cities by predominantly white suburban communities that contain and control a substantial share of metropolitan area resources.[5] In 1970, 59 percent of the black population but only 28 percent of the white population lived in central cities. The geography of black America is to an alarming extent an archipelago of central cities strung out across the land.[6] This is the departure point for what may constitute the next major social and spatial transformation of the black population.

This chapter provides a brief overview of the pace and magnitude of recent black suburbanization at the national scale. This introductory discussion serves to establish the context: questions of disaggregation, and of the processes underlying these national trends, are examined in subsequent chapters. The first issue is that of documenting the magnitude of the phenomenon, and we examine fluctuating suburban black growth rates through the mid-1970s. Regional variations in the scale and pace of black suburbanization are considered next, followed by an assessment of the role of black migration both into and out of the nation's suburbs. Important income differences between suburban black in- and out- migrants are seen to contribute to the changing definition of the black population in place in the suburbs.

SUBURBANIZATION TRENDS SINCE 1960

In 1977, 4.6 million blacks, or 18.8 percent of the national black population, resided in the non-central-city "suburban" portion of metropolitan areas (Exhibit 2-1). At the same time, 55 percent (13.5 million) resided in central cities, and 26.2 percent (6.4 million) lived in nonmetropolitan areas. In contrast, 41.9 percent, or 77.2 million, of the national white population resided in suburban areas, while 24.4 percent (45 million) lived in central cities and 33.7 percent (62.2 million) were in nonmetropolitan areas. Blacks were consequently vastly underrepresented in suburban areas, overrepresented in central cities, and somewhat less than proportionally present outside SMSAs.

While substantial imbalances, therefore, remained at the end of the 1970s, the period from 1960 to 1977 had witnessed some substantial changes. In 1960, just 2.7 million blacks lived in the suburbs. Ten years later, 3.4 million blacks resided

EXHIBIT 2-1
POPULATION CHANGE BY RACE AND METROPOLITAN STATUS, 1960-1977

| | WITHIN METROPOLITAN AREAS[a] | | | |
	Total	*Inside Central Cities*[b]	*Outside Central Cities*	*NONMETROPOLITAN*
A. Population (in thousands)				
Black				
1960	12,311	9,636	2,675	6,037
1970	16,342	12,909	3,433	5,714
1977	18,048	13,451	4,596	6,427
White				
1960	104,176	48,845	55,331	52,182
1970	118,938	48,909	70,029	56,338
1977	122,177	44,951	77,226	62,158
B. Percent Change[c]				
Black				
1960-70	32.7 (2.87)	34.0 (2.97)	28.3 (2.53)	-5.4 (-0.55)
1970-74	9.4 (2.27)	6.7 (1.64)	19.5 (4.55)	0.6 (0.15)
1974-77	1.0 (0.32)	-2.4 (-0.79)	12.1 (3.87)	11.8 (3.79)
White				
1960-70	14.2 (1.33)	0.1 (0.01)	26.6 (2.38)	7.8 (0.77)
1970-74	2.5 (0.61)	-4.4 (-1.12)	7.3 (1.77)	5.8 (1.43)
1974-77	0.2 (0.08)	-3.9 (-1.31)	2.8 (0.93)	4.2 (1.39)

Notes: a. Standard Metropolitan Statistical Areas are defined by their 1970 boundaries.
      b. Central city data for 1974 exclude annexations since 1970.
      c. Numbers in parentheses are average (compounded) annual rates of change.

Source: U.S. Bureau of the Census, Current Population Reports, Special Studies, Series P-23, Nos. 37, 55 and 75, *Social and Economic Characteristics of the Metropolitan and Nonmetropolitan Population*, 1971, 1975, and 1978.

in the suburban zone. The increase of 1.9 million suburban blacks between 1960 and 1977 represented a growth of 71.8 percent, although it should be remembered that the initial base was quite small.[7] The proportion of all blacks who resided in suburbs increased slowly yet consistently over the period, from 14.6 percent in 1960 to 18.8 percent in 1977. The proportion of the metropolitan-area black population living in the suburbs remained constant at 21 percent in both 1960 and 1970, and then increased to 22.9 percent in 1974 and to 25.5 percent by 1977.

Suburban black increases have their counterparts in relative nonsuburban decreases. Both metropolitan and nonmetropolitan growth rates fluctuated significantly between 1960 and 1977. From 1960 to 1970, metropolitan areas gained blacks while nonmetropolitan areas showed decreases. The average annual compounded rate of black increase in metropolitan areas (2.87 percent) stood in striking contrast to the average annual black *loss* rate (–0.55 percent) in nonmetropolitan areas (Exhibit 2-1). Within SMSAs during the 1960s, annual black growth rates were nearly identical in central cities (2.97 percent) and suburbs (2.53 percent).

Since 1970, however, there has been a remarkable shift. From 1970 to 1974, the longstanding decline of the nonmetropolitan black population was reversed as the annual rate of black nonmetropolitan change rose to 0.15 percent a year while the annual rate of black metropolitan increase fell to 2.27 percent. These trends accelerated dramatically in the ensuing three years. Metropolitan areas approximated zero black population growth during 1974-77 as the annual rate of metropolitan black increase fell to just 0.32 percent per year. In contrast, the rate of nonmetropolitan black increase rose precipitously to 3.79 percent per year.

But while these shifts in metropolitan and nonmetropolitan rates of change are significant, a far more dramatic transition has occurred within metropolitan areas. First, the average annual rate of central city black increase has fallen from 2.97 percent during 1960-70, to 1.64 percent in the period from 1970-74, and subsequently to an annual *loss* rate of – 0.79 percent during 1974-77 (Exhibit 2-1). Suburban rates of increase have varied more irregularly in recent years. The average annual rate of black suburban increase rose from 2.53 percent during 1960-70 to 4.55 percent during 1970-74, and then fell to 3.87 percent between 1974 and 1977. The emerging picture is one of absolute annual black declines in central cities, primarily due to accelerating rates of net out-migration from the largest central cities, while both suburban and nonmetropolitan areas experienced comparably high rates of black increase.

Since 1960, black and white trends have generally been similar in direction but not in degree. Both racial groups have moved toward zero metropolitan population growth, while the annual rate of black nonmetropolitan growth exceeds the white by a factor of almost three. White decline in the central city is somewhat greater than that of blacks, but in the suburbs, the black population is increasing four times as rapidly as the white.

REGIONAL VARIATIONS

Aggregate national statistics tend to conceal significant interregional differences regarding racial composition and rates of change. These differences issue from unique regional histories and their structural by-products in the form of social and economic relations within which the black community is positioned. The majority of black Americans trace, some through several generations, back to the South, a region that still claims over half (53.7 percent in 1977) of the national black population. The Northeast (17.1 percent) and the North Central (20.4 percent) states claim 37.5 percent, while the West, a region distinguished by many dimensions of diversity, claims just 8.8 percent. This interregional distribution has held almost constant since 1960 despite a substantial exchange of migrants among the regions.

Black configurations are similar in both the Northeast and North Central states. In both, about three-quarters of the black population resides in central cities, and about four in five of these live in central cities of SMSAs having in excess of one million persons in 1977. In the Northeast, 16.9 percent of all blacks live in suburbs of SMSAs whose total populations exceed one million, while just 3.3 percent live in the suburbs of SMSAs having fewer than one million persons. In the North Central states, 11.8 percent of all blacks live in the suburbs of SMSAs exceeding one million persons, while 3.3 percent live in the suburbs of the smaller SMSAs.

The West offers a distinct contrast. There, 34.3 percent of all blacks resided in suburbs by 1977, and over four in five suburban blacks were in the suburbs of SMSAs having over one million total population. But if the black population of the West is the most suburban of the major census regions, that of the South is the most nonmetropolitan. Fully 44.3 percent of the black population of the South resides in nonmetropolitan areas, and four in five of these are in rural counties having no urban place over 25,000 population. Just 8.0 percent of southern blacks reside in suburbs of SMSAs having over one million population, while 9.2 percent reside in the suburbs of SMSAs having fewer than one million persons. In sum, regarding blacks, the Northeast and North Central states are the most "urban," the West most "suburban," and the South most "rural."

Given these interregional disparities, rates of black suburbanization can be expected to differ substantially across regions (Exhibit 2-2). As indicated earlier, the nation's suburban black population increased by just over a third between 1970 and 1977, within suburban boundaries as delineated in 1970. This rate was shared in the North Central (38.4 percent) and South (34.4 percent) regions. In contrast, the Northeast recorded the slowest rate of increase, 12.6 percent, while the West had the highest, 61.2 percent.

Nationally, the rate of black population growth between 1970 and 1977 was higher in the suburbs of SMSAs with a population of a million or more (44.2 percent) than in the suburban rings of SMSAs of less than a million (18.6 percent). This appears to reflect basic demographic differences between the

EXHIBIT 2-2

SUBURBAN BLACK POPULATION, BY REGION, 1977 and 1970

(in thousands)

Region	SUBURBS IN ALL SMSAs				SUBURBS IN SMSAs OVER ONE MILLION				SUBURBS IN SMSAs UNDER ONE MILLION			
	1977	1970	Change 1970-77 Number	Percent	1977	1970	Change 1970-77 Number	Percent	1977	1970	Change 1970-77 Number	Percent
Northeast	841	747	94	12.6	704	654	50	7.6	137	93	44	47.3
North Central	760	549	211	38.4	593	442	151	34.2	167	107	60	56.1
South	2,260	1,681	579	34.4	1,046	573	473	82.5	1,214	1,108	106	9.6
West	735	456	279	61.2	613	381	232	60.9	122	75	47	62.7
U.S. Total	4,596	3,433	1,163	33.9	2,956	2,050	906	44.2	1,640	1,383	257	18.6

Source: U. S. Bureau of the Census, Current Population Reports, Special Studies, Series P-23, No. 75, Social and Economic Characteristics of the Metropolitan and Nonmetropolitan Population, 1977 and 1970, 1978, Table 3.

South and the rest of the country.[8] In the South, the black population increased by 82.5 percent in the suburbs of large SMSAs and by only 9.6 percent in small metropolitan areas (Exhibit 2-2). These proportions were nearly reversed in the Northeast, where the 7.6 percent suburban black growth rate in large SMSAs was eclipsed by an increase of 47.3 percent in smaller SMSAs. The North Central pattern was closer to that of the Northeast than the South, while the rate of suburban black increase was nearly identical in large and small metropolitan areas in the West.

Blacks constitute a proportionally larger share of total population in the South than in other regions, setting it apart in several further respects from the rest of the country. In the non-South regions, the proportion of the suburban population that was black in 1977 was greater in the suburban rings of large SMSAs than in small SMSAs. The black proportion of the suburban population in large metropolitan areas ranged from 4.2 to 4.9 percent in the Northeast, North Central, and West regions, but reached 10.8 percent in the South. In the smaller SMSAs, between 1.7 and 2.3 percent of the suburban population was black in the non-South regions, compared to 11.2 percent in the South. Thus, the proportion black in the South was relatively invariant in the suburbs of large and small SMSAs, while outside of the South, metropolitan size appears more important than region in influencing the black proportion of the suburban population.

MIGRATION AND SUBURBAN CHANGE

In recent decades, migration has been the prime dynamic of change within the suburban black population. Between 1970 and 1975, net migration to suburbs of persons five years old or over in 1975 accounted for a 15 percent increase in black population, or 381,000 additional persons (Exhibit 2-3). Between 1975 and 1978, the increase due to the net arrival of persons who were three years old or over in 1978 was 13 percent or 461,000 persons, indicating an accelerating rate of annual increase.

Population flows affecting suburban racial composition are a complex inter-weaving of movements within a national matrix of origins and destinations.[9] Of the 827,000 blacks moving to suburbs from within the nation during 1970-75, 87 percent previously resided in central cities and 13 percent originated in nonmetropolitan areas (Exhibit 2-3). Seven in ten of those arriving from central cities moved to a suburb within the same SMSA, while three in ten migrated from the central city of one SMSA to the suburbs of another. A similar pattern is evident for the 1975-78 period.

In contrast to the prevalent impression, black suburbanization is not a simple product of in-migration. Substantial numbers of blacks are simultaneously departing the suburbs. During 1970-75, one black departed for every two who arrived: most migrated to central cities, and less than 15 percent moved to nonmetropolitan areas. Similar trends prevailed between 1975 and 1978. The

EXHIBIT 2-3

MOBILITY STATUS OF THE BLACK POPULATION, BY FAMILY STATUS
AND INCOME, 1970-75 AND 1975-78

(persons in thousands)

| | TOTAL PERSONS[a] | | FAMILIES OF TWO OR MORE | | | |
| | | | 1970-1974 | | 1975-1977 | |
	1970-75	1975-78	Persons	Mean Family Income	Persons	Mean Family Income
Persons residing in suburbs over entire period	2,480	3,564	2,485	$10,367[c]	3,332	$14,108[c]
Total moving to suburbs[b]	827	939	677	$10,567[d]	614	$12,966[d]
From central cities	718	780	573	NA	559	NA
From nonmetro areas	109	159	104	NA	55	NA
Total moving from suburbs[b]	446	478	406	$ 9,165[e]	251	NA
To central cities	382	409	344	NA	201	NA
To nonmetro areas	64	69	62	NA	50	NA
Net migration to suburbs	381	461	271		363	

Notes: a. Persons at end of interval who were born before it began. Years as of March.
b. Excludes movers between residences in suburbs of the same or different SMSAs.
c. Based on nonmovers plus movers within suburbs of same SMSA.
d. Based on movers from central city of same SMSA only.
e. Based on movers to central city in same SMSA only.
(NA) Base less than 75,000 families.

Sources: U.S. Bureau of the Census, Current Population Reports, Series P-20, No. 285, *Mobility of the Population of the U.S., March 1970 to March 1975,* 1975, Tables 1, 28; Series P-20, No. 331, *Geographical Mobility: March 1975 to March 1978,* 1978, Table 1: Series P-23, No. 55, *Social and Economic Characteristics of the Metropolitan and Nonmetropolitan Population: 1974 and 1970,* 1975, Table 8; and Series P-23, No. 75, *Social and Economic Characteristics of the Metropolitan and Nonmetropolitan Population: 1977 and 1970,* 1978, Table 8.

evidence suggests that as a group, blacks are maintaining longstanding rural-to-urban migration patterns while simultaneously accelerating the centrifugal process of decentralization.

There is evidence of important differences between suburban black in- and out-migrants. During 1970-74, the mean income of black families arriving from central cities was 15 percent greater than that of families departing for central cities, and 2 percent greater than that of families already residing in the suburbs (Exhibit 2-3). This discrepancy is pertinent to the discussion in Chapter 4 where it is seen that the largest suburban black losses are occurring in outlying rural suburban communities while black increases are concentrated in higher-income residential suburbs and communities adjacent to the central cities.

ECONOMIC STATUS OF THE SUBURBAN BLACK POPULATION

Income differences of black migrants to and out of the suburbs, as well as internal transformations within the suburban black population, have yielded substantial improvements in the economic status of suburban black households. In 1960, 44 percent of blacks in suburbs lived in poverty; by 1970, only 27 percent did so, and by 1977, just 20 percent were beneath the poverty threshold. SMSA size seems to have become less influential over this period in determining suburban black poverty rates. In 1970, the percentage of blacks in poverty was 1.8 times higher in the suburbs of SMSAs of over a million than in SMSAs of less than a million. By 1977, one in five suburban blacks lived in poverty in both large and small metropolitan areas.

Median black family income in constant dollars increased by 12 percent in the suburbs between 1970 and 1977, and fell by 8 percent in central cities (Exhibit 2-4). Central city and suburban income distributions were strikingly similar in 1970. Since then they have become increasingly dissimilar as the percentage of suburban black families earning less than $6,000 has fallen and the percentage earning $15,000 and over has risen.

Increases in median family incomes have been accompanied by the increasing spatial segregation of income classes among suburban blacks. One indication of this is the changing proportional distribution within suburban poverty areas of the suburban black population above and below the poverty level.[10]

First, consider the suburban rings of SMSAs having a million persons or more (Exhibit 2-5). In these large SMSAs, 26 percent of nonpoverty suburban blacks lived in poverty areas in 1970, while only 2 percent of comparable whites did so. Fifty percent of suburban blacks below the poverty level resided in poverty areas, whereas just 7 percent of comparable whites did so. By 1977, the proportion of suburban blacks not in poverty but residing in poverty areas had fallen substantially, from 26 to 14 percent, although nonpoverty whites were still far less likely to reside in poverty areas. The proportion of suburban blacks beneath the poverty level who lived in poverty areas had also decreased by 1970, from half to just over a third.

EXHIBIT 2-4

BLACK FAMILY INCOME DISTRIBUTION IN
CENTRAL CITIES AND SUBURBS, 1977 AND 1970
(percents)

Total Money Income	SUBURBS		CENTRAL CITIES	
	1977	1970	1977	1970
Less than $3,000	7.1	12.7	9.5	12.8
$3,000 to 5,999	15.3	14.3	22.9	15.9
$6,000 to 9,999	19.6	19.3	20.5	20.3
$10,000 to 14,999	15.3	21.7	14.8	22.1
$15,000 to 24,999	30.3	24.4	25.5	22.1
$25,000 and over	12.4	7.6	6.8	6.7
Total	100.0	100.0	100.0	100.0
Number of families (in thousands)	1,147	746	3,242	2,919
Median income ($)	12,037	10,745	9,361	10,188
Mean income ($)	13,727	12,245	11,398	11,712

Note: Income in constant 1976 dollars.

Source: U.S. Bureau of the Census, Current Population Reports, Special Studies, Series P-23, No. 75, *Social and Economic Characteristics of the Metropolitan and Nonmetropolitan Population, 1977 and 1970,* 1978, Table 20.

A shift in a similar direction occurred in the suburban rings of smaller SMSAs (Exhibit 2-5). Here in 1970, 47 percent of nonpoor suburban blacks and fully 71 percent of blacks below the poverty level lived in poverty areas. By 1977, proportions within suburban poverty areas of these smaller SMSAs were still higher than in the large SMSAs, but nonetheless had dropped to 29 and 66 percent among suburban blacks above and below the poverty level, respectively.

In sum, suburban blacks above and below the poverty level are far more likely to reside in poverty areas than are their white counterparts. The degree of black concentration in suburban poverty areas was higher in the suburban rings of SMSAs having fewer than one million persons than in those of SMSAs having more than one million persons. This disparity existed in both 1970 and 1977 and applied to blacks both above and below the poverty level. The rate of decline in the proportion of blacks residing in poverty areas was greater during the period from 1970 to 1977 for nonpoverty suburban blacks than for blacks residing in poverty. Overall, blacks residing in suburbs in 1977 were geographically more dispersed than those in suburbs in 1970. That is, the proportions of both the poor and the nonpoor residing in suburban poverty areas have declined since 1970.

Despite these gains, however, disparities persist in the socioeconomic characteristics of suburban blacks and whites (Exhibit 2-6). Suburban blacks are on

EXHIBIT 2-5

POPULATION IN SUBURBAN POVERTY AREAS, BY RACE, METROPOLITAN SIZE, AND POVERTY STATUS, 1977 AND 1970

	SUBURBAN POPULATION ABOVE POVERTY LEVEL				SUBURBAN POPULATION BELOW POVERTY LEVEL			
	Total (in thousands)		Percent in Poverty Areas		Total (in thousands)		Percent in Poverty Areas	
	1970	1977	1970	1977	1970	1977	1970	1977
SMSAs of 1,000,000 or more								
Black	1,569	2,294	26	14	455	642	50	36
White	40,016	44,327	2	1	2,487	2,370	7	5
SMSAs of less than 1,000,000								
Black	832	1,288	47	29	547	340	71	66
White	24,688	28,244	7	7	2,396	2,220	24	17

Note: Poverty areas are census tracts in which more than 20 percent of the population was below poverty level in 1970.

Source: U. S. Bureau of the Census, Current Population Reports, Special Studies, Series P-23, No. 75, *Social and Economic Characteristics of the Metropolitan and Nonmetropolitan Population: 1977 and 1970,* 1978, Table 21.

average younger and live in larger families than their suburban white counterparts, and are more likely than whites to live in female-headed families. The proportion of suburban blacks under eighteen is some ten percentage points higher than the proportion of whites, and this difference is uniform in both large and small metropolitan areas. While about 10 percent of all suburban white families are female-headed households, a fourth of black families in the suburbs of small SMSAs and nearly a third of those in the suburbs of large SMSAs are female-headed.

Although educational attainment of both blacks and whites is higher in large SMSA suburbs than in the suburbs of small SMSAs, black educational levels are lower than those of whites in both types of suburbs. The mean income of suburban blacks is only about 70 percent of suburban white mean income, again regardless of SMSA size.

These disparities reflect the characteristics of the black and white populations in place in suburbia at the end of the 1970s. They are subject to the continuing effect of the sifting and sorting process encapsulated in the migration patterns described above. The income differences of black migrants to and from suburbia suggest that black/white discrepancies might be expected to diminish further over time. The discussion in Chapter 6 reveals striking similarities in the characteristics of new black and white homebuyers in a diversified set of suburban case study communities.

EXHIBIT 2-6

SELECTED CHARACTERISTICS OF THE SUBURBAN
POPULATION, BY RACE, 1977

| | SUBURBS IN METROPOLITAN AREAS OF: | | | |
| | 1,000,000 or more | | Less than 1,000,000 | |
	Black	White	Black	White
AGE DISTRIBUTION				
(percent)				
Under 18	39.0	29.8	41.4	30.8
18 to 64	57.0	61.3	53.1	60.8
Over 64	4.0	9.0	5.5	8.4
FAMILY STATUS				
Average size (persons)	3.7	3.4	4.1	3.4
Families with female				
head (percent)	30.7	10.3	24.5	9.4
EDUCATION[a]				
(percent)				
High school grad.	59.6	74.6	48.4	70.2
College, 4 or				
more years	13.2	20.4	9.4	16.3
MEAN INCOME (dollars)[b]				
All workers	$ 9,211	$12,893	$ 8,050	$11,050
Families	14,115	20,917	12,952	17,925
INCOME DISTRIBUTION OF				
FAMILIES (percent)				
Under $10,000	41	18	45	24
$10,000 to 14,999	19	16	18	22
$15,000 and over	40	66	37	54

Notes: a. Persons 25 years and over.
          b. According to incomes in 1976.

Source: U.S. Bureau of the Cenuss, Current Population Reports, Series P-23, No. 75, *Social and Economic Characteristics of the Metropolitan and Nonmetropolitan Population: 1977 and 1970,* 1978, Tables 1, 7, 9, 10, and 17.

SUMMARY

Black suburbanization is clearly not a monolithic process. Rather, it comprises several distinct though interrelated avenues of movement, distinguished by the nature, mix, and pace of suburban migration. This chapter has sketched the broad national context, summarizing the accelerating pace of black suburbanization in the 1970s. The turn-around in longstanding patterns signaled by the loss of black population in the nation's central cities in recent years suggests that suburbanization is more than a transient phenomenon. Blacks resident in the suburbs still lag behind whites according to several measures of socioeconomic well-being. The characteristics of the black migrant streams entering and leaving the suburbs, however, give reason to expect the continued diminution of these disparities as suburbanization progresses. The suburbs are the new racial frontier, and the pattern and process of black suburbanization will likely determine the prospects of many black Americans for years to come. In the following chapter, we begin to assess these prospects by examining the housing units occupied by suburban blacks and the transition of suburban housing units from white to black occupancy.

NOTES

1. Kathryn P. Nelson, *Recent Suburbanization of Blacks: How Much, Who, and Where?* (Washington, D.C.: Office of Policy Development and Research, U.S. Department of Housing and Urban Development, 1979); Eunice Grier and George Grier, *Black Suburbanization at the Mid-1970s* (Washington, D.C.: The Washington Center for Metropolitan Studies, 1978); Thomas A. Clark, *Blacks in Suburbs: A National Perspective* (New Brunswick, N.J.: Center for Urban Policy Research, 1979).

2. U. S. Bureau of the Census, *Social and Economic Characteristics of the Metropolitan and Nonmetropolitan Population, 1977 and 1970* Current Population Reports, Special Studies, Series P. 23, No. 75, 1978.

3. Wesley C. Calef and Howard J. Nelson, "Distribution of the Negro Population in the United States," *Geographical Review,* 46 (January 1956): 82-97; F. Henri, *Black Migration: Movement North 1900-1920* (Garden City, N.Y.: Doubleday, 1975); R. B. Grant, *The Black Man Comes to the City* (Chicago: Nelson-Hall, 1972); John Fraser Hart, "The Changing Distribution of the American Negro," *Annals of the Association of American Geographers* 50 (September 1960): 242-66.

4. Allan H. Spear, *Black Chicago: The Making of a Ghetto, 1890-1920* (Chicago: University of Chicago Press, 1967); Gilbert Osofsky, *Harlem: The Making of a Ghetto, Negro New York 1890-1930* (New York: Harper, 1963); Chicago Commission on Race Relations, *The Negro in Chicago: A Study of Race Relations and a Race Riot* (New York: Arno Press and The New York Times, 1968; orig. publ. 1922).

5. Bennett Harrison, *Urban Economic Development: Suburbanization, Minority Opportunity, and the Condition of the Central City* (Washington, D.C.: The Urban Institute, 1974); Norman Fainstein and Susan Fainstein, *Urban Political Movements: The Search for Power by Minority Groups in American Cities* (Englewood Cliffs, N.J.: Prentice-Hall, 1974); H. Paul Friesema, "Black Control of Central Cities: The Hollow Prize," *Journal of the American Institute of Planners* 35 (March 1969): 75-79; Frances Fox Piven and Richard A. Cloward, "Black Control of Cities," *The New Republic,* September 30 and October 7, 1967.

6. *Report of the National Advisory Commission on Civil Disorders* (New York: Bantam, 1968); Morton Grodzins, *The Metropolitan Area as a Racial Problem* (Pittsburgh, Pa.: University of Pittsburgh Press, 1958); Reynolds Farley, et al. "Chocolate City, Vanilla Suburbs: Will the Trend Toward Racially Separate Communities Continue?" *Social Science Research* 7 (December 1978): 319-44.

7. Reynolds Farley, "Components of Suburban Population Growth," in *The Changing Face of the Suburbs,* ed. Barry Schwartz (Chicago: University of Chicago Press, 1976), pp. 3-38; Leo F. Schnore, et al. "Black Suburbanization, 1930-1970," in *The Changing Face of the Suburbs,* pp. 69-94; Harry Sharp and Leo F. Schnore, "The Changing Color Composition of Metropolitan Areas," *Land Economics* 38 (May 1962): 169-85.

8. Avery M. Guest, "The Changing Racial Composition of Suburbs, 1950-1970," *Urban Affairs Quarterly* 14 (December 1978): 195-206.

9. Kathryn P. Nelson, *Recent Suburbanization of Blacks;* William H. Frey, "Black Movement to the Suburbs: Potentials and Prospects for Metropolitan-Wide Integration," in *The Demography of Racial and Ethnic Groups,* ed. Frank D. Bean and W. Parker Frisbie (New York: Academic Press, 1978), pp. 79-118.

10. Poverty areas include all suburban Census tracts in which more than 20 percent of the population was below the poverty level in 1970. Census tracts that exceed this poverty threshold in subsequent years but not in 1970 are excluded from consideration. See also Ann B. Schnare, *Residential Segregation by Race in U.S. Metropolitan Areas: An Analysis Across Cities and Over Time* (Washington, D.C.: The Urban Institute, 1977); Karl E. Taeuber, "Racial Segregation: The Persisting Dilemma," *Annals of the American Academy of Political and Social Science* 422 (November 1975): 87-96.

3

RACIAL TRANSITION AND BLACK HOMEOWNERSHIP

INTRODUCTION

Analysts have long stressed the importance of existing housing stocks, as opposed to new construction, as a source of housing opportunities for blacks and other minorities.[1] The transfer of housing units from white to black occupancy is thus a necessary concomitant of suburban black population growth. As Long and Spain point out, the turnover of individual housing units from white to black is the "primary process" behind the changing racial composition of neighborhoods.[2] It is therefore instructive to consider the extent to which the transition of suburban housing units from white to black is synonymous with increased black homeownership, and secondly, whether black suburban homeownership is synonymous with equity accumulation and the generation of wealth.

This chapter examines the extent of suburban housing unit transition from white to black or from black to white occupancy as a mediator of homeownership opportunities for blacks in the suburbs. Data made available through the U.S. Census Bureau's *Annual Housing Survey* permit year-to-year tracing of unit and household characteristics in a national sample of housing units resurveyed each year.[3] Utilizing these data for 1974 and 1975, three aspects of suburban racial and tenure transition are analyzed in terms of their impact on black homeownership in the suburbs.

First, what is the magnitude of transition from white to black occupancy in suburban housing units? Disaggregating this overall transition rate into renter and owner components provides a measure of availability of homeownership opportunities for blacks in the suburbs.

Second, what are the characteristics of suburban housing units acquired by blacks? Here, differentiation between units initially occupied by whites and those units that turn over within the black housing market provides evidence of the significance of white-to-black transition as a source of good quality owner-occupied suburban units. Census Bureau demographers have examined the socio-economic characteristics of households involved in the transition of units from white to black, and earlier studies described the neighborhoods experiencing racial succession, but data on the individual housing units involved have heretofore not been analyzed.[4]

Third, what are the housing dynamics confronting the suburban black home-owner seeking to recapture stored equity through resale? The accumulation of equity through homeownership is perhaps the most widespread and successful means of wealth generation available to the American middle class. The inflation of housing values in the post-World War II era has been a particular boon to the largely suburbanized homeowning middle-class white population. The nation's black population, however, disproportionally comprised of renters rather than owners and generally confined to portions of older urban areas that have not experienced the inflation of housing values characteristic of suburbia, has been less able to benefit from the wealth-generative potential of suburban home-ownership. Earlier studies not focused primarily on suburbia have demonstrated that a black-occupied housing unit infrequently reverts to white occupancy.[5] If this pattern is replicated in the suburbs, then black homeowners wishing to sell will be at a distinct disadvantage: adequate market demand is required if home-ownership is to function as a path to capital accumulation. The suburban dream will be less golden if otherwise equivalent units owned by blacks and whites are funneled into dual resale markets, leaving blacks with inferior rates of economic return and equity recapture. An analysis of housing value and equity accumulation based on detailed case study data is provided in Chapter 8. Here we examine national data to further establish a context for the case study analysis.

Initial findings suggest that white-to-black transition in suburban rental units far outpaces that in owner-occupancy, extending the central city disparity in homeownership rates for whites and blacks into the suburbs. Those black suburbanites who do own their own homes are far more dependent on black replacements than are whites; black owners wishing to sell are saddled with the consequences of lesser black buying power. The findings suggest the need for policy initiatives aimed at stimulating the demand for black-owned suburban units, for it is only in this way that suburban homeownership will provide blacks with the wealth generative function it has traditionally served for earlier aspirants to the middle class.

In assessing these trends, the following discussion focuses first on the increase in the number of suburban housing units occupied by blacks and on the characteristics of suburban black housing units. We then address in turn the magnitude of racial transition of individual suburban housing units, the characteristics of those housing units, and the conditions of equity recapture in black-owned housing in the suburbs.

THE SUBURBAN BLACK HOUSING STOCK

The increase in black-occupied housing units since 1970 reflects the black population trends described in the preceding chapter. Between 1970 and 1976, the number of black suburban households increased by 49 percent to a total of 1.4 million, compared to a 21 percent increase (to 25.8 million) in white suburban households.[6] Black owner-occupied units in the suburbs increased by 39 percent (compared to 23 percent for whites) while black renter-occupied units increased by 62 percent (versus 16 percent for whites). As with the data for population reported earlier, a somewhat larger proportion of total metropolitan area black households lived in the suburbs in 1976 (23 percent) than was the case in 1970 (19 percent). Among metropolitan area blacks in owner-occupied units, the suburban share increased marginally from 27 to 28 percent between 1970 and 1976. Among black renter households, the suburban share increased from 14 percent in 1970 to 19 percent in 1976.

Two sets of comparisons help clarify the nature of the black suburban niche within the current metropolitan structure.[7] Compared to suburban white households, suburban blacks on average continue to receive short shrift. Compared to central city blacks, however, suburban residence represents a substantial improvement in both housing and neighborhood quality (Exhibit 3-1).

Considering tenure and housing type in 1975, for example, just under half (49.4 percent) of black suburban households were owners, compared to almost three-fourths (71.2 percent) of white suburbanites and about one-third (35.4 percent) of black central-city households. Conversely, some 17 percent of black suburbanites lived in structures of ten or more units, compared to only 9 percent of white suburban households and 23 percent of black city dwellers. Turning to property value, 11 percent of black suburban households, versus 2 percent of white suburbanites and 15 percent of black city residents lived in units whose property value was less than $10,000. At the same time, 10 percent of black suburbanites lived in homes valued at $50,000 or more, in contrast to 24 percent

EXHIBIT 3-1

SELECTED HOUSING CHARACTERISTICS OF HOUSEHOLDS, BY RACE AND INTRAMETROPOLITAN LOCATION, 1975
(in thousands)

Housing Characteristics	HOUSEHOLDS[a]					
	White Suburban		Black Suburban		Black Central City	
	Number	Percent	Number	Percent	Number	Percent
TENURE						
Own	14,259	71.2	491	49.4	1,346	35.4
Rent	5,788	28.9	502	50.6	2,456	64.6
STRUCTURE TYPE						
One-unit detached	13,920	69.5	540	54.4	1,263	33.2
Ten units or more	1,823	9.1	165	16.6	863	22.7
PROPERTY VALUE						
Less than $10,000	226	1.8	49	11.2	165	14.7
$50,000 or more	2,970	23.7	45	10.2	34	3.0
HOUSING RATING						
Excellent	8,376	42.0	229	23.2	562	14.9
Poor	299	1.5	52	5.3	351	9.3
NEIGHBORHOOD RATING						
Excellent	8,514	42.7	197	19.9	427	11.3
Poor	239	1.2	38	3.8	336	8.9

Note: a. Households in fifty SMSAs for which intrametropolitan location of housing units is indicated on Annual Housing Survey national public use tapes. See note 3.

Source: U.S. Bureau of the Census, *Annual Housing Survey: 1975,* national public use tapes.

of white suburban households but only 3 percent of black central-city residents. In terms of overall housing satisfaction, black suburbanites were only half as likely as white suburbanites, but one and a half times more likely than black city dwellers, to rate their housing unit as excellent. Ratings of overall neighborhood quality are distributed similarly.

These findings are in accord with those of Roof and Spain on the changing socioeconomic characteristics of suburban residents.[8] Two general conclusions can be drawn from this brief overview. First, compared to white households in the suburbs, black suburban households occupy less satisfactory, lower-value units in less desirable neighborhood settings, and have attained lower proportions of owner-occupancy. Secondly, the data lend support for extension to the suburbs of patterns previously documented for central cities: it is on average the more affluent, higher-status blacks who are the first to move into previously all-white areas, thereby improving their housing and neighborhood quality.

With this brief introduction to the relative characteristics of black suburban households within the metropolitan setting, we turn now to an examination of racial transition in the existing suburban housing stock.

RACE AND TENURE CHANGE IN
THE SUBURBAN HOUSING STOCK

Data from the *Annual Housing Survey* national samples provide information on 15.9 million suburban housing units for which race and tenure can be identified in both 1974 and 1975. Utilization of this data set permits identification of the magnitude of racial and tenure change within the suburban housing stock, and analysis of changes in household characteristics attendant on turnover in the housing inventory.

Total Inventories

We begin by comparing the racial and tenure characteristics of the suburban inventory in 1974 with the identical units in 1975 (Exhibit 3-2). As indicated above, the total suburban inventory is divided approximately 70/30 between owner and renter occupancy, and some 5 percent of total units in both years are black. The overwhelming share of units, of course, evidences no change in tenure or race from one year to the next. Relative shifts within this framework, however, provide initial evidence of differences in black and white experiences in the suburban housing market.

First, considering racial transition within the entire suburban inventory, 0.64 percent (101,000 units) of the entire 1974 supply shifted from white to black in the one-year period. Disaggregating by 1974 tenure, 0.23 percent (26,000 units) of the owner-occupied stock and 1.63 percent of the renter-occupied units (75,000 units) shifted from white to black during the period. This suggests that owner-occupancy units in the white inventory become available to black buyers at a slower rate than do renter-occupancy units, although whether this is due to supply restrictions or differential demand functions is unclear.

Second, considering tenure change within each racial category, 1.59 percent of the black-occupied stock (11,000 units) changed from renter- to owner-occupancy between 1974 and 1975 but 1.88 percent (13,000 units) reverted from owner- to renter-occupancy. Within the white-occupied inventory, in contrast, 1.30 percent (195,000 units) changed from renter to owner while 1.20 percent (180,000 units) reverted from owner- to renter-occupancy. In all, focusing here on tenure changes *within* each racial inventory and ignoring for the present the extent of racial transition, the 1974 white inventory registered a net gain of 15,000 owner-occupied units while the black inventory registered a net loss of 2,000 owner-occupied units. While these tenure changes are not substantial in absolute terms, it appears that the net white increase in owner-occupied units was not duplicated within the black inventory.

EXHIBIT 3-2
TENURE AND RACIAL CHARACTERISTICS OF THE SAME-UNIT SUBURBAN HOUSING INVENTORY[a]
(in thousands)

1974 TENURE AND RACE (HOUSEHOLDS)	Total	1975 TENURE AND RACE (HOUSEHOLDS) Owner-Occupied[b]				Renter-Occupied[c]			
		Total	White	Black	Other	Total	White	Black	Other
ALL UNITS	15,899	11,307	10,793	369	143	4,592	4,136	362	94
White	14,989	10,813	10,757	23	32	4,176	4,050	78	49
Black	692	363	18	345	0	329	48	278	3
Other	218	131	18	1	111	87	38	6	42
OWNER-OCCUPIED[b]	11,295	11,099	10,602	360	135	196	178	10	7
White	10,798	10,618	10,569	22	26	180	170	4	6
Black	365	352	15	337	0	13	7	6	0
Other	132	129	18	1	109	3	1	0	1
RENTER-OCCUPIED[c]	4,604	208	191	9	8	4,396	3,958	352	87
White	4,191	195	188	1	6	3,996	3,880	74	43
Black	327	11	3	8	0	316	41	272	3
Other	86	2	0	0	2	84	37	6	41

Notes: Colums might not add to totals because of rounding.
  a. U.S. Suburbs = non-central city portions of fifty SMSAs for which intrametropolitan location of unit is reported on AHS national survey tapes. See note 3.
  b. Owner-occupied = Owner-occupied + Condominium + Cooperatives.
  c. Renter-occupied = Renter-occupied + Rented, no cash rent.

Source: U.S. Bureau of the Census, Annual Housing Survey: 1974 and 1975, national sample public use tapes.

Housing Market Turnover

Of the 15.9 million suburban units described above, we have identified 2,250,000 units within the white and black suburban housing inventories that turned over between 1974 and 1975 (Exhibit 3-3). This figure represents a 14.3 percent turnover rate. (Excluded from further discussion are the 218,000 units—1.4 percent of the total—occupied by "other races" in 1974.) Units occupied by a different household in 1974 and 1975 were identified as those which in the latter-year survey responded to questions asked only of "recent movers," i.e., households that moved in within the twelve-month period preceding the survey. These units form the data base for our analysis of market turnover and racial transition.[9]

Considering turnover by tenure, 5.8 percent of owner-occupied units in 1974 turned over during the year, while the equivalent rate for renter-occupied units was 34.8 percent. Not surprisingly, in other words, rental units in the suburbs change hands at a faster rate than owner-occupied units.

The turnover rate in owner-occupied units is essentially identical for blacks and whites: 6.0 percent of black owner-occupied units and 5.8 percent of white. In the rental market, however, the turnover rate in white renter-occupied units (35.8 percent) exceeds that in black renter-occupied units (30.6 percent). Going somewhat beyond the data, these findings may suggest that suburban rental occupancy for whites is typically a temporary stop en route to homeownership, while it is a far more stable and permanent tenure arrangement for blacks confronted with racial barriers to homeownership.

Racial Change

The final question in this section focuses on the role of racial change within the more general picture of housing turnover. Again drawing on the data in Exhibit 3-3, four observations can be made.

First, although blacks comprise only five percent of all suburban households, blacks replace other blacks nearly as frequently as they replace whites. Of the 161,000 units with a new black occupant in 1975, 84,000 (52 percent) were transferred from white to black occupancy while 77,000 (48 percent) were already black-occupied in 1974. Thus, while in a color-blind market blacks would replace blacks one time in twenty, the actual frequency is one time in two.

Second, white-to-black transition far outweighs black-to-white transition in both absolute and relative terms. As noted above, white-to-black change amounted to 84,000 units; in contrast, only 45,000 suburban units transferred from black-to-white between 1974 and 1975. Of the resulting net gain of 39,000 new black-occupied units, 10,000 were owner-occupied and 29,000 were renter-occupied in 1975.

The third question focuses on the probability of ownership for new black occupants. If a new occupant of a suburban housing unit is black rather than

EXHIBIT 3-3

1974-75 TENURE CHANGE BY RACIAL CHANGE, SUBURBAN HOUSING UNITS OCCUPIED BY RECENT MOVERS IN 1975[a]

(in thousands of units)

Tenure Transition[b] 1974-75	All Units		RACIAL TRANSITION 1974-75							
			White-to-White		Black-to-Black		White-to-Black		Black-to-White	
	Number	Percent	Number	Percent	Number	Percent	Number	Percent	Number	Percent
All Units	2,250	100.0	2,044	100.0	77	100.0	84	100.0	45	100.0
Own-to-Own	516	22.9	491	24.0	4	5.2	16	19.0	5	11.4
Rent-to-Rent	1,506	67.0	1,348	65.9	64	83.1	63	75.0	31	70.5
Own-to-Rent	133	5.9	116	5.7	6	7.8	4	4.8	7	15.9
Rent-to-Own	95	4.2	89	4.4	3	3.9	1	1.2	2	4.5

Notes: Columns might not add to totals due to rounding.

a. Suburban units are those in the non-central city portion of fifty SMSAs for which intrametropolitan location of units is specified on AHS national survey tapes. See note 3. Recent movers are those households that moved into the unit within the twelve-month period prior to 1975 AHS enumeration.

b. Owner-occupied units = Owner-occupied + Condominiums + Cooperatives.
Renter-occupied units = Renter-occupied + Rented, no cash rent.

Source: U.S. Bureau of the Census, *Annual Housing Survey: 1974 and 1975,* national sample public use tapes.

white, the likelihood is greater that the black household will rent rather than buy, regardless of the race of the initial occupant. This finding is revealed by the tenure characteristics of the units within each racial transition category (Exhibit 3-3). Focusing on the race of household in the second year, a transfer within the rental market constitutes 83.1 percent of black-to-black and 75.0 percent of white-to-black turnover, but only 70.5 percent of black-to-white and 65.9 percent of white-to-white turnover. Combining these figures with those for transfers from ownership to rental status, units rented in 1975 (rent-to-rent plus own-to-rent) constitute 86 percent of all turnovers to a new black occupant and only 72 percent of turnovers to a new white occupant.

What is the probability of a black owner-occupied unit in the initial year remaining within the owner inventory or shifting to rental status during turnover? We find that a black-owned unit is more likely than a white-owned unit to shift to renter-occupancy, again regardless of the race of the new occupant. Of white-owned transition units in 1974, 19 percent of those turned over to a white household and 20 percent of those turned over to a black household shifted to renter-occupancy in 1975. Of black-owned units, in contrast, 58 percent and 60 percent of those turned over to, respectively, a white and black household shifted into the rental market. This indicates the relative weakness of the market for black-owned suburban housing. The implications for equity recapture in black versus white-owned suburban units are evident.

Summary of Transition Findings

The principal findings thus far can be summarized briefly. New black occupancy in the suburbs involves a unit already within the black inventory as frequently as it involves a unit shifted from white to black occupancy. Such transition as does occur is predominantly a one-way transfer: white-to-black transition far outweighs transfers from black to white. Largely due to differential turnover rates, owner-occupancy units in the suburbs become available to potential black occupants at a slower rate than do rental units. Black units turn over faster than those occupied by whites, largely because blacks are more concentrated in rental units, which turn over faster than owner units do. Black rental units, however, turn over at a slower rate than do white rental units, suggesting that black rental occupancy in the suburbs—perhaps due to fewer available options—is less temporary and more stable than white rental. While white-to-black transition results in a net gain in black suburban owner-occupied units this gain is in part offset by a loss of owner units through tenure change to rental within the black inventory. The present data suggest but do not allow definitive testing of the hypothesis that many black owner-units gained through racial transition are subsequently lost by an inability to sustain adequate demand within a dual housing market context. Further evidence on this point must await data on turnover chains over a longer time period than presently available. In sum, black suburbanites are less likely than their white counterparts to own their own homes, and those who do are more likely than white owners to transfer their unit to rental status in the event of turnover of the unit.

CHARACTERISTICS OF TRANSITION UNITS

The discussion thus far has focused on the magnitude of turnover and transition within racial segments of the suburban housing market. What of the characteristics of the housing units comprising these racial submarkets? Are housing units transferred from white to black substantially different from those transferred within the white housing market? Do units in these categories differ in turn from those transferred within the black housing market?

To examine these questions, we compare units in each of the suburban racial transition categories in terms of four basic characteristics: age of structure, median value, median rent, and overall evaluation of housing and neighborhood quality. For this segment of the discussion, we focus on those housing units for which tenure type (own or rent) is maintained both before and after the move. Units that changed tenure type (own-to-rent, rent-to-own) are eliminated from further discussion due to small sample sizes and the resulting ambiguity of generalizations based on a relatively small number of observations.

Age of Structure

Transfers within the black suburban housing market tend on average to involve substantially older units than transfers within the white market. White-to-black turnover appears concentrated in relatively newer units, reflecting perhaps the comparatively greater buying power of those black households who can gain access to the formerly white segment of the suburban market. In contrast, black-to-white transfers appear to encompass both the newest and the oldest suburban units.

Among all suburban transition units in 1975, about a third (31.3 percent) of white-to-white transfers but only a fourth (26.5 percent) of black-to-black transfers were built in the preceding six years (1969-74). A higher proportion (34.2 percent) of units transferred from white to black were built in this period, as were over half (51.1 percent) of black-to-white units. Another third (29 percent) of black-to-white units were built prior to 1939.

Among owner-occupied units, fully two-thirds of the suburban units transferred between black owners were built between 1950 and 1959, making them between 16 and 25 years old. In contrast, well over half (56.7 percent) of the units transferred between white owners were 15 years old or less, i.e., built since 1960. Within the rental market, recently built units (1969-74) are again underrepresented among black-to-black transfers (28.9 percent), followed in frequency by turnover within the white market (32.9 percent), from white to black (39.4 percent), and overwhelmingly represented among black-to-white transfers (72.6 percent). In all, the data suggest that blacks replacing blacks are concentrated in suburban areas with older housing units, while white-to-black transition results in improvement in the black-occupied suburban housing stock.

Median Value

The median value of suburban units transferred within the white market in 1974-75 was $40,000, compared to a median value of $36,200 for units transferred from black-to-black. Units transferred from white-to-black ownership were yet lower in value on average ($30,400). White replacement of a black household is clearly confined to the highest value units, as indicated by a median value of $55,000 for units shifting from black-to-white.

Transfer of a unit within the black submarket appears to provide relatively inexpensive housing, as the median value-to-income ratio in this market segment is only 1.8. Black purchase of a previously white-owned unit results in a median value-to-income ratio of 2.4 while the figure for white-to-white transfers is 2.1. Clearly, black home purchase requires a significantly larger proportion of income when purchasing a white-owned unit than when the previous owner is black.

Median Rent

Suburban rent levels within the all-white market ($175) are the highest among the various market segments examined; conversely, rents in black-to-black units are on average the lowest ($145). In contrast to the situation in owner-occupancy, however, these comparatively low rents in the black rental market are coupled with the highest measure of rent as a percent of income, 30.6 percent, substantially above the 25 percent benchmark generally accepted as reasonable. Average rent levels are identical in white-to-black and black-to-white units ($170). In the former segment, however, this rent level amounts to 27 percent of income, just above the 25 percent norm, while in the latter segment the same median rental amounts to only 23 percent of income, just below the norm. Indeed, suburban white renters are on average burdened with a 23 percent rent/income ratio regardless of the race of the previous renter, while black renters in the suburbs pay substantially more than one-fourth of their income for housing.

Comparing rent levels with rents paid in the household's previous unit, blacks renting a previously white-occupied unit experience the highest average increase in rent ($61) over what they were paying in their previous unit. Blacks renting previously black-occupied units experience an average rent increase of $47, while whites renting previously white-occupied units increase their rent by only $20.

Housing and Neighborhood Quality

The distribution of responses on overall ratings of the housing unit and the neighborhood are essentially identical, and therefore can be discussed together. Fully twice the proportion of households in the white-to-white market (30 percent) as those in the black-to-black market (15 percent) rated their house and neighborhood as excellent. Black households replacing whites were more likely to offer an "excellent" rating (25 percent) than were black households replacing blacks. Similarly, households in black-to-black units were most likely (40 percent) to evaluate house and neighborhood as only fair or poor. Only 16 percent of whites in previously white units but 26 percent of blacks in previously white units offered this low rating.

Summary

The above discussion furnishes a brief sketch of the housing available in each of the suburban racial submarkets.[10]

Suburban units that turn over from white to white are on average recently built units, of higher value than those transferred to black occupancy, and yield a below-average value-to-income ratio. Rental units in the white-to-white market command the highest rent but nonetheless require the lowest proportion of their residents' income.

A direct contrast is evident in the suburban units that turn over from black to black. Such units are on average older and of lower value than white-to-white units. Rent levels in this market segment are the lowest but nonetheless constitute the largest percentage of income. Black suburban renters experience the largest increase in rent over rentals paid in their previous units, regardless of whether the new rental unit was previously occupied by a black or white. Black-to-black units and their neighborhoods are least likely to be rated excellent by their residents and most likely to be rated fair or poor.

Units transferred from white to black occupy a position somewhere between these two extremes. These are generally newer units, contributing to an upgrading of the black-occupied suburban housing stock. However, owner-occupied units in this category have the lowest median value. Black renters of previously white-occupied units experience the largest increase in rent over their previous unit. While blacks replacing whites pay the same for rent as do whites replacing blacks, this amount represents a larger proportion of income for the former group than for the latter. Black-occupied units formerly occupied by whites, however, are more likely than those previously occupied by blacks to receive satisfactory ratings of housing and neighborhood quality.

Finally, units transferred from black-to-white occupancy are in general among either the newest or the oldest portions of the suburban inventory and command the highest median value and relatively high rent levels. It is likely that the few cases comprising this category (2 percent of all transition units) represent relatively isolated black suburbanites whose units are transferred to whites within predominantly white communities.

BLACK HOMEOWNERSHIP AND WEALTH

The final question focuses on the efficacy of suburban homeownership as a means of equity accumulation. Numerous studies have pointed to the significance of homeownership as the principal source of savings for the lower and middle-income population, and equity accumulated in the home has traditionally served as the launch vehicle for upward mobility among many immigrant ethnic groups.[11] What has been the recent experience of black suburban homeowners?

A direct comparison of sale price changes over time in a sample of suburban housing units sold by blacks and whites is undertaken in Chapter 8. Before assessing the case study data, however, we may obtain substantial insight into black suburban housing market dynamics by considering several indirect sources: (1) change in estimated value of black- and white-owned suburban units; (2) the pattern of racial and tenure change in black-owned units; and (3) the previous tenure of suburban black homebuyers.

From the standpoint of the aspiring homebuyer, the inflation of housing prices in recent years has caused considerable concern. From the seller's standpoint, however, such inflation simply magnifies the significance of homeownership as an investment. To what extent have black suburban homeowners shared in this equity-building inflation of housing prices?

To answer this question, we compared reported property value in owner-occupied suburban units for 1974 to property value in the same units reported in 1975. According to Census Bureau definitions, these value figures represent "the respondent's estimate of how much the property (house and lot) would sell for if it were for sale." The results of this comparison are tabulated in Exhibit 3-4.

At all levels of housing value, suburban units occupied by blacks in both 1974 and 1975 were less likely to increase and more likely to decrease in estimated value than units occupied by whites. Among the lowest-value properties (those valued less than $20,000 in 1974), 41 percent of white-occupied units but only 25 percent of black-occupied units had increased in value in 1975. Among the highest-value properties (those valued $50,000 or more), 13 percent of white-occupied units but 24 percent of black-occupied units had decreased in value by 1975. At intervening value levels, black-owned units were less likely than white-owned units to increase in value and were up to twice as likely to decrease in value. For example, among suburban units valued from $20,000 to $34,999 in 1974, 20 percent of black-owned units versus 27 percent of white-owned units had increased in value by 1975, while 9 percent of black units but only 5 percent of white units decreased in value. Similarly, increases were reported for 22 percent of white-owned but 18 percent of black-owned units valued between $35,000 and $49,999, while 24 percent of black units and 10 percent of white units in this value category decreased between 1974 and 1975.

In sum, when comparing reported property value of identical suburban units at two points a year apart, units owned by blacks in both years were less likely to increase and more likely to decrease in value than white-owned units matched by value in the initial year. If inflation in housing prices is producing windfalls for some, the data suggest that such beneficial effects are less likely to accrue to

EXHIBIT 3-4

1975 PROPERTY VALUE BY 1974 PROPERTY VALUE, IN IDENTICAL BLACK- AND WHITE-OWNER-OCCUPIED SUBURBAN UNITS
(percents)

Property Value in 1975	PROPERTY VALUE, 1974							
	Less than $20,000		$20,000 - 34,999		$35,000 - 49,999		$50,000 or more	
	White-White	Black-Black	White-White	Black-Black	White-White	Black-Black	White-White	Black-Black
Less than $20,000	59.3	75.0	4.9	8.7	0.9	6.7	0.6	12.1
$20,000-34,999	34.5	20.9	68.4	71.6	9.0	17.1	2.3	0.0
$35,000-49,999	4.5	4.1	24.6	17.8	67.8	58.5	10.4	11.9
$50,000 or more	1.8	0.0	2.1	1.9	22.3	17.7	86.8	76.0
Total	100.0	100.0	100.0	100.0	100.0	100.0	100.0	100.0
Number of Units (in thousands)	1,123	98	3,763	138	2,499	47	1,857	11

Note: U.S. Suburbs = non-central city portions of fifty SMSAs for which intrametropolitan location of units is reported on AHS national survey tapes. See note 3.

Source: U.S. Bureau of the Census, *Annual Housing Survey: 1974 and 1975,* national sample public use tapes.

a suburban homeowner who is black than to one who is white.

The disproportionate value increase of white-owned and black-owned units may be due to weaker demand for the latter. The data suggest extremely limited white demand for units sold by blacks. The probability that a black-owned suburban unit will turn over to a black household is far higher than that of a white-owned unit. With black households comprising five percent of the suburban population, roughly that proportion of housing turnovers would go to blacks in an unbiased market. Indeed, of all 649,000 owner-occupied suburban units that turned over between 1974 and 1975, 4.6 percent were black-occupied in 1975. Disaggregating this total picture by race, however, reveals a significant pattern: fully 46 percent of the suburban black-owned units that turned over but only 3.2 percent of the suburban white-owned units that turned over went to a black household. In short, the probability that a suburban black owner will be replaced by another black is fourteen times that of a white owner. As a result, black home sellers are confined to a restricted pool of buyers and are far more likely than their white counterparts to bear the burden of lower black purchasing power.

The previous tenure of black home buyers is one indicator of their weaker purchasing ability. Previous tenure impacts on home purchase through the availability of equity to apply to the downpayment. First-time homebuyers must be able to draw from personal savings, relatives, or similar sources for the downpayment that second-time buyers typically obtain from the equity accumulated in the previous unit. Equity accumulated through previous homeownership greatly facilitates home purchase, and racial differences in tenure of previous unit influence downpayment ability.

Fully 60 percent of black purchasers of suburban housing units in 1975, but 49 percent of white purchasers, rented their previous unit. Thus, white homebuyers were more likely than black buyers of suburban units to draw on previous equity to help finance their suburban home purchase.[12]

Further, white suburban homebuyers were more likely to own than rent their previous unit, regardless of whether it was located in a central city or a suburb. Among black suburban homebuyers, however, an interesting pattern emerges when location of the previous unit is considered along with tenure. Eight out of ten black suburban homebuyers whose previous residence was in a central city rented that unit; six out of ten already in the suburbs, however, were owners. Thus, while black homebuyers already in the suburbs are somewhat more likely to be previous owners when compared to their white counterparts, this former group constitutes a considerably smaller share of black homebuyers than white. In sum, central city renters comprise the largest share (42 percent) of black suburban homebuyers; another 18 percent were suburban renters, and only 40 percent were owners. Among white suburban homebuyers, in contrast, only 17 percent were central city renters, and 51 percent were previous owners. The implication of these figures for this discussion is clear. Black suburban homeowners, more dependent than whites on finding a black buyer to achieve a sale, are significantly confined to a segment of the market characterized by a weaker asset position as measured by equity accumulated in a previous home.

SUMMARY

Although a growing share of the nation's black population is located in the suburbs, suburbanization per se is neither synonymous with equal housing opportunity nor is it likely to automatically serve the wealth-accumulative function it has provided for previous suburbanizing ethnic groups. Progress toward these goals requires continued monitoring of the housing market conditions governing the black suburbanization process that is underway.

This initial look at the nature of black suburbanization has focused on three broad elements of the process: the magnitude of white-to-black transition as a source of suburban housing, the characteristics of the housing units involved, and the potential of homeownership thus achieved as a means of equity accumulation. As of the mid-1970s, we found that rental units become available to blacks at a faster rate than owner-occupied units, that black suburbanites are less likely than whites to own their own homes, and that those who do are more likely than whites to see their units transfer to rental occupancy with subsequent turnover. Compared to suburban units transferred within the white submarket, units that turn over from white to black are on average older, are of lower value, and are assigned lower ratings of housing and neighborhood quality. Owner-occupied units within the black suburban submarket are less likely to increase in value and more likely to decrease in value than equivalently priced units within the white submarket.

If these trends continue unchecked, we will have yet further evidence of the disparity between the black experience in America and that of other ethnic and immigrant groups. For the latter, dispersion into the suburbs was typically synonymous with assimilation, the breaking down of ethnic enclaves, and unfettered upward mobility. Evidence to date raises the issue of whether the equivalent process will hold for the suburbanizing black population. The specter of "two societies" so often hailed to describe black cities and white suburbs may simply be replicated at a new metropolitan scale.

The following chapters begin to disentangle the overall patterns that have emerged thus far. The transition dynamics uncovered here take on additional meaning in Chapter 4, where we consider the spatial variations in the location of black population growth within the suburban realm.

NOTES

1. John F. Kain, "Theories of Residential Location and Realities of Race," in *Essays in Urban Spatial Structure* (Cambridge: Ballinger, 1975).
2. Larry Long and Daphne Spain, *Racial Succession in Individual Housing Units,* U.S. Bureau of the Census, Current Population Reports, Special

Studies, Series P-23, No. 71, 1978.

3. Our discussion of post-1970 suburban housing characteristics is based on published and unpublished data from the U.S. Bureau of the Census *Annual Housing Surveys* for 1974, 1975, and 1976. The *Annual Housing Survey* comprises a national sample of some 84,000 housing units resurveyed each year and weighted to represent the national housing stock.

The Census Bureau's confidentiality requirements restrict identification of intrametropolitan location of sampled housing units in some cases. Unless otherwise indicated, our analysis of "suburban" housing units is therefore limited to units in the non - central city portions of fifty SMSAs, for which intrametropolitan location is identified on AHS computer tapes. These fifty SMSAs, which contained 74.8 percent of the nation's black metropolitan occupied housing units in 1970, are: Akron, Albany - Schenectady - Troy, Anaheim - Santa Ana - Garden Grove, Atlanta, Baltimore, Birmingham, Boston, Buffalo, Chicago, Cincinnati, Cleveland, Columbus, Dallas, Denver, Detroit, Fort Worth, Gary - Hammond - East Chicago, Greensboro - Winston Salem - High Point, Honolulu, Houston, Indianapolis, Jersey City, Kansas City, Los Angeles - Long Beach, Louisville, Miami, Milwaukee, Minneapolis - St. Paul, New Orleans, New York City, Newark, Norfolk - Portsmouth, Oklahoma City, Paterson - Clifton - Passaic, Philadelphia, Phoenix, Pittsburgh, Portland (Ore.), Providence - Warwick - Pawtucket, Rochester, Sacramento, St. Louis, San Bernardino - Riverside, San Diego, San Francisco - Oakland, San Jose, Seattle - Everett, Tampa - St. Petersburg, Toledo, and Washington, D.C.

4. Long and Spain, *Racial Succession in Individual Housing Units;* Karl E. Taeuber and Alma F. Taeuber, *Negroes in Cities: Residential Segregation and Neighborhood Change* (New York: Atheneum, 1969).

5. For example, Chester Rapkin and William Grigsby, *The Demand for Housing in Racially Mixed Areas* (Los Angeles: University of California Press, 1960).

6. This discussion, utilizing published data sources, covers the suburban portions of *all* metropolitan areas identified in the 1970 census. See U.S. Bureau of the Census, Current Housing Reports, Series H-150-76, *General Housing Characteristics for the United States and Regions: 1976.* Annual Housing Survey: 1976, Part A, Table A-1, 1978.

7. Data based on a limited sample of suburban housing units. See note 3.

8. Wade Clark Roof and Daphne Spain, "A Research Note on City-Suburb Socio-economic Differences Among American Blacks," *Social Forces* 56 (September 1977): 15-20.

9. Discrepancies between totals in Exhibits 3-2 and 3-3 result from the procedures utilized to identify housing units occupied by different households in 1974 and 1975. Exhibit 3-2 includes all suburban housing units for which race, tenure, and suburban location could be identified in both 1974 and 1975. Exhibit 3-3 includes only that subset of Exhibit 3-2 units occupied by "recent movers" at the time of the 1975 survey. As a result, some units

shown as having turned over in Exhibit 3-2 are not identified as "recent movers" in Exhibit 3-3. "Recent movers" are defined by the Census Bureau as households that moved into the unit during the twelve-month period preceding the survey. Since AHS national surveys are conducted between October and December of each year, some units may be resurveyed as much as fifteen months apart. Some households could thus move into a unit subsequent to the 1974 survey and not be counted as "recent movers" in 1975. Further discrepancies are introduced in cases where the race of the household head changes through marriage, separation, or divorce but the household continues to occupy the same dwelling unit. The effect of these accounting procedures is to decrease the within-category totals reported in Exhibit 3-3 compared to Exhibit 3-2. There is no evidence, however, that relationships between categories in Exhibit 3-3 are skewed in any systematic way.

10. Spain, et al., substantiate these findings in their recent analysis of the socioeconomic characteristics of transition households. See Daphne Spain, John Reid, and Larry Long, *Housing Successions Among Blacks and Whites in Cities and Suburbs*, U.S. Bureau of the Census, Current Population Reports, Special Studies, Series P-23, No. 101, 1980.

11. See, for instance, John Kain and John Quigley, *Housing Markets and Racial Discrimination* (New York: National Bureau of Economic Research, 1975).

12. U.S. Bureau of the Census, Current Housing Reports, Series H-150-17D, *Housing Characteristics of Recent Movers*, Annual Housing Survey: 1975, Part D, 1977.

4

SPATIAL PATTERNS OF SUBURBAN BLACK GROWTH

INTRODUCTION

The preceding two chapters have focused on the growth rate of the suburban black population and on the characteristics of suburban housing units transferred from white-to-black occupancy. The discussion, however, has dealt with aggregate national statistics in which the suburbs are viewed jointly as all non-central-city portions of metropolitan areas. Given the heterogeneity of suburbia thus defined, national data undoubtedly obscure variations in the distribution of black growth within the suburban zone. Spatial variations in the location of black population increase may be indicative of suburban resegregation. Further, as Harold Rose has suggested, the spatial distribution of black growth within the suburbs has implications for the extent to which suburbanization yields access to an improved quality of life.[1]

This chapter addresses two related questions in examining the geographic distribution of recent black population growth within the suburbs. First, is the increase in the suburban black population evenly distributed throughout suburbia or concentrated in particular community types? For earlier suburbanizing ethnic groups, the move to the suburbs often meant assimilation and the dispersion of identifiable spatial concentrations.[2] Alternately, evidence of the spatial concentration of black suburbanization would suggest the repetition of segregated central city patterns within the suburbs. Second, given the variability and heterogeneity of the suburban zone, how does the spatial distribution of black population growth correlate with the distribution of housing and neighborhood characteristics? If black suburbanization is indeed spatially concentrated in particular community types, then the characteristics of those communities are likely to explain much of the pattern of white-to-black transition described in the preceding chapter.

In shifting focus to variations *within* suburbia, we turn from the aggregate national data to consider patterns of black residence and growth in the New Jersey suburbs. Because of its highly suburbanized character and the diversity of its black population, New Jersey is an appropriate setting for the study of black suburbanization. In 1970, blacks accounted for 11.1 percent of the American population and 11.4 percent of the population of New Jersey.[3] Black migration patterns to and within the state are the result of a wide variety of influences, such as employment opportunities in agriculture and industry and the growth and decline of the state's largest cities. Measured by population density and percent of the population living in places of 2,500 or more, New Jersey ranks as one of the nation's most urbanized states, and as such may provide a portent of urbanization trends elsewhere in the country.[4] Seventeen of the twenty-one counties in the state lie within metropolitan (SMSA) boundaries. With the central cities of these SMSAs excluded, this leaves nearly 70 percent of the state's total land area categorized as suburban.

Beginning with suburban communities with above-average black concentrations, we develop a community typology based on a priori observations of the factors contributing to the distribution of blacks in the New Jersey suburbs. In the absence of intercensal racial data for the period since 1970, recent patterns are identified by analysis of changes in public school enrollment by race between 1971 and 1976.[5] We then assess the proportion of overall suburban black growth accounted for by each category of the community typology. In the final section, changes in school enrollment are related to community land use and census characteristics in a multivariate analysis that confirms and substantiates the basic elements of the typology.

The findings reveal that black suburbanization is multidimensional, encompassing a range of community types, of initiating mechanisms, and of dynamics of growth. Aggregate data showing an overall black increase conceal a redistribution of the suburban black population, in which some suburban communities are gaining and others losing black population. To a large extent, black suburbanization is not synonymous with residential integration. Suburban black increase is most closely associated with the outward expansion of central city black concentrations: the largest share of black growth is occurring in older, densely populated suburban municipalities adjacent to the central cities.

A TYPOLOGY OF BLACK SUBURBANIZATION

Several attempts have been made to identify in general terms the types of suburban communities with evidence of black residence or growth. Harold Connolly characterized black suburbanization as "the physical expansion of inner-city ghettos into contiguous [suburban] areas" and the "expansion of an already existing, distinctly suburban, black concentration into a more visible ghetto."[6] More explicitly, Reynolds Farley described three general types of suburban communities where black population increased during the 1960s: "older, densely settled suburbs often containing or near employment centers," "new suburban development(s) . . . built exclusively for Negroes," and quasi-rural "areas lacking adequate sewer and water facilities, containing dilapidated homes of low value, and having exclusively black populations."[7] Harold Rose contrasted the exclusively black outer-suburban community with the community formed through outward expansion of the central city ghetto, characterizing the former as "colonizing" and the latter as "ghettoizing" forms.[8]

The distribution of the New Jersey suburban black population as measured by 1976 public school enrollment encompasses each of these community types (Exhibit 4-1). Primary black concentrations are found in ring-like zones adjacent to central cities: Newark, Trenton, New Brunswick, Long Branch-Asbury Park, and Atlantic City. A second cluster includes the small, old industrial towns on the Delaware River in Burlington, Camden, and Gloucester Counties. A third concentration is in the largely agricultural southern part of the state. This pattern, which subsumes a broad range of community types throughout the suburban portion of the state, underscores the need for systematic specification of a typology of suburban black concentrations.

Defining a Community Typology

In an effort to systematize these general observations, the typology focuses on the factors contributing to initial black entry into the suburban zone. This approach has the advantage of subsuming the broadest possible range of suburban black settlement types, including communities with a stable or decreasing black population, as well as ones where the black population is increasing. Six factors likely to influence black suburban migration can be identified: expansion of central city black concentrations beyond corporate boundaries into contiguous suburban municipalities; individual selection by black households of traditional suburban dormitory residence; agricultural employment in rural areas subsumed by the expansion of metropolitan areas; employment in small, satellite industrial towns also subsumed by the expansion of suburbia; development of

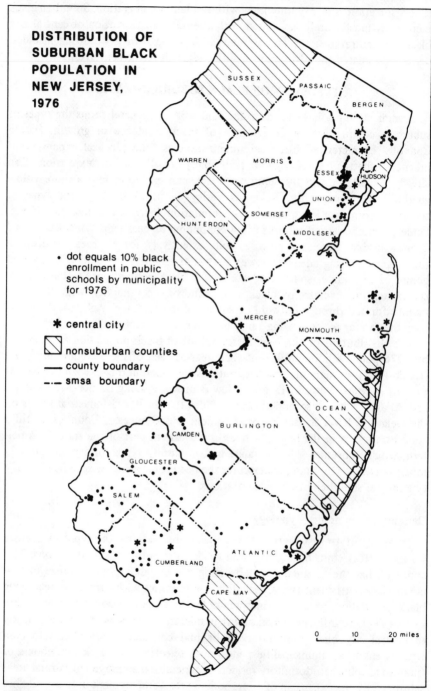

DISTRIBUTION OF SUBURBAN BLACK POPULATION IN NEW JERSEY, 1976

· dot equals 10% black enrollment in public schools by municipality for 1976

✳ central city

▧ nonsuburban counties

— county boundary

—·— smsa boundary

Exhibit 4-1. Distribution of Suburban Black Public School Enrollment in New Jersey, 1976.

affordable housing under state and federal subsidy programs that at times is marketed predominantly to blacks; and residual factors that are not included in the first five categories, such as employment opportunities afforded by large commercial concentrations, large-scale private or public institutions, military bases, and other governmental installations. A typology of suburban communities reflecting these factors can be defined based on locational, land use, and density criteria, using statewide averages (means) as thresholds for selection (Exhibit 4-2). The definitions we have used are as follows:

Classified as *central-city spillover* are municipalities contiguous to a central city and urban in character. For a suburban municipality to be designated in this category, the adjacent central city must have had a 1970 black population of 1,000 or more. Urbanized character is indicated by a population density in persons per square mile greater than or equal to the statewide mean.

A *dormitory* community corresponds most closely to the popular image of suburbia. Land use in communities of this type is predominantly residential. The percentage of total assessed valuation in residential use (excluding multifamily structures) is greater than the statewide mean, and the proportions of land in nonresidential uses are below state averages.

A *metropolitan rural* suburb is termed metropolitan since it is within an SMSA boundary, but it is rural in character and land use. An above-average percentage of assessed valuation in communities of this type is derived from farm land. Low density character is further reflected by below-average assessed valuation in land devoted to apartments and below-average population density.

The *outer-industrial* category comprises small industrial satellites enveloped by expanding suburbanization. These communities are defined as municipalities with above-average assessed valuation in industrial land use, below-average proportions of land in residential and farm uses, and a location not adjacent to a central city.

A *subsidized* community is one that falls into none of the previous four categories but in which federal or state housing subsidies play a distinctive role. The overwhelming majority of suburban municipalities in New Jersey contains no subsidized housing units. Subsidized rental units average 6 percent of total units in the 35 suburban municipalities containing such housing. Thus, a subsidized community is defined here as a municipality in which 6 percent or more of total housing units are subsidized.

Mixed-use suburbs are all those that correspond to none of the criteria designated for the previous categories. Municipalities in this group are generally mixed residential-commercial or residential-industrial communities and in several cases are the sites of large governmental or military facilities.

All suburban black concentrations within a sixteen-county suburban portion of the state have been assigned to categories of this typology. The suburban area encompasses the entire state with the following exceptions: omitted are the four nonmetropolitan counties of Ocean, Cape May, Hunterdon, and Sussex, all outside SMSA boundaries. Hudson County, coterminous with the Jersey City

EXHIBIT 4-2

A TYPOLOGY OF SUBURBAN BLACK COMMUNITIES

Community Type	Criteria[a]	Frequency Number	Percent
Central-city spillover	adjacent to a central city with a 1970 black population of 1000 or more; population density 953 or more persons per square mile	10	10.8
Dormitory	1971 total assessed valuation 63 percent or more residential, less than 14.2 percent commercial, less than 10.7 percent industrial, and less than 1.6 percent farm	22	23.7
Metropolitan rural	1971 total assessed valuation 1.6 percent or more farm and less than 6 percent apartments; population density less than 953 persons per square mile	28	30.0
Outer-industrial	1971 total assessed valuation 10.7 percent or more industrial, less than 63 percent residential, and less than 1.6 percent farm; location not adjacent to a central city	9	9.7
Subsidized	6 percent or more housing units with state or federal subsidy; not in above catagories	6	6.5
Mixed-use	all others	18	19.4
Total		93	100.0

Note: a. All density and land use criteria represent the New Jersey statewide mean.

Sources: Thirty-fourth Annual Report of the Division of Local Government Services, Statements of Financial Conditions of Counties and Municipalities (Trenton: New Jersey Department of Community Affairs, Division of Local Government Services, 1971); and New Jersey Directory of Subsidized Rental Housing (Trenton: New Jersey Department of Community Affairs, Division of Housing and Urban Renewal, 1978).

SMSA, is excluded owing to its highly urbanized character: the county comprises the densely populated municipalities of Jersey City, Bayonne, Hoboken, Secaucus, West New York, Weehawken, and Union City. Also excluded are the fourteen urban areas in the state designated as central cities by the Bureau of the Census, and the cities of Camden and Elizabeth, which each had a 1970 total population of over 100,000.

Identifying Suburban Black Concentrations

Population patterns within this suburban area incorporate both existing black concentrations and areas experiencing recent black increases or decreases. Three different data sources have been used to identify both static and dynamic black communities for inclusion in the analysis. Suburban communities with an existing resident black population are defined as those with a population at least 11.4 percent black (the statewide mean) according to the 1970 census. Communities with above-average black concentrations since 1970 are defined as those with public school enrollment above the statewide average of 16.9 percent black in 1976. Finally, a statewide survey of 122 local community informants was used to identify communities with low absolute numbers of black residents that appear to be attracting a disproportionate share of recent black in-migration. Respondents were selected and interviewed on the basis of the likelihood of their knowledge of local population and housing trends. The respondents included representatives of county and local planning boards, fair housing groups, the Urban League, the NAACP, and the League of Women Voters, as well as members of county and local real estate boards, school boards, churches, local newspaper staffs, and community and civic organizations.[9] Each respondent first was asked the question: "Are there any areas or communities in _____County where black households live or into which blacks are moving?" The respondent was then administered a structured questionnaire designed to elicit descriptive information on the characteristics of each community that was identified. A municipality was included in the analysis if it was identified by two or more survey respondents as a community in which black households reside or to which blacks are currently moving. Municipalities meeting this criteria but having neither of the minimum black concentration thresholds (i.e., based on 1970 population or 1976 school enrollment) were labeled "perceptual" or "incipient" black suburbs.

Ninety-three suburban communities, or 21 percent of the 440 suburban municipalities in New Jersey, met at least one of the above criteria for black concentrations and were assigned to categories of the community typology (Exhibit 4-2). Nearly one-third are classified as metropolitan rural communities, clustered mainly in the southern, less industrial, portion of the state (Exhibit 4-3). Second in frequency (23.7 percent) are the dormitory suburbs, concentrated in the northern, urbanized part of the state focused on Newark and New York City, and also in the portions of Gloucester, Camden, and Burlington counties that are linked to Philadelphia. Central-city spillover communities

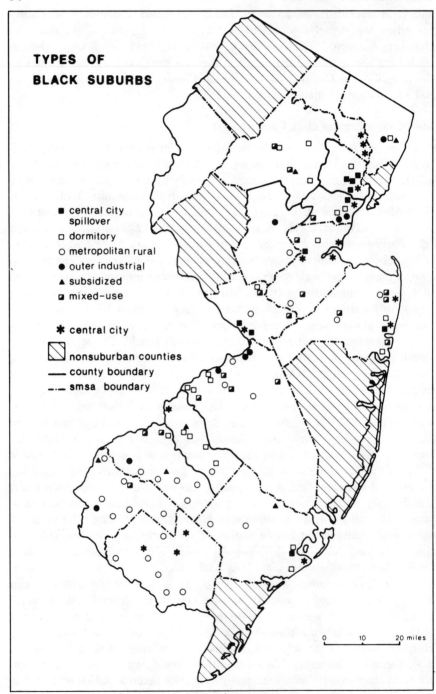

TYPES OF BLACK SUBURBS

- ■ central city spillover
- □ dormitory
- ○ metropolitan rural
- ● outer industrial
- ▲ subsidized
- ◪ mixed-use

- ✳ central city
- ▨ nonsuburban counties
- —— county boundary
- ·_·_ smsa boundary

0   10   20 miles

Exhibit 4-3. Types of Black Suburbs in New Jersey.

account for 11 percent of the total; five of the ten municipalities in this category are adjacent to Newark, which was 56 percent black in 1970 and is the state's largest city. Another 10 percent of the municipalities are categorized as outer-industrial suburbs. This group includes a number of small industrial centers whose status predates the Revolutionary War, as well as the refinery com-munities of Linden and Rahway in Union County and the newer industrial development in central Somerset County. The six subsidized communities, 6.5 percent of the total, present no easily discernable locational pattern. Their status is most likely the result of the industriousness of individual local sponsors of subsidized housing and thus lacks any identifiable spatial regularity. Finally, the eighteen remaining communities comprise the mixed-use category, a diverse group of commercial-industrial centers and institutional sites distributed throughout New Jersey's central corridor.

Community Characteristics

The diversity of black suburbanization is displayed in a comparison of selected characteristics of the six community types (Exhibit 4-4). Central-city spillover communities are the largest in total population and rank highest in population density. Second in size are the outer-industrial suburbs but even these communities are on average less than half the total size of the former group. Metropolitan rural communities occupy the low end of the scale in both total population and density. These patterns are expected because population density is a component of the definition of community types. Change in total population between 1970 and 1975 conforms to the broad nationwide patterns that have been identified for the post-1970 period.[10] Central-city spillover com-munities have experienced a net loss of total population, echoing the long-term losses in the adjacent central cities. The dormitory suburbs, in contrast, continue to gain population, perhaps an indication of the persisting desirability of these communities as residential settings. The highest growth rate for total population is in the metropolitan rural suburbs. This may be explained in part by the relatively small 1970 base population in these communities, but it also coincides with national data that indicate a rapid acceleration in the growth of outer-suburban and nonmetropolitan communities. The outer-industrial suburbs, how-ever, have maintained a relatively stable total population, decreasing by 0.9 percent between 1970 and 1975.

The average percent black in 1970 ranges from a low of 13.3 percent in dormitory municipalities to a high of 32.1 percent in subsidized communities. These averages include the 23 "perceptual" communities that were below the 1970 statewide average black population of 11.4 percent, or the 1976 average black public school enrollment of 16.9 percent, but were identified by survey respondents as communities to which blacks are moving. The 1970 average black population in the 70 remaining communities was 21.8 percent. Given that many New Jersey suburban municipalities were less than 1 percent black in 1970,

EXHIBIT 4-4

BLACK SUBURBAN COMMUNITY CHARACTERISTICS[a]

Community Type	Total Population 1975	Population Density, 1970 (Persons/sq. mile)	Percent Change in Total Population, 1970-75	Percent Black, 1970	Median Black Family Income, 1969 (dollars)	Black/ Total Family Income Ratio, 1969	Black Percent Homeowners 1970	Black/White Homeowner Ratio, 1970	Median Black Housing Value, 1970 (dollars)	Black/ Total Median Housing Value Ratio, 1970
Central-city spillover	39,336	9,246	-1.3	17.6	8,266	.91	58.6	1.02	17,610	.90
Dormitory	15,776	3,996	8.2	13.3	8,309	.74	59.2	.81	17,619	.79
Metropolitan rural	7,801	238	10.9	20.0	7,122	.79	71.8	.90	12,057	.78
Outer-industrial	17,975	4,124	-0.9	19.0	7,590	.85	48.9	.79	14,314	.82
Subsidized	11,779	3,557	6.7	32.1	7,164	.88	56.4	.83	15,320	.79
Mixed-use	14,313	4,163	-2.2	13.7	6,422	.82	49.5	.79	15,306	.75

Note: a. All values are unweighted averages (means) of individual observations for each community type.

Source: Calculated from Census Bureau data.

these figures indicate black concentrations significantly above the norm. Blacks comprise a relatively high proportion of the total population in a number of individual municipalities. Among these are East Orange, a central-city spillover community adjacent to Newark that was 54 percent black in 1970, the mixed-use community of Plainfield that was 40 percent black, and the subsidized community of Lawnside that was 90.5 percent black in 1970.

Black median family income as reported in the 1970 census was highest in the dormitory communities, a statistic supporting the inference that this community type is favored by suburban blacks who are able to express their residential preferences through mobility. Median income among black families in central-city spillover communities is also relatively high, a reflection of the higher incomes and higher living expenses of urban areas. The lowest median family incomes are found in metropolitan rural and mixed-use communities.

The relatively high black income in dormitory suburbs is less impressive when the median income for black families is expressed as a ratio to the median income for the total population. Although black families in dormitory suburbs have the highest median income, this income level is only three-fourths of median family income for the total population in this community category. All other community types have less disparity between black and total incomes, with income for blacks being more than 90 percent of total income in central-city spillover suburbs. This finding may suggest that black residents of spillover communities have experienced an increase in income that achieves parity with the total population. Another interpretation, however, supported by data on population growth patterns, is that parity has been achieved by the selective out-migration of upper-income white households from the older suburbs adjacent to the central cities rather than by a rise in black incomes.

Almost three-fourths of black households in metropolitan rural suburbs are homeowners, probably a reflection of the absence of rental units in these areas. In no other case does the average rate of homeownership exceed 60 percent, and barely half of black households in outer-industrial and mixed-use suburbs are homeowners. As with the income data, these rates of black homeownership have additional significance when they are expressed relative to the rates for whites. The black ownership rate is almost identical in central-city spillover and dormitory communities. Comparison with the white rate, however, reveals that black households in the former community type are more likely to be homeowners than are their white neighbors; in dormitory suburbs, the black homeownership rate is only 80 percent of that achieved by whites. The data provide additional evidence that black households in central-city spillover communities may be financially better off than the remaining white population, while the opposite holds in dormitory suburbs.

The data on median housing values generally reflect income patterns. Although black households in metropolitan rural suburbs have the highest probability of homeownership, housing units in these communities have the lowest median value. The highest values are found in central-city spillover and dormitory suburbs. In the former communities, ownership of relatively high value units places black households almost on par with total median housing value in the community. The same high housing value in dormitory suburbs, however, brings black-occupied units only within 80 percent of the median value of all units.

In sum, comparison of characteristics across community types reveals the broad variety of residential settings encapsulated in the suburban black experience. Black households in central-city spillover suburbs live in relatively large, high-density communities, at income and housing-value levels on par with the remaining, but decreasing, white population. Dormitory communities provide housing for the highest-income segment of the suburban black population but in a setting where blacks represent a relatively low proportion of the total population, and their income, their rate of homeownership, and the value of the houses they own are all low in comparison to those of whites. Metropolitan rural suburbs are low in total population size and density, and they contain a black population with a relatively low average income and the lowest value of homes owned. Outer-industrial suburbs combine relatively higher total population size and density with relatively lower income and housing value. The highest concentrations of black population are found in subsidized communities. Mixed-use suburbs are characterized by the lowest level of black family income.

POPULATION GROWTH PATTERNS

The diversity of characteristics among black suburban communities raises the issue of the relative importance of each community type in the overall distribution of the suburban black population. A concentration of black population growth in a particular community type may have implications for the meaning of black suburbanization in providing access to desired components of the suburban environment. Two related aspects of the question are considered here: first, the likelihood of each community type to increase or decrease in percent black since 1970, and second, the actual net contribution of each community type to changes in total black school enrollment between 1971 and 1976.

Growth Categories

In a manner analogous to the community typology, we have defined five distinct categories of black population growth (Exhibit 4-5).

Existing stable black suburban communities are ones with above-average black concentrations in both 1970 (measured as a percentage of total population) and 1976 (measured as a percentage of total public school enrollment). Although the black proportion of total population is relatively high at both dates, the black growth rate is relatively moderate over the period, limited to an increase in black school enrollment of less than 25 percent.

New black suburban municipalities had a below-average black proportion of total population in 1970 but were above the statewide average percent black public school enrollment in 1976.

Growing black communities reported an increase in black public school enrollment of 25 percent or more between 1971 and 1976. These include municipalities that had an above-average percentage of blacks in 1970, that is—percentage black high and increasing—and also those that attained above-average black school enrollment by 1976, that is, percentage black increasing to a high level.

Declining black suburbs are those that had an above-average percentage of blacks in 1970 but had a below-average percentage black public school enrollment in 1976.

Perceptual black suburbs had below-average black concentrations in both years but were identified by two or more community informants as current reception areas of suburban black in-migration.

The number of communities in each growth category varies from six to fifty (Exhibit 4-5 and 4-6). Existing stable communities are clearly the most numerous, a verification of related findings of the stability of black suburban concentrations.[11] Six municipalities qualify as "new" black suburbs, and an additional six as "growing" black communities. These twelve communities are combined into a single category in subsequent analysis. Eight municipalities, clustered in the southern half of the state, are identified as "declining" black suburbs. Finally, the "perceptual" black suburbs comprise nearly a fourth of the total number of communities considered.

The association between growth category and community type reveals striking patterns in the distribution of suburban black population growth (Exhibit 4-7). Fewer than one-third of dormitory suburbs and only 40 percent of central-city spillover communities fall into the existing stable growth category. In contrast, this category contains eight of the nine outer-industrial suburbs. New or growing black suburbs comprise fully one-third of the central-city spillover and the subsidized communities and less than half that proportion in all other types. None of the outer-industrial suburbs and only 3.6 percent of metropolitan rural suburbs are characterized as new or growing. The declining growth pattern is clearly most salient among metropolitan rural suburbs, where 17.9 percent are so categorized. Dormitory communities evidence the greatest likelihood (45.5 percent) of being termed perceptual black suburbs. Only 10.7 percent of metropolitan rural suburbs, 11.1 percent of outer-industrial suburbs, and none of the subsidized suburbs are in this category. This may stem in part from the respondents' untutored definition of "suburban" in replies to survey questions, but also reflects incipient trends in the community types experiencing recent black suburbanization. In sum, at the community level of analysis, suburban black population increase appears to be closely associated with central-city spillover and subsidized communities. Decline is associated with metropolitan rural suburbs, and stability with outer-industrial suburbs. Local perceptions of black population increase appear focused on dormitory suburbs.

EXHIBIT 4-5

GROWTH CATEGORIES OF SUBURBAN BLACK COMMUNITIES

Community Growth Category	Criteria[a]	Number	Percent
Existing-stable	1970 population more than 11.4 percent black; 1976 public school enrollment more than 16.9 percent black; 1971-76 increase in black public school enrollment less than 25 percent	50	53.8
New	1970 population less than 11.4 percent black; 1976 public school enrollment more than 16.9 percent black	6	6.5
Growing	1971-76 increase in black public school enrollment more than 25 percent; 1970 population more than 11.4 percent black or 1976 public school enrollment more than 16.9 percent black	6	6.5
Declining	1970 population more than 11.4 percent black; 1976 public school enrollment less than 16.9 percent black	8	8.6
Perceptual	Not in preceding categories but identified by two or more survey respondents as a suburban community with resident or incoming black population	23	24.7
Total		93	100.0

Note: a. 1970 and 1976 criteria represent the New Jersey statewide mean.

Source: U.S. Census of Population, 1970: General Population Characteristics, Final Report PC(1)-B32, New Jersey (Washington, D.C.: Bureau of the Census, 1971); and data provided by the New Jersey Department of Education, Trenton.

Net Changes in Black and White School Enrollment

The relative share of total suburban black increase attributable to each community type reflects the extreme imbalance in the distribution of black suburbanization (Exhibit 4-8). Black public school enrollment in the municipalities in the typology increased by 13.2 percent between 1971 and 1976, but the rate of increase was far more rapid in some community types than in others. Simultaneously, white public school enrollment in these selected suburban communities decreased by 17.4 percent. Most strikingly, the communities with the highest rates of white loss generally coincide with the communities with the highest rates of black gain, and moderate white decreases are found in areas with moderate black increases. White enrollment in all other (predominantly white)

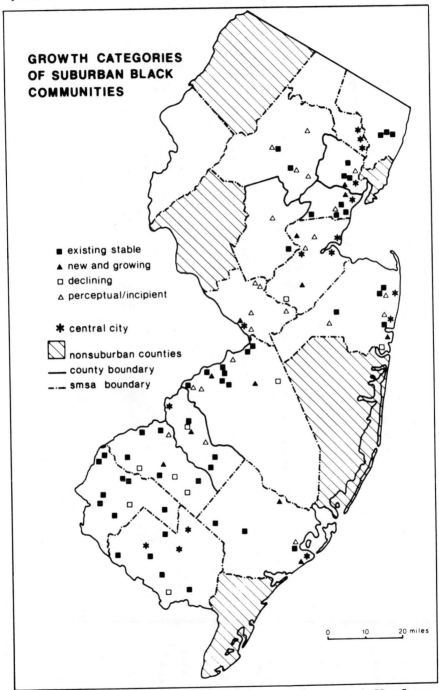

GROWTH CATEGORIES OF SUBURBAN BLACK COMMUNITIES

■ existing stable
▲ new and growing
□ declining
△ perceptual/incipient

✳ central city

▨ nonsuburban counties
—— county boundary
—·— smsa boundary

0   10   20 miles

Exhibit 4-6. Growth Categories of Suburban Black Communities in New Jersey.

EXHIBIT 4-7
GROWTH CATEGORY BY COMMUNITY TYPE
(percents)

Growth category	Central-city spillover (N=10)	Dormitory (N=22)	Metropolitan rural (N=28)	Outer— industrial (N=9)	Subsidized (N=6)	Mixed-use (N=18)
Existing-stable	40.0	31.8	67.9	88.9	66.7	44.4
New or growing	30.0	13.6	3.6	0.0	33.3	16.7
Declining	0.0	9.1	17.9	0.0	0.0	5.6
Perceptual	30.0	45.5	10.7	11.1	0.0	33.3
Total	100.0	100.0	100.0	100.0	100.0	100.0

suburbs not included in the typology decreased by 9.4 percent over the five-year period. If this is viewed as the normal rate of white contraction related to shrinking family size, then the white loss rates in the typology communities are unusually high (Exhibit 4-8). Independently of possible black-white differences in the rate of family formation and the number of school-age children, white and black households are responding to different influences affecting the suburban distribution of the two groups.

The highest rate of black gain (27.2 percent) is found in central-city spillover communities (Exhibit 4-8). The ten communities in this category account for fully 62.1 percent of the entire five-year increase in black public school enrollment recorded in all of the communities in the typology, and for over half of the black increase in all 405 suburban communities in the state.[12] Within the central-city spillover category, three municipalities characterized as new or growing more than doubled their black public school enrollment during the five-year period, increasing by 105 percent and accounting for one-third of the total increase recorded for the typology communities.

Black school enrollment in dormitory suburbs increased by 14.2 percent between 1970 and 1976, or by just under half the rate of growth recorded in central-city spillover communities. The twenty dormitory suburbs with full enrollment data accounted for the second largest share of black increase: 17 percent of the increase within the typology and 13.8 percent of total suburban black growth.

The black growth rate of 26.5 percent in subsidized communities was nearly as high as that in the central-city spillover category, and with only a few communities contributing yielded a relatively high average increase per community. In contrast, both outer-industrial and mixed-use communities showed essentially no change in black school enrollment.

Metropolitan rural suburbs recorded the lowest rate of white loss (-2.8 percent), while black enrollment increased by a moderate 10.1 percent. Indeed, these figures conceal the fact that white enrollment actually increased in nine metropolitan rural communities, virtually the only community type to experience any such increase in white public school enrollment. Simultaneously, sixteen of the metropolitan rural suburbs for which enrollment data are available experienced an absolute decrease in black enrollment. To the extent that public school enrollment figures reflect broad demographic patterns, it appears that the longstanding black population in metropolitan rural suburbs might be decreasing just as renewed white growth is reaching these outer suburban communities.

The average rate of white enrollment decrease in all other categories equals that in the central cities (-22.7 percent) but is substantially greater than in the remaining predominantly white suburbs (-9.4 percent). It appears that communities experiencing suburban black growth are marked by white out-migration that is not being replaced with other whites.

The pattern of black gains and white losses adjacent to central cities, coupled with white gains and black losses in outlying metropolitan rural suburbs, suggests

EXHIBIT 4-8

CHANGE IN PUBLIC SCHOOL ENROLLMENT
BY RACE AND COMMUNITY TYPE, 1971-76

Community Type[d]	WHITE ENROLLMENT			BLACK ENROLLMENT		
	Enrollment Change Number	Percent	Share of Suburban Change	Enrollment Change Number	Percent	Share of Suburban Change
Typology Communities						
Central-city spillover (N=10)	−8,097	−18.6	8.7	6,019	27.2	51.5
Dormitory residential (N=20)	−11,503	−20.4	12.3	1,613	14.2	13.8
Metropolitan rural (N=25)	−838	−2.8	0.9	848	10.1	7.3
Outer-industrial (N=7)	−2,953	−17.3	3.2	90	1.3	0.8
Subsidized (N=4)	−1,152	−25.7	1.2	735	26.5	6.3
Mixed-use (N=13)	−6,685	−23.1	7.1	386	3.1	3.3
Consolidated[b] (N=12)	−998	−3.4	1.1	825	22.7	7.1
All other suburbs (N=314)	−61,300	−9.4	65.5	1,168	8.8	10.0
Suburban Total (N=405)	−93,526	−10.9	100.0	11,684	14.5	100.0
Central Cities (N=16)	−19,031	− 22.7	NA	−1,917	−1.6	NA

Notes: a. Includes all New Jersey municipalities within SMSA boundaries excluding Hudson County. Numbers in parentheses indicate the number of communities for which both black and white school enrollment figures were available for both 1971 and 1976.

b. Indicates municipalities combined into consolidated school districts where constituent municipalities are assigned to different categories of the community typology.

Source: Data provided by the New Jersey State Education Department, Trenton.

that black suburbanization may be contributing little to convergence in the residential distributions of blacks and whites.

CORRELATES OF SUBURBAN BLACK GROWTH

The discussion thus far has been limited to actual or perceived black concentrations that have been categorized in a typology based on a priori observations. It remains to assess the validity of the typology by examining the community and land use characteristics correlated with black population increase throughout the suburbs as a whole. Our concern is with replicating the preceding descriptive analysis in a multivariate analysis of the types of communities most closely associated with black suburbanization.

Several studies have attempted to predict the rate and direction of black suburbanization. These have generally considered such factors as suburban employment opportunities and the socioeconomic characteristics of the central city black population as determinants of black suburban migration. Marshall and Stahura, for instance, differentiate between push and pull factors influencing black suburbanization, where the former include central city housing, demographic, and socioeconomic characteristics and the latter include the age, size, and status of suburban destination areas.[13] In contrast to this approach, our concern is not with predicting the flow of black suburban migration but rather with identifying the community types with which it is associated. Public school enrollment data are again used to approximate suburbanization trends between 1971 and 1976, and are related to community land use and housing stock characteristics measured in 1970, at the beginning of the period.

Three measures of the extent and direction of black suburbanization have been developed using black enrollment in public school (grades 1-12) for the years 1971-72 and 1976-77. The *magnitude* of black suburban concentrations is indicated by the absolute total black enrollment in 1976. The mean black enrollment in 403 suburban school districts (municipalities) in that year was 229, and the median was 16. Fifty-seven suburban communities had no black students, and an additional 120 had fewer than 10. In all, 44 percent of the 403 suburban New Jersey school districts had fewer than 10 black students in 1976, and 6 percent had 1,000 or more.

Suburban black *increase* is measured by both the absolute and relative change in black school enrollment between 1971 and 1976. Absolute change ranged from -289 to 2,070, with a mean of 28 and a median of zero: most communities experienced no change over the period, 19 percent lost 10 or more black students and 23 percent increased by 10 or more. The *growth rate* in black school enrollment was calculated as the absolute change divided by the initial year enrollment times 100, but due to the volatile nature of change measures, it required several transformations for use in the analysis.[14]

Data on community characteristics reflect those used in defining the suburban typology.[15] For each municipality, data published by the New Jersey

Department of Community Affairs indicate the percent of parcels and the percent of total assessed valuation in each of six land use categories: vacant (unimproved), residential, farm, commercial, industrial, and apartments. These data define the preponderant land use characteristics of each municipality in 1970. Characteristics of the housing stock, obtained from the 1970 census, include the age of structures, the percent of owner-occupied units and of units in multifamily structures, median rent and value, median number of rooms and bedrooms, and the percent of crowded units and units lacking complete plumbing facilities. Measures of turnover in the housing stock include the percent of 1970 households who lived in the same house in 1965, and the percent who moved into their present unit prior to 1950. A final set of measures pertains to municipal taxes and expenditures: total property valuation, the total and municipal tax rate, and the level of municipal expenditures.

In all, thirty-two variables measuring the land use, housing stock, and municipal finance characteristics of 392 suburban communities were submitted to principal components analysis and yielded eight factors summarizing the basic dimensions of suburban community types (Appendix Exhibit 4A-1). The eight factors, accounting for 81.5 percent of the variation in the original variables, are unambiguously defined:

Apartments factor— multifamily rental units; high proportion of parcels and valuation in apartments; small units.

High value factor— high total property valuation and municipal expenditures; high rent and housing value; low incidence of crowded units.

Stability factor— few units built 1960-70 and many built prior to 1950; high proportion of households who moved in before 1950 and who lived in the same house in 1965 as in 1970

Farm factor— high percentage of parcels and assessed valuation in farm use and low percentage in residential use; high incidence of substandard housing units.

Residential factor— high percentage of parcels in residential use and low percentage of undeveloped (vacant) parcels; low incidence of crowded or substandard units.

Tax rate factor— high total and municipal tax rates in both 1970 and 1975.

Industrial factor— high proportion of parcels and valuation in industrial uses and low percentage residential.

Commercial factor—high proportion of parcels and assessed value in commercial land use.

Factor scores provide a measure for each community on each of these eight dimensions of community type. Three additional variables have also been computed and related to black school enrollment change: number of total housing units in 1970, an indicator of size of place; absolute change in white public school enrollment between 1971 and 1976; and population potential. The last is a measure of the distance decay property of migration and measures the interaction between the available population pool and distance. For our purposes, population potential is the product of the 1971 black enrollment in the suburb times the 1971 black enrollment in the nearest central city divided by the distance between them, in miles. It is thus an interaction term measuring the combined effect of the size of the black population in both origin and destination areas and the intervening effect of distance.[16]

The relationship between these community characteristics and suburban black school enrollment confirms the earlier descriptive analysis (Exhibit 4-9). The eleven measures explain between 40 and 50 percent of the variation in the level and rate of change in black suburbanization. More important, the pattern of significant coefficients mirrors the categories of the suburban typology.

Focusing first on the magnitude of black enrollment, large suburban black concentrations are found in large communities dominated by multifamily and commercial land uses and marked by high tax rates. High tax rates are generally indicative of communities with an aging physical plant and depreciated property values. Large black enrollments are also positively associated with farm communities and negatively associated with residential dormitory suburbs. This pattern confirms earlier work characterizing existing black suburbs as either central-city spillover ghettoes or outlying rural substandard enclaves, and suggests additionally that the black presence in largely residential suburbs is relatively small in scale.

Community characteristics associated with absolute change in black enrollment similarly reflect expectations. Positive increases are found in large communities with large resident black concentrations and high tax rates close to central cities. Large absolute black increases are also associated with high rates of housing turnover and absolute decreases in white enrollment. Again, this is consistent with earlier findings of substantial white enrollment decreases in central-city spillover communities, suggesting that suburban black growth is funneled into older suburban communities (indicated by high tax rates), adjacent to central cities, being vacated by whites.

The most significant factors explaining the rate of suburban black growth are again community size and age: the largest positive coefficients are for total housing units and the tax rate factor. Reflecting the influence of initial population on growth rates, the population potential measure is negatively related to the black growth rate. The highest rates of increase over the 1971-76 period are found in suburban communities with low initial black concentrations. As suggested earlier, both farm communities and those with commercial concentrations reflect the highest rates of black decrease (or the lowest rates of increase) and residential dormitory communities similarly attained low rates of black growth.

EXHIBIT 4-9

COMMUNITY CHARACTERISTICS RELATED TO THE LEVEL AND CHANGE IN BLACK PUBLIC SCHOOL ENROLLMENT

Independent Variables	Total Black School Enrollment, 1976	Absolute Change in Black School Enrollment, 1971-76	Percent Change in Black School Enrollment, 1971-76
Total housing units, 1970	.443** (10.482)	.132* (2.151)	.312** (2.789)
Absolute change in white enrollment, 1971-76	na	−.139* (2.508)	−.099 (1.369)
Population potential	na	.455** (9.596)	−.482** (4.465)
Apartment factor	.128** (3.311)	.049 (1.133)	.089 (0.953)
High-value factor	.036 (0.918)	.011 (0.285)	−.010 (0.179)
Stability factor	.010 (0.279)	−.089* (2.287)	−.266** (5.238)
Farm factor	.171** (3.061)	.038 (0.630)	−.426** (4.492)
Residential factor	−.221** (3.817)	−.089 (1.390)	−.235** (2.679)
Tax rate factor	.441** (11.142)	.134** (2.868)	.491** (4.892)
Industrial factor	.008 (0.148)	.070 (1.302)	.296** (4.369)
Commercial factor	.098* (2.067)	−.004 (0.071)	−.334** (5.366)
R^2	.511**	.452**	.386**

Notes: See text for variable definitions. Values are standardized regression coefficients with absolute t-values in parentheses. Two-tailed significance test: (**) indicates coefficient significant at .01, (*) indicates coefficient significant at .05.

na = variables deleted from this regression: white enrollment change was used only in the black change regressions; population potential includes total black enrollment in its definition.

N = 387.

SUMMARY

National data on aggregate black suburbanization obscure the diversity of suburban black residential patterns. Suburban New Jersey municipalities with a resident or an incoming black population fall into six mutually exclusive categories. Major suburban black concentrations are found predominantly in multifamily housing in older, larger municipalities adjacent to the central cities as well as in agricultural communities marked by substandard housing conditions.

Suburbanization trends since 1970 reveal a redistribution process in which rural suburbs are losing blacks while central-city spillover communities register the largest increases. This latter category accounts for over half of the recent black population increase recorded in all suburban communities in the state. Dormitory residential suburbs, corresponding most closely to the stereotypical suburban ideal, when taken as a whole have very few, if any, black residents. Those dormitory communities with black concentrations, however, account for the second-largest absolute black population increase of the six categories. Given the dominant role of central-city spillover suburbs, however, the large size, high density, and rapid rate of white out-migration characterizing communities of this type suggest that black suburbanization may offer less than full realization of the stereotypical American dream.

To the extent that the New Jersey data reflect broader national trends, these findings help elucidate the discussion in the preceding chapters. The higher family income of suburban black in-migrants compared to out-migrants is expected if the out-migration is predominantly from rural suburbs to central cities while city-to-suburb flows are to spillover and dormitory communities. The characteristics of transition units described in Chapter 3 are similarly clarified by the community setting. Black-to-black transfers, found to involve units with the lowest average value and lowest quality ratings, are most likely to occur in communities with major black concentrations: central-city spillover and metropolitan rural suburbs. White-to-black transfers have the highest probability of occurrence in central-city spillover communities, since these report the highest rates of white decrease and black increase. The high median value of black-to-white transfers may be explained if these are concentrated in dormitory suburbs with low proportions of black population.

These findings on the variety of suburban black communities inform the selection of case study municipalities that provide the focus for the discussion in Part II.

APPENDIX EXHIBIT 4A-1
LAND USE DIMENSIONS OF
NEW JERSEY SUBURBAN COMMUNITIES
(N=392)

Community characteristics[a]	I Apartments	II High Value	III Stability	IV Farm	V Residential	VI Tax Rate	VII Industrial	VIII Commercial
Percent units in structures with five units or more	.871							
Percent units owner-occupied	-.863							
Percent valuation apartments	.829							
Median number of bedrooms	-.791							
Median number of rooms	-.746							
Percent parcels apartments	.674							
Percent parcels commercial	.410							.706
State equalized total property valuation, 1970		.905						
State equalized total property valuation, 1975		.832						
Annual municipal expenditures, police		.716						
Median housing value		.689						
Annual total municipal expenditures		.639						
Median gross rent		.480						
Percent units with more than one person per room		-.464			-.413			
Percent units built 1960-70			-.894					
Percent units built pre-1950			.876					
Percent moved in pre-1950			.799					

APPENDIX EXHIBIT 4A-1 (continued)

	I Apartments	II High Value	III Stability	IV Farm	V Residential	VI Tax Rate	VII Industrial	VIII Commercial
Percent in same house in 1965			.619					
Percent parcels farm				.931				
Percent valuation farm				.923				
Percent parcels residential				-.582	.765			
Percent units lacking plumbing				.439	-.450			
Percent valuation residential				-.437			-.542	
Percent parcels vacant					-.932			
Percent valuation vacant					-.621			
State equalized total tax rate, 1975						.827		
State equalized total tax rate, 1970						.776		
State equalized municipal tax rate, 1975						.718		
State equalized municipal tax rate, 1970						.688		
Percent valuation industrial							.936	
Percent parcels industrial							.651	
Percent valuation commercial								.815
Percent of common variance	26.8	25.5	14.7	12.2	6.8	6.0	4.1	3.8

Note: a. All data are for 1970 unless otherwise indicated. Only factor loadings greater than .40 or less than -.40 are reported in this exhibit.

Sources: Census of Population: 1970. *General Population Characteristics*, Final Report PC (1)-B32, New Jersey; State of New Jersey, Department of Community Affairs, Division of Local Government Services, *Thirty-Third Annual Report of the Division of Local Government Services, 1970*, and *Thirty-Eighth Annual Report of the Division of Local Government Services, 1975*.

NOTES

1. Harold M. Rose, *Black Suburbanization: Access to Improved Quality of Life or Maintenance of the Status Quo?* (Cambridge, Mass.: Ballinger, 1976); Rodney A. Erickson and Thedore K. Miller, "Race and Resources in Large American Cities: An Examination of Intraurban and Interregional Variations," *Urban Affairs Quarterly,* 13 (June 1978): 401-20.

2. Stanley Lieberson, *Ethnic Patterns in American Cities* (Glencoe, Ill.: Free Press, 1963); Stanley Lieberson, "The Impact of Residential Segregation on Ethnic Assimilation," *Social Forces* 40 (October 1961): 52-57.

3. U.S. Census of Population: 1970. *General Population Characteristics,* Final Report PC(1)-B1 United States Summary, 1972.

4. *The Social Economy of Cities,* ed. Gary Gappert and Harold M. Rose (Beverly Hills, Calif.: Sage Publications, 1975), pp. 43-44.

5. Wilson and Taeuber found a correlation of .87 between school segregation and residential segregation in their analysis of California school districts. Franklin D. Wilson and Karl E. Taeuber, "Residential and School Segregation: Some Tests of Their Association," in *The Demography of Racial and Ethnic Groups,* ed. Frank D. Bean and W. Parker Frisbie, (New York: Academic Press, 1978), pp. 51-78.

6. Harold X. Connolly, "Black Movement into the Suburbs: Suburbs Doubling Their Black Population During the Sixties," *Urban Affairs Quarterly* 9 (September 1973): 91-111.

7. Reynolds Farley, "The Changing Distribution of Negroes Within Metropolitan Areas: The Emergence of Black Suburbs," *American Journal of Sociology* 75 (January 1970): 512-29.

8. Rose, *Black Suburbanization;* Harold M. Rose, "The All-Negro Town. Its Evolution and Function," *Geographical Review,* 55 (July 1965): 362-81; Harold M. Rose, "The All-Black Town: Suburban Prototype or Rural Slum?" in *People and Politics in Urban Society,* ed.Harlan Hahn (Beverly Hills, Calif.: Sage Publications, 1972), pp. 397-431; and Leonard Blumberg and Michael Lalli, "Little Ghettoes: A study of Negroes in the Suburbs," *Phylon* 27 (Summer 1966): 117-31.

9. A similar procedure was utilized in a national study designed to identify and analyze integrated neighborhoods. Norman M. Bradburn, et al, *Racial Integration in American Neighborhoods: A Comparative Study* (Chicago: National Opinion Research Center, 1970).

10. Brian J.L. Berry and Donald C. Dahmann, *Population Distribution in the United States in the 1970s* (Washington D.C.: National Academy of Sciences, 1977); George Sternlieb and James W. Hughes, "New Regional and Metropolitan Realities of America," *Journal of the American Institute of Planners* 43 (July 1977): 227-41.

11. Avery M. Guest, "The Changing Racial Composition of Suburbs," *Urban Affairs Quarterly* 14 (December 1978): 195-206.

12. Forty-seven of the 440 suburban municipalities are combined within twenty-three regional or consolidated elementary school districts. In these cases, census and land use data for the individual municipalities have been combined, making the school district the unit of analysis. Another eleven municipalities, largely legal entities with minimal population, maintain no schools and have been deleted. Municipalities and school districts are coterminous in all other cases, making a total of 405 cases for the analysis.

13. Harvey H. Marshall and John M. Stahura, "Determinants of Black Suburbanization: Regional and Suburban Size Category Patterns," *The Sociological Quarterly* 20 (Spring 1979): 237-53; Harvey H. Marshall and John M. Stahura, "Black and White Population Growth in American Suburbs: Transition or Parallel Development?" *Social Forces* 58 (September 1979): 305-27; Thomas A. Clark, "Race, Class, and Suburbanization: Prior Trends and Policy Perspectives," unpublished paper (New Brunswick, N.J.: Rutgers University Department of Urban Planning and Policy Development, 1979).

14. Cases with zero black enrollment in 1971 were changed to one to avoid dividing by zero. Cases that were zero in both years were changed to one in the latter year as well, to avoid artificially showing a decrease. Then, because even relatively small increases from a very small base (say an increase from 1 to 10) would appear as extremely high growth rates, a fifth root transformation was applied (an odd-root transformation was required to accommodate negative changes). Finally, analysis of the change rate measure was weighted by total black enrollment in 1971 to further minimize distortions introduced by relatively small initial numbers.

15. Autocorrelation prohibits using community socioeconomic characteristics such as income or occupation in the analysis: there is no way of determining whether black increase is occurring because of a community's socioeconomic characteristics or whether these characteristics are due to the increasing black population.

16. Gunnar Olsson, *Distance and Human Interaction: A Review and Bibliography* (Philadelphia, Pa.: Regional Science Research Institute, 1965).

PART

II

PROCESS:

THE SUBURBAN
BLACK EXPERIENCE

5

THE CASE STUDY SETTING:
FIVE COMMUNITIES

INTRODUCTION

In this chapter we begin to narrow our attention to a finer focus, from broad national and statewide patterns to the richer complexity of the case study. The change in scale permits a shift from a description of trends to clarification of the processes that give rise to the trends. In this second part of the book, we seek to examine the communities within which black suburbanization is progressing and to compare the housing market experiences of black and white homebuyers within these communities.

Selection of case study communities was guided by the typology of suburban black communities described above and by the overall goals of the study. Comparison of the homebuying experiences of blacks and whites required identification of suburban communities in which black households are purchasing homes in sufficient numbers to be located and surveyed. The suburban typology delineates the types of communities likely to meet this criterion. Based on the analysis in Chapter 4, five suburban municipalities were selected as case study sites, encompassing a broad range of housing prices, income levels, proportion black population, and geographic location within the state (Exhibit 5-1). Three are central-city spillover communities, clearly the paramount black community category in the typology. These are Franklin Township, adjacent to New Brunswick; Ewing Township, adjacent to Trenton; and Pleasantville, adjacent to Atlantic City. The two remaining municipalities represent dormitory residential communities with relatively higher income and housing price levels. While most of the state's dormitory suburbs have no significant black population, those containing black concentrations account for the second largest recent absolute increase in suburban black population. Case study communities in this category include Teaneck Township, a suburb of New York City, and Montclair, located within the Newark metropolitan area. This chapter provides a profile on each of these communities as an introduction to the discussion in the remainder of the book. The Recent Buyers Survey conducted within these communities is described in Chapter 6.

The five communities encompass a substantial degree of diversity (Exhibit 5-2). Total population (1977) ranges in size from 40,000 in Montclair and Teaneck to 14,161 in Pleasantville, and ranges in percent black (1970) from 33 percent in Pleasantville to 9.3 percent in Ewing. Per capita income in 1977 was $9,648 in Montclair and only $4,515 in Pleasantville.[1] The communities also represent substantial historical variation: Franklin was incorporated in 1798, Teaneck in 1895, and Pleasantville in 1914. White response to integration varies similarly among the communities, from active integration management in Teaneck to defensive withdrawal in Franklin and benign neglect in Ewing.

While the communities are therefore economically, socially, and historically diverse, we have unavoidably omitted several components of the suburban black population by limiting analysis to these five sites. One such element is rural poverty-area black households within metropolitan boundaries. The preceding chapter, however, showed that while this group is relatively large in absolute terms, it is declining in numbers since 1970 and does not represent a focus of new black suburbanization. A second element not represented is the set of isolated affluent black pioneer households moving into all-white communities. As will be shown in Chapter 6, however, the analysis does include black households moving into all-white neighborhoods within each of the case study communities. A final caveat concerns the biracial nature of the five communities. These towns are not typical of all suburban communities if for no other reason than that they are all regionally identified as suburban communities

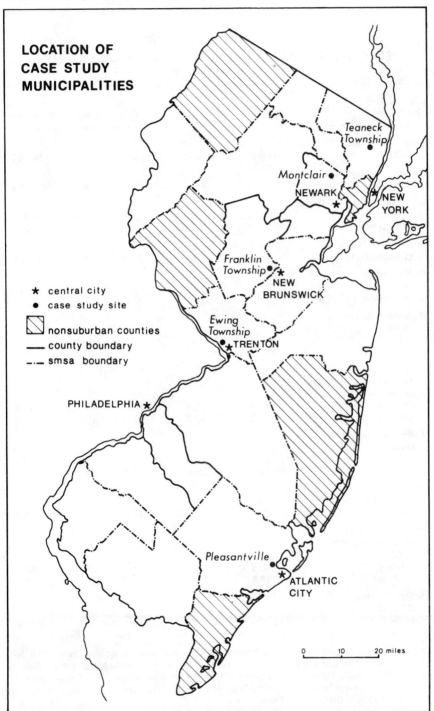

LOCATION OF
CASE STUDY
MUNICIPALITIES

Teaneck
Township

Montclair

NEWARK

NEW
YORK

Franklin
Township

NEW
BRUNSWICK

Ewing
Township

TRENTON

★ central city
● case study site
▨ nonsuburban counties
━ county boundary
─·─ smsa boundary

PHILADELPHIA

Pleasantville

ATLANTIC
CITY

0   10   20 miles

Exhibit 5-1. Location of Case Study Municipalities in New Jersey.

EXHIBIT 5-2
SELECTED SUMMARY CHARACTERISTICS OF CASE STUDY
COMMUNITIES

Community Characteristics	Montclair	Teaneck	Franklin	Ewing	Pleasantville
Total population, 1977	41,000	40,084	30,727	34,937	14,161
Percent change in total population, 1970-77	−6.9	−5.4	1.1	6.4	1.1
Black population, 1970					
Number	11,932	6,232	4,376	3,054	4,626
Percent of total	27.1	14.7	14.4	9.3	33.0
Percent black school enrollment, 1976	40.9	32.7	31.1	21.8	64.2
Percent change in black school enrollment, 1971-76	−9.9	18.5	15.3	2.1	10.5
Median family income, 1970					
Black	$ 8,981	$12,825	$ 9,973	$10,402	$ 7,024
White	17,897	16,603	13,701	12,722	8,395
Percent employed as professionals, managers, or administrators, 1970					
Black	17.4	25.1	15.5	12.7	11.1
White	45.2	40.9	33.9	28.0	14.9
Median school years completed, 1970					
Black	10.7	12.4	10.3	12.2	10.1
White	13.0	12.6	12.4	12.3	10.1
Percent of housing units in 1970 built since 1960	7.4	6.2	38.5	29.0	8.9
Percent of housing units owner-occupied, 1970					
Black	40.9	82.0	53.1	84.1	66.4
White	57.4	78.2	77.7	77.8	68.4
Median sale price of houses sold, 1978	$59,000	$54,500	$52,500	$41,500	$20,500

Sources: U.S. Bureau of the Census, Population Estimates and Projections, Series P-25, No. 843; Census of Population: 1970, General Population Characteristics, Final Report PC(1)-B32; New Jersey Department of Community Affairs, U.S. Census Data for New Jersey Townships, 1970; New Jersey State Treasury Department, Division of Taxation, Usable Sales Tapes.

to which blacks can move. While therefore largely atypical of the suburbs in general, taken together they are representative of communities involved in black suburbanization. By implication, disparities in the experiences of whites and blacks within these municipalities would be magnified severalfold in other, more exclusionary, suburbs.

Anticipating the discussion in Chapter 6, we have mapped neighborhood racial composition by census block for each of the five communities. Four neighborhood categories are defined on the basis of 1970 census block data by race and the race of new homebuyers moving into the block during the survey period, as described in Chapter 6. These neighborhood categories are as follows:

All-White: 1970 census block population less than 5 percent black; only white in-movers. Mean 1970 percent black on these blocks was 0.51.

Black-Entry: 1970 census block population less than 5 percent black; black in-movers during the study period. Mean 1970 percent black on these blocks was 0.63.

Inter-Racial: 1970 census block population more than 5 percent and less than 80 percent black. Mean 1970 percent black population was 29.3 percent.

All-Black: 1970 census block population more than 80 percent black. Mean 1970 percent black population on these blocks was 86.1.

TEANECK TOWNSHIP: MANAGING INTEGRATION

Located in Bergen County fifteen minutes by car from New York City via the George Washington Bridge, Teaneck is a pleasant dormitory suburb with attractive Tudor-style houses and an extensive system of parks and open space. Teaneck was the first suburban New Jersey community to voluntarily desegregate its public school system (in 1964), and it has attained a regional reputation as an integrated community. With a 14.7 percent black population in 1970 and sizable concentrations of Asian-Americans, East Indians, and Orthodox Jews, the community prides itself on its multi-ethnic character.

Teaneck experienced its peak population growth between 1920 and 1940, increasing from 4,192 to 25,275 in conjunction with the major thrust of suburban development in northern New Jersey occasioned by the opening of the George Washington Bridge in 1931. Total population reached 42,085 by 1960 but then increased by only 270 between 1960 and 1970 and declined to 40,089 by 1977. Median family income was above both county and state levels in 1970: $15,794 versus $13,597 and $11,407, respectively.[2] Nearly three-fourths of the work force is employed in white-collar occupations, and a third commutes to New York City for work.

The town exudes an air of residential respectability, with well-maintained, architecturally diverse homes on tree-lined streets. Effective use of zoning and land use planning has excluded heavy industry and confined commercial activities to several attractive neighborhood clusters. Teaneck has successfully avoided the strip commercial development characteristic of the suburban communities surrounding it and places great stock on maintaining a high level of aesthetic and environmental quality. The town can accurately be described as a middle-class, dormitory residential suburb graced with attractive homes, extensive recreational facilities, an excellent school system, and a high degree of participation in a wide array of civic and private clubs and organizations.

Teaneck is in Bergen County, whose 24,915 blacks comprised only 2.8 percent of the total county population in 1970. Eighty-two percent of the county's black population was located in Teaneck and the two adjacent communities of Englewood and Hackensack; the remainder was distributed over the other 67 municipalities in the county.[3] The population of Teaneck was less than 1 percent black until 1950. By 1960, it was 4.2 percent black and the percentage grew to 14.7 percent by 1970. The increase in proportion black during a period when total population was remaining stable and then decreasing suggests that white population is declining and that housing units are transferring from white to black occupancy.

The history of black residence in Teaneck is one of initial strenuous white resistance to the entry of black families, extended community conflict centering on the issue of school desegregation, eventual acceptance of integration, and recently, attempts to manage integration by continuing to attract white homebuyers to the community.[4]

A small number of black families lived in Teaneck in the 1920s, in the northeast corner of the town adjacent to the predominantly black Fourth Ward of Englewood, the neighboring municipality (Exhibit 5-3). Englewood's black population was initially composed of servants and domestics who, beginning at the turn of the century, arrived to work on the estates in the area. The few black families living in Teaneck were socially and economically tied to the larger black population in adjacent Englewood.

In 1945, the Teaneck Town Council erected a buffer zone, known as Argonne Park, between the all-white, developed section of Teaneck and the black families on the northeast border and in Englewood. The barrier of trees was planted over streets that had already been laid out with curbs, sewers, and sidewalks. In 1951, a black family bought land and built a house on the Teaneck side of Argonne Park. Several more black families moved in and, by 1954, extensive panic selling had ensued, fueled by block-busting activities of real estate agents who urged whites to sell before their property values dropped. Since few white families would buy homes in the northeast, and since white brokers within Teaneck would not represent black buyers, whites in the northeast wishing to sell listed their homes with black brokers in Englewood, accelerating the transition. Several informal block meetings of white homeowners were held in an attempt to allay fears and counter rumors being spread by brokers, and these informal networks joined to form the Teaneck Civic Conference in 1955. Efforts to improve inter-

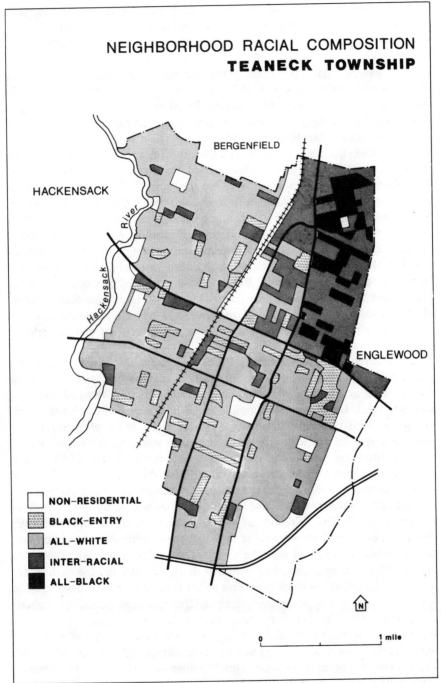

Exhibit 5-3. Neighborhood Racial Composition, Teaneck Township, New Jersey, 1978.

racial relations and encourage whites not to leave were largely unsuccessful. Whites in the northeast sector of Teaneck continued to move out, in spite of a lack of overt racial incidents, crime, or other evidence of neighborhood disintegration.

The Teaneck Civic Conference petitioned the town council to appoint a Human Relations Commission in 1956. This request was refused on the grounds that there was no problem. An Advisory Board on Community Relations was established the following year, however. Lacking enforcement powers, it served a public information function and publicized unethical practices of brokers. In 1959, the Civic Conference, the Bergen County Ethical Society, and clergymen of the National Council of Churches formed the Bergen County Fair Housing Committee, shifting the emphasis from the township to the county. The objective was to seek out white homeowners who were willing to sell their homes to blacks and list them with the Fair Housing Committee that, in turn, facilitated home inspection by black families. Monthly forums, sponsored by the Ethical Society, took up such issues as discrimination in housing. These early efforts of the Fair Housing Committee were unsuccessful. In three years they found a home for only one black family. Black demand continued to rise in the northeast section of Teaneck, since very few whites in other areas consented to sell to blacks. Also, blacks preferred not to move into all-white areas, and whites proved to be unreceptive to education about the virtues of integrated neighborhoods.

Racial tensions intensified and by 1961 began to coalesce around the issue of school desegregation. A referendum for a school addition to ease overcrowding was defeated on largely racial grounds and the superintendent resigned. The new superintendent, Dr. Harvey B. Scribner, came into a divided and hostile community in 1961. Instead of avoiding the racial issue, as his predecessors had done, he convinced the school board to establish a voluntary desegregation plan whereby black families in the northeast could transfer their children to any elementary school outside the black area, but whites could transfer their children only to the all-black Bryant Elementary School. The voluntary program was attacked by conservatives and liberals alike, as well as by the black community. Black families felt that the program placed an unfair burden on their children since they alone were asked to forfeit the benefits of the neighborhood school. Scribner was faced with the defeat of the voluntary desegregation plan and in 1963 drew up a mandatory plan that sought to centralize the sixth grades at Bryant School in the black area. This meant that the burden of desegregation was distributed among all families, since children had to be bussed throughout the community. The anti-integration, antibussing forces concentrated their efforts in an attempt to block Scribner's plan. Their organization of black and white families, the Neighborhood School Association, sought to gain support for the preservation of neighborhood schools. Other parents formed the Teaneck Citizens for the Public Schools, which campaigned vigorously for active integration, not merely in defense of the mandatory desegregation plan. The thrust of their argument was that quality education meant integrated education. They charged the opposition with being anti-education and argued that a good school system was the best guarantee of stable and rising property values.

Despite a large, vocal, and well-organized opposition, the Board of Education adopted the desegregation plan in 1964, and that fall Bryant School became the township school for all the sixth grades. The board argued that segregated housing patterns created imbalance in the schools, and that voluntary desegregation was better than waiting for a state-mandated plan. Teaneck was thus the first school district in the state to voluntarily desegregate its schools.

As a result of continued block busting and panic selling, the northeast sector had become predominantly black by the mid-1960s. The town council passed an antisolicitation ordinance in 1966, requiring real estate brokers to notify the town clerk in advance of any intended canvassing or solicitation aimed at encouraging owners to sell.[5] Block-busting activities and panic selling ceased under the combined impact of local ordinances and monitoring undertaken by the renamed Bergen County Fair Housing Council. Many of the most prejudiced whites left during the school desegregation conflict, and Teaneck in fact began to attract whites committed to the ideal of integration during the period of civil rights popularity in the sixties.

By the 1970s, organized community efforts had shifted to promoting Teaneck as an integrated community and managing the integration process. A voluntary organization called Teaneck Together was founded in 1972 with the primary objective of maintaining the attractiveness of Teaneck for white homebuyers. It induced the town council to budget $25,000 for a report by a New York City public affairs consulting firm that recommended ways "to attract to Teaneck many homeseekers who might otherwise fail to consider Teaneck as a place to live."[6] As a result of this report and the support of Teaneck Together, the town has established a Housing Information Office within the municipal government with a full-time paid public relations coordinator responsible for preparing and disseminating publicity about the advantages of living in Teaneck. The third principal accomplishment of Teaneck Together was the establishment of the Teaneck Housing Center. Financed by Community Development Block Grant Funds and a grant from the County Board of Freeholders, the Housing Center provides tours of Teaneck's neighborhoods and facilities for prospective homebuyers, publicizes the township's advantages with local employers, coordinates referrals of homebuyers to real estate brokers, and counsels minority residents about housing discrimination.[7] While these activities are being pursued within the community, the Bergen County Fair Housing Council has recently switched its focus to encouraging blacks to search for housing in the predominantly white communities outside of Teaneck, Englewood, and Hackensack.

A major attraction that Teaneck has consistently been able to offer is its exceptionally high quality public education system. Some 70 percent of 1978 high school graduates went on to college, and in 1976 Teaneck had the highest percentage of National Merit Scholarship semifinalists in the state. Residents today feel that the elementary schools are truly integrated, not simply desegregated. Social segregation is extremely strong among the teenage adolescent cohort, however. At the high school, there is an informally declared "white door" and a "black door," where each group enters the school and congregates during recesses and after school. Social activities at the high school are attended by blacks only, and neighborhood recreation centers and swimming pools geared to adolescents are de facto racially segregated.

Teaneck continues to attract both blacks and whites, and residents affirm a commitment to integration. The northeast section remains predominantly black; although blacks now have unimpeded access to the entire town, few whites, if any, are interested in or are shown houses in the northeast. The lack of social integration remains a challenge to Teaneck's residents.

MONTCLAIR: AFFLUENT SUBURB

Montclair is a well-to-do residential community located on the slopes of the Watchung Mountains two-and-one-half miles northwest of Newark. Residents differentiate informally between Upper Montclair, with large expensive homes and often palatial estates on the slopes and ridges, and Montclair proper, with smaller homes and the town's commercial center, on the flats. Montclair offers a stock of older, exceptionally well-built homes augmented by a rich store of community resources including an art museum (dating from 1914), a repertory theater, a local symphony orchestra, Montclair State College (a branch of the New Jersey State College system), and an excellent public school system. Wealthy black families in the Newark area tend to view Montclair as the pinnacle of social and geographic mobility: one moves from Newark to an apartment in East Orange to a home in Montclair as one climbs the social ladder. The area southeast of the business district, however, contains a concentration of low-income black households in substandard housing units. Montclair's black community is not only the largest but also the most heterogeneous of the five case study communities.

The development of suburban Montclair began in 1854 when the first railroad was built from Newark. It became a fashionable resort and residential area as wealthy families moved from the New York metropolitan area in search of fresh air and pleasant surroundings. The opening of the Greenwood Lake branch of the Erie-Lackawanna Railroad in 1873 resulted in rapid population growth, spurred further by the opening, despite vehement opposition from the wealthy older residents, of a trolley-car line from Newark in 1899. Total population, which was 2,853 in 1870, doubled by 1880 and increased fourfold between 1880 and 1910.[8] In-migration of middle-income white-collar workers continued until 1930, when total population reached 42,017. Population stabilized with the onset of the Depression, reaching only 44,043 by 1970, and declined by 6.9 percent between 1970 and 1977.

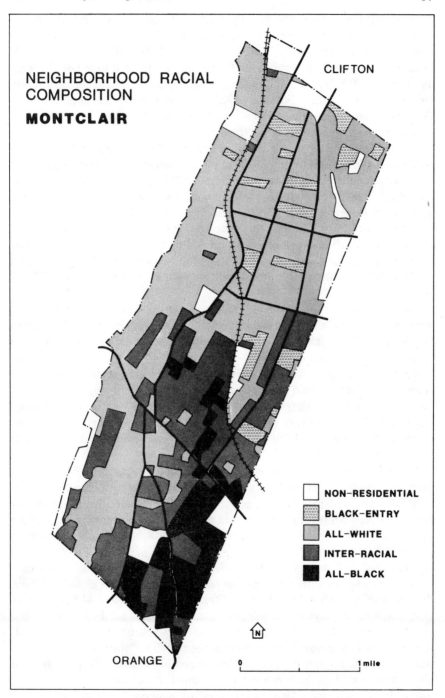

NEIGHBORHOOD RACIAL COMPOSITION

MONTCLAIR

CLIFTON

□ NON-RESIDENTIAL
▦ BLACK-ENTRY
▨ ALL-WHITE
▨ INTER-RACIAL
■ ALL-BLACK

N

ORANGE

0 _____ 1 mile

Exhibit 5-4. Neighborhood Racial Composition, Montclair, New Jersey, 1978.

Montclair remains a predominantly residential community with over 60 percent of its land area devoted to housing, only 3.3 percent in industry and commercial uses, and nearly 7 percent in parks. Fully 78 percent of its 1970 housing units were built prior to 1940, and only 7.4 percent were built between 1960 and 1970.[9] Housing values are generally higher in Montclair than in surrounding municipalities, but the housing stock varies from large architect-designed mansions in the affluent neighborhoods to older homes with incomplete plumbing facilities in the town center.

Unlike the relatively recent arrival of blacks in Teaneck, blacks first migrated to Montclair in the 1860s and 1870s to work as servants on the white estates.[10] The black population increased from 36 in 1870 to 1,344 in 1900, when blacks comprised 9.6 percent of the total population. This proportion increased steadily, to 15 percent in 1930, 20.7 percent in 1950, 24.1 percent in 1960, and 27.8 percent in 1970. The regional concentration of blacks in Montclair parallels that of Teaneck. Blacks comprised 31 percent of the total population of Essex County in 1970: of these, 74 percent resided in Newark, and 24 percent resided in Montclair and three other municipalities, each with more than 1,000 black residents.

According to a 1935 study by the New Jersey Conference of Social Work, some 90 percent of employed blacks in Montclair at that time worked as domestics. Most black households lived in the southeast section but a few blacks lived throughout the town, some as live-in domestics and some as a result of employers willing property to their servants. The 1935 survey revealed "great overcrowding in the colored districts of Montclair" and "a great amount of unemployment and a relatively low wage level for those who were employed." Educational levels were very low ("seventy-two percent had taken some elementary school training") and "fifty-seven percent of the families receiving relief in Montclair were Negroes."[11]

In 1947, a report on racial conditions in Montclair prepared for the Presidential Commission on Civil Rights motivated the town to perform a community audit of assets and liabilities in race relations. Cosponsored by the Montclair Forum, a liberal white reform group, and the American Veterans Committee, the audit documented the inequalities between black and white residents in the areas of education, housing employment, public health, public facilities, religious organizations, and recreation. The audit showed that most blacks held only menial jobs, that restaurants and private recreational clubs were closed to blacks, that the YMCA and YWCA had separate facilities for blacks and whites, and that local hospitals employed discriminatory hiring practices for both doctors and nurses. Blacks could not buy homes in white neighborhoods, and the schools were effectively segregated, since through the so-called "optional area" system, white parents could transfer their children to another school if the proportion of black children in the neighborhood school seemed unacceptable.

The 1947 audit had a gradual effect in lessening overt discrimination. The police force hired additional black personnel, discrimination in restaurants and retail stores decreased "under the spotlight of publicity," and by 1953 the YM-YWCA abolished its policy of racial separation and combined its facilities.[12] Also as a result of the 1947 audit, the Montclair Town Commission established a Civil Rights Commission in 1949 to enforce compliance with state anti-discrimination laws.

An updating of the 1947 audit was undertaken in 1964, inspired by the 1960s national civil rights movement. A member of the YWCA Board of Directors returned from the 1963 "Freedom March" in Washington, D.C. inspired to "do something" about racial inequality in Montclair. The 1964 audit followed a public policy statement by the Town Commission supporting an end to racial discrimination, and was cosponsored by representatives of the YWCA, the NAACP, the Montclair Civil Rights Commission, B'nai B'rith, and several other local religious and civic organizations.[13] The survey found some improvement since 1947 as well as substantial evidence of continuing racial inequality. While the optional area plan in the schools had been abolished, most elementary schools were highly segregated as a result of residential segregation. Private and parochial schools in Montclair were all white. Seemingly harking back to an earlier era, the 1964 audit noted that "the Health Department in 1962 reported that 71 percent of the tuberculosis cases and 70 percent of the infant mortality were located in the 18 percent of the Town area where 84 percent of the non-white population live." The Montclair Fair Housing Committee, established by the Town Commission to counter racial discrimination in housing, was proving relatively ineffectual. The few blacks who succeeded in buying homes in white neighborhoods did so privately, without a broker's services. The 1964 audit reported that "it is almost impossible for a Negro to rent an apartment in an all-white apartment building. There are apartment houses, some of them fine ones, wholly Negro occupied but there is only one integrated apartment house . . ."

An antiblockbusting ordinance was passed in 1963, and although whites continue to fear concentrations of blacks, there has been little evidence of panic selling in newly integrated neighborhoods. The high value, architectural distinctiveness, and exceptionally high quality of Montclair's older housing would be difficult to duplicate elsewhere and may provide a disincentive to white out-migration. The 1964 community audit credits a few Montclair real estate brokers with serving as a stabilizing influence in newly integrated neighborhoods, in some cases discouraging panic selling among whites by calling homeowners and urging them to remain. Montclair brokers have formed a separate Montclair Multiple Listing Service that effectively keeps information about housing availability within the confines of the town.

Montclair continues to attract higher-income black families from the Newark and New York metropolitan areas, most of whom commute to white-collar jobs in New York City. Present black residents claim that blacks can now purchase homes anywhere in the community that they can afford.

Montclair leads the county and state in per capita expenditures for education.

Under a 1977 state mandate to correct racial imbalance, the school system instituted an innovative desegregation magnet plan involving a combination of voluntary transfers and managed racial balance. The plan redrew district lines and reorganized grades K-4. A "gifted and talented" magnet school was located in the heavily black southeast section and a "fundamental" magnet school, emphasizing basic skills, was located in the north. Under a freedom-of-choice option, parents apply to the elementary school of their choice. Admission is granted as long as no overcrowding results and the racial balance is maintained. The racial distribution in the schools is carefully monitored: in September 1977, no school had less than 32.5 percent or more than 50.5 percent black enrollment. Of an elementary school population of 2,800, approximately 1,700 have chosen the magnet programs. More than half the children are voluntarily bussed, and there has been an overall increase in school enrollment.

Despite the racial balance in the schools and the increasing neighborhood integration, Montclair, as with Teaneck, is socially divided. No blacks belong— and probably have not applied—to the Montclair Country Club. Respective black and white elites have established separate organizations and mutually exclusive social networks. While the pressure for desegregation in Teaneck grew initially from a faction within the white community, the longstanding black community in Montclair provided—and continues to provide—its own leadership. The existence of separate elites within Montclair, however, has perpetuated a sense of mutual coexistence and noblesse oblige rather than social acceptance.

FRANKLIN TOWNSHIP: WHITE DEFENSIVENESS

Franklin Township, a rapidly developing community adjacent to the central city of New Brunswick, began the transition from rural to suburban in the 1950s. Eighty percent of developable land in the township is still vacant, and nearly three-fourths of housing units in 1970 were built since 1950. The densest development is in the northern and eastern portions of the township nearest New Brunswick, which gives way to farmland and open space to the south (Exhibit 5-5). Containing moderately priced housing units, located near several large corporate employers (AT&T, Johnson and Johnson, etc.), and well-served by a network of interstate highways and commuter railroads, Franklin is a popular destination for mid-level, white-collar corporate relocatees. The prevalence of corporate transfers and the high rate of new housing construction account for an exceptionally high rate of population turnover: a fourth of all households in 1970 lived in their current unit less than three years.[14]

Originally settled by the Dutch and incorporated in 1798, Franklin gained early prominence through its location on the major highway and canal route between New York and Philadelphia. Franklin has throughout its history been the home of several national and ethnic groups that formed separate and distinct communities within the township. Seventy acres of land were bought in 1925 by a group of Norwegian longshoremen from Brooklyn who formed a community

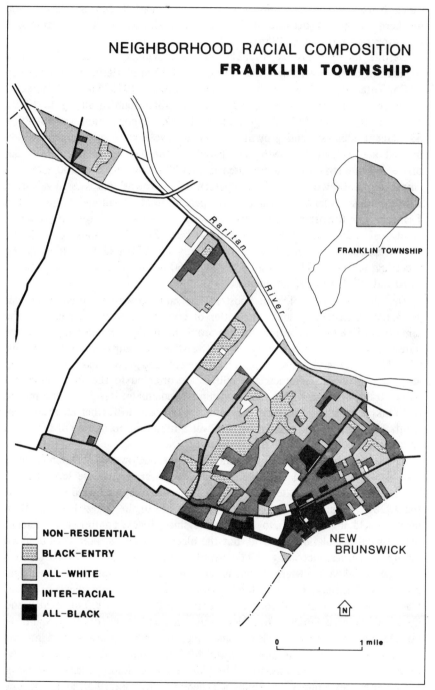

Exhibit 5-5 Neighborhood Racial Composition, Franklin Township, New Jersey, 1978.

called Norseville.[15] Many residents of the northeast section are eastern and southern Europeans; because of these ties, Franklin served as a reception area for Hungarian refugees in 1956.

Despite its early history, Franklin was overwhelmingly rural and the total population of the township remained under 3,000 until 1930, when it reached 5,675. Total population grew by 42 percent between 1930 and 1940, increased 62 percent from 1940 to 1950, and then more than doubled during the 1950s, reaching 19,858 by 1960. Ten years later, Franklin's population was 30,389, a 53 percent increase, and growth appears to have slowed subsequently. Commercial and industrial growth have paralleled the increase in population. Six office and industrial parks are located in Franklin, covering over 900 acres and employing 2,500 workers.[16] Eleven percent of the township's assessed valuation is from industrial land, compared to 0.1 percent in Montclair and 2.3 percent in Teaneck. The township's Industrial Committee is actively engaged in attracting additional industrial employment and ratables. Franklin's housing stock has grown apace: 38.5 percent of housing units in 1970 had been built in the preceding ten years. The township added 1,460 net new housing units between 1970 and 1977, a 17 percent increase.[17]

Despite the claims of local boosters, the rapid growth in recent years has given rise to instability and is a matter of concern to many residents. At the same time, Franklin is confronted with problems of physical deterioration in the oldest and most densely populated northeast section adjacent to New Brunswick. Municipal services are at times hard pressed, and growth has been criticized as poorly planned. Commercial facilities are oriented to the automobile and public transportation within the township is inadequate. Residents who moved to Franklin because of its rural character are opposed to further rapid development. The high rate of population turnover inhibits the formation of social ties and weakens commitment to the community.

The earliest black residents of Franklin were slaves owned by Dutch farmers, and blacks who arrived later were employed as farmers, house servants, and blacksmiths. Blacks migrated to Franklin as part of the northward migration of the 1920s, but in 1923 the township was the site of the largest Ku Klux Klan meeting held in the North to that date or since. Blacks comprised 10 percent of the total population in 1960, but the black population more than doubled during the sixties, increasing 159.6 percent between 1960 and 1974. Part of this increase is linked to deterioration, urban renewal, and displacement in neighboring New Brunswick during the period. An additional component of recent black growth is attributed to the accelerated influx since 1960 of middle- and upper-middle class families from New Brunswick and New York City, and from outside the region. Black employees and executive personnel transferred into the area are often directed to the township by both employers and corporate relocation services that have identified Franklin as a community amenable to black entry. Somerset County was only 4.2 percent black in 1970, and only one municipality in the county in addition to Franklin had more than 1,000 black residents in that year.[18] By 1974, the 5,168 blacks in Franklin comprised 16.2 percent of the township's total population.

Initial racial conflict in Franklin's "suburban" era centered on the housing issue. Pine Grove Manor, a 398-unit cooperative apartment development insured under Section 213 of the 1949 Housing Act, opened the first of four sections in 1957. Under the cooperative arrangement, tenants bought shares in the cooperative association and signed an occupancy agreement equivalent to a lease. The apartments were relatively affordable: the initial downpayment fee required for the two- and three-bedroom units was approximately $500. Because FHA regulations required a certain percentage of units to be subscribed prior to construction, Pine Grove's four sections were divided into four separate corporations with autonomous tenant selection and governing powers. Advertisements for the apartments were concentrated primarily in New York City; all residents of the first section to open were white, and many were Jewish. The cooperative was a highly active community that published its own newspaper, established the town's first cooperative nursery and day care center, and founded the first library.

The initial rate of black entry to Pine Grove Manor was slow, and the managing board followed a policy of avoiding concentrations of black households in particular sections of the development. At the time that the fourth section opened in 1959, some 5 to 7 percent of residents were black. In 1960, the oldest section of Pine Grove was cited for discrimination by the state Human Rights Commission for rejecting a nonwhite applicant. The board of Section One signed a consent decree agreeing to nondiscriminatory tenant selection and the boards of the other three sections followed suit. The rate of racial transition increased sharply thereafter and by 1963 10 percent of total units were vacant and 12 percent of occupied units were black. The proportion black increased to 22 percent in 1966, and in the following year, financial problems stemming from high turnover and high vacancy rates led to foreclosure of the mortgage that was assumed by FHA.

The change in fortunes of Pine Grove Manor was closely tied to developments in the surrounding area. In December 1958, the Franklin Housing Authority opened 100 units of public housing on a site adjacent to Pine Grove. The Park Side housing project was the only public housing built in Franklin and was nearly 100 percent black from its inception. An attractive, low-cost alternative to Pine Grove became available in 1963 (the same year that vacancies in the cooperative increased dramatically) with the opening of a 1,400-home Levitt development within a radius of two miles of Pine Grove. The low downpayment requirements and perceived advantages of homeownership were competitive with the two- and three-bedroom apartments and induced many white residents to move from Pine Grove. Finally, white flight from Pine Grove may have been accelerated by rapid racial transition occurring simultaneously in a single-family subdivision adjacent to the cooperative known as Hollywood Homes. Opened in 1952, Hollywood Homes was the first postwar subdivision developed in Franklin, with fifty small, inexpensive single-family homes. The first black family purchased a home there in 1956, but rapid transition began in 1960 and the development was approximately one-third black by 1966.

The combination of an increasing proportion of blacks in surrounding areas, the agreement barring discrimination in tenant selection, and the availability of affordable alternatives close at hand prompted white abandonment of Pine Grove Manor, which led to its ultimate foreclosure. In 1970, the agent managing Pine Grove for HUD was charged with discrimination after twelve black families were threatened with eviction. All twelve had been active in complaining about poor maintenance and services. Investigations by the Franklin Human Relations Commission, the State Division of Civil Rights, and HUD led to reinstatement of the tenants. Pine Grove was sold in 1974 to a private developer; the apartments are poorly maintained, rents are federally subsidized, and 82 percent of the units are black-occupied.

Increased residential segregation has had its counterpart in segregated schools. Franklin was among the 103 New Jersey school districts mandated by the State Office of Equal Educational Opportunity (OEEO) to desegregate its elementary schools in 1977. Emotional debate flared over alternative plans to satisfy the state mandate, and more than thirty desegregation proposals were considered.[19] The final plan was implemented without incident, but many white families have enrolled their children in private or parochial schools. Periodic fights and racial incidents continued to erupt during the 1960s and early 1970s, especially in the high school. The resumption of high school social activities in September 1974 after a three-year ban was cause for comment in local newspapers, but renewed conflict broke out again the following February.[20] Both blacks and whites are concerned about the quality of education in the Franklin school system, and complaints about lack of discipline in the schools have become a euphemism for racial conflict.

Continuing conflict over both schools and housing have led to polarization and a sense of defensiveness. The pervasive sense is one of careful monitoring of racial balances with little commitment to either the overall community or the solution of its problems. Most residents of Franklin are recent arrivals, and few have established strong ties to the community. The absence of higher-value housing within the township leaves no anchor to hold the upwardly mobile, and these families leave for more affluent communities. Many white residents, particularly those transferred to the area, are in Franklin more of necessity than by choice. The Levitt and similar developments provide affordable housing with complete appliances and a convenient location, and the unit can be resold easily at the next transfer. An additional factor may be that Franklin provides housing for short-term transferees that white families seeking a more permanent residence may avoid. The resulting instability breeds a lack of commitment. Private or parochial school enrollment provides a short-term expedient that obviates the need to work for quality public schools. In the housing arena, whites tend to monitor the turnover of units in their neighborhood and white-to-black transition proceeds on a block-by-block basis. The extent of continued racial conflict in Franklin appears to be largely dependent on the future black growth rate.

EWING TOWNSHIP: THE INVISIBLE MINORITY

Ewing Township is adjacent to Trenton, New Jersey's state capital and fourth largest city. Ewing's black population is smallest in absolute numbers (3,054 in 1970) and lowest in proportion to total population (9.3 percent) of the five case study communities. As in Franklin Township, Ewing's history antedates the Revolutionary War—as part of Trenton Township it was considered as a site for the national capital until Washington opted for proximity to Virginia—but its present character is a product of postwar suburbanization. A General Motors production plant, opened in 1938, provides a third of the private-sector employment within the township. Proximity to the state capital, however, sets Ewing's predominant traits: 29 percent of the land area is owned by the municipal, state, and federal governments and 32 percent of employed residents are government workers. Public facilities located in Ewing include the State Police Training School, the State School for the Deaf, the State Mental Hospital, the State Home for Girls, Trenton State College, Mercer County Airport, and an adjacent Naval Air Station. The mid-priced housing stock in Ewing is commensurate with the predominantly blue-collar and government employment characteristic of township residents.

Ewing's total population of 6,942 in 1930 increased steadily for the next three decades, growing by increments of 50 to 60 percent in each ten-year period. Total population reached 26,628 by 1960 but then increased by only 23 percent between 1960 and 1970. Unlike the other case study communities, which have shown no growth or a decrease since 1970, Ewing's population increased by a further 6.4 percent between 1970 and 1977.

Ewing's black population increased at nearly double the rate of the white population between 1950 and 1970. The greatest discrepancy occurred during the 1960s, when black growth outpaced that of whites by a factor of four. The initial base was quite small, however, and although black population increased by 169 percent over the twenty-year period, the black proportion of the total population remained less than 10 percent. Ewing's black population in 1970 was the largest in absolute terms of all municipalities in Mercer County with the exception of Trenton. While Princeton had a slightly higher proportion of blacks (10 percent vs. 9.3 percent in Ewing), Ewing exceeded Princeton in absolute numbers of blacks by nearly three to one.

A large supply of four- to five-room ranch sytle homes was built in Ewing during World War II to house workers at the GM plant and in related defense industries. These wartime tract homes sold for approximately $4,000 when built in the 1940s and sell for perhaps $25,000 today. This inexpensive stock provided affordable housing for upwardly mobile black families moving from Trenton in the postwar period. The black families who moved from Trenton to Ewing beginning in the 1950s were skilled workers and small entrepreneurs with steady incomes and respected positions within the black community. Among them were workers at the GM plant, teachers, those who owned their own businesses such as beauty shops that catered to a black clientele, domestics for private families in nearby Princeton, and waiters and maitre d's in exclusive clubs, the latter considered a prestigious position in the black community. In 1970, 36.2 percent of employed blacks in Ewing were government workers.[21] Ewing's black population has traditionally been upwardly mobile, internally cohesive, and socially independent of the white community. In 1970, a higher proportion of black housing units (84 percent) than white units (78 percent) were owner-occupied.

Early black population growth in Ewing was confined to three small neighborhoods that by the mid-1950s were almost entirely black (Exhibit 5-6). The first of these was an approximately eight-block area in the extreme southeastern corner of Ewing directly adjacent to Trenton. Separated from the rest of the township by a railroad line and warehouse district, this small area of low-value housing was more an extension of Trenton than an integral part of Ewing. The adjacent neighborhood of Prospect Park, also in the southeast corner of the township, was occupied by higher-status black families representing the remains of southern black bourgeoisie in the Trenton area. Prospect Park has maintained its status within the black community over time. The third black concentration was in the blue-collar neighborhood of Ewing Park in the central, densely developed section of the township. Black growth in Ewing Park occurred through in-filling on vacant land rather than outward growth. New residents of this area have tended to be of higher income and occupational status than existing residents, resulting in an upgrading of socioeconomic status over time. Recent trends have seen a slight relaxation of territorial restrictions on black residence in Ewing. Two newer postwar housing developments to the east and west of the central black neighborhood of Ewing Park have become predominantly black since the 1960s. Most neighborhoods are said to have achieved at least token integration in recent years.

As in each of the other case study communities, residential segregation in Ewing was reflected in segregated schools. The school issue became the primary arena for racial conflict in a community in which both blacks and whites maintained otherwise self-sufficient independent lives with little basis for interaction. Ewing received its desegregation notification from the state Office of Equal Educational Opportunity (OEEO) in late 1969, setting an implementation deadline of September 1971 under threat of losing approximately $1 million in state and federal aid. A 65-member Citizens Advisory Committee, representing as many community and civic organizations, was formed in January 1970 to prepare recommendations for desegregation strategies for the Board of Education.[22] The plan finally implemented maintained neighborhood elementary schools for grades K-5 and established a community-wide "middle school" (grades 6 and 7) and a "central school" (grades 8 and 9).[23] The only bussing instituted for maintaining a racial balance is from the central all-black Ewing Park area to two

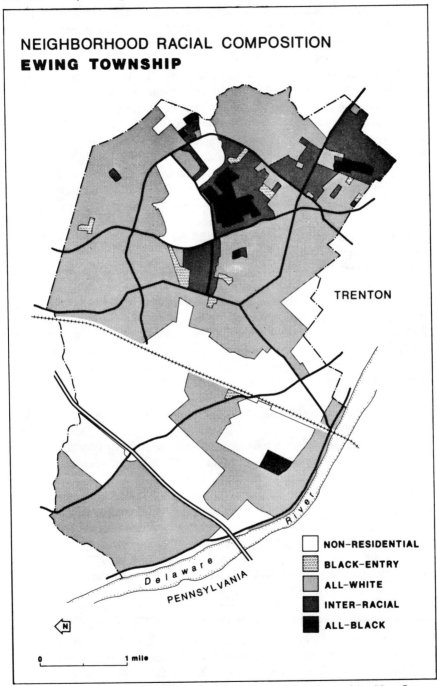

Exhibit 5-6. Neighborhood Racial Composition, Ewing Township, New Jersey, 1978.

newer all-white schools in high-income subdivisions in the western part of the township. The desegregation plan won acceptance by not requiring the bussing of white school children.[24]

Black political involvement in the township is generally restricted to the schools, in part indicative of the commitment to education on the part of the upwardly mobile and also reflecting the role of the schools as one of the few common meeting grounds for whites and black. Currently, two members of the nine-member board of education are black, and one or two positions on the board have traditionally been claimed by the black community. Often half of the attenders at board of education meetings are black, a proportion far in excess of black representation in the total population. At the same time, there are no blacks on the Township Committee, and according to community informants none have run for election to the committee. Social and civic organizations in Ewing are segregated, as are the churches with one exception.

With the single significant exception of the schools, the black and white communities in Ewing are substantially separate. The general absence of overt racial conflict is largely attributable to minimum contact between the two groups. Ewing's black population is small in numbers compared to the other case study communities, and while it has increased gradually over time, blacks have maintained roughly the same proportion of total population for several decades. Black families moving to Ewing in recent years are on average higher in socioeconomic status than existing whites, somewhat mitigating white fears of neighborhood deterioration. To an even greater extent than the other four sites, Ewing is a biracial rather than an integrated community.

PLEASANTVILLE: BLUE-COLLAR SEPARATISM

Pleasantville, the nearest mainland community to Atlantic City, has seen its fortunes rise and fall in lockstep with those of the resort city across the causeway. A blue-collar community, one-third black in 1970, with low-value housing and a deteriorating commercial core, Pleasantville has traditionally served as the service hinterland for Atlantic City. Pleasantville lost a fourth of its white population during the 1960s, a period of decline in the nearby resorts, while the black population increased by nearly 70 percent. Retailing, wholesaling, and services dominate the employment opportunities for residents and 1977 per capita income in Pleasantville was one-third less than in the state as a whole.

Early settlers of the area, most of whom were English, were employed in fishing and whaling and carted oysters and clams to Philadelphia, sixty miles away. Although the area was settled as early as 1660, the City of Pleasantville was not incorporated until 1914. Pleasantville grew as railroad lines were built first from Philadelphia in 1854 and then from the north as the popularity of the beach and resort communities increased. The town's population doubled between 1900 and 1910, reaching a total of 4,390. The period of greatest growth followed World War I, with the population doubling again from 5,887 to 11,580 between 1920 and 1930. Both Pleasantville and Atlantic City suffered a net loss of population during the Depression years, showed a slight increase during the 1940s and 1950s, and then declined during the 1960s. Pleasantville's 7.7 percent decrease in total population between 1960 and 1970 masked a substantial exchange of whites and blacks: the loss of 3,046 whites during the decade was only partially offset by a gain of 1,881 blacks.[25]

The first blacks to live in Pleasantville were slaves in the 1700s, and the black population increased gradually in proportion to the growth of the town. Many present black families are third or fourth generation residents. Black maids and service employees working in Atlantic City came to live in Pleasantville in the 1920s, further reinforcing the town's biracial character. Residential patterns, however, traditionally have been strictly segregated, with whites living to the east (the bay side) of Main Street, the principal north-south thoroughfare, and blacks concentrated on the west or inland side (Exhibit 5-7). The population shifts of the 1960s tended to blur this boundary somewhat when blacks began to move into formerly all-white neighborhoods as the black proportion of the total population increased from 18 to 33 percent.

Pleasantville's role as transportation terminal and service base for Atlantic City has dominated the town's development. The railroad lines built through Pleasantville in 1854 provided the initial spur to growth. (The railroad connection to Philadelphia was duplicated in the 1960s with construction of the Atlantic City Expressway through Pleasantville.) Infrastructure development was boosted with construction in Pleasantville in 1893 of the Atlantic City Water Company pumping facilities. The surge of population growth at the beginning of the century caused a real estate boom. Four of the town's five elementary schools date from before 1925, and the high school (now the junior high) was built in 1916. Although the city was subdivided in the 1920s, houses were constructed individually as residents bought lots and built on them. Initial development was consequently scattered, and a few small Cape Cods were built on vacant in-fill lots during the brief period of rejuvenation during the postwar years in the 1950s. Sixty-four percent of total housing units were built before 1940; only 440 units were built in Pleasantville during the entire decade of the 1960s, and 38 percent of these were rental units. Housing units in Pleasantville are of very low value. The median value of units in 1970 ($11,000) was 25 percent below the median for Atlantic County ($14,700) and less than half the median for the state as a whole ($23,400). The median value of all homes sold in Pleasantville in 1978 was only one-third the value of homes sold in Teaneck, Montclair, and Franklin, and half the value of homes sold in Ewing.

The occupational characteristics of residents reflect the town's position as compared to the nearby resorts. The largest categories among whites (1970) are sales and clerical (27.5 percent), craftsmen (20.2 percent) and service workers (16.0 percent). Service employment accounts for nearly one-third (31.3 percent) of Pleasantville's black workforce, followed by operatives (22.8 percent) and sales and clerical workers (16.8 percent). Nearly 6 percent of blacks (only 0.1

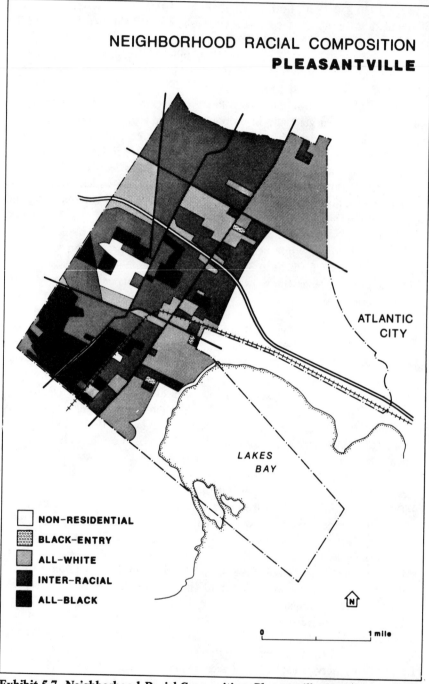

Exhibit 5-7. Neighborhood Racial Composition, Pleasantville, New Jersey, 1978.

percent of whites) are still employed as private household workers, but nearly equal proportions of blacks and whites (8.3 percent) have professional or technical positions. These proportions are unlikely to have changed considerably since 1970; the largest employment increases in the first nine months of 1979 for Atlantic County as a whole were in the construction and service categories.[26] The preponderance of resort-oriented employment in Pleasantville has traditionally led to great season fluctuations, and crime rates rose during the winter in step with unemployment. Year-round employment provided by recent casino development in Atlantic City is expected to dampen seasonal unemployment; the larger hotels no longer lay off their workforce during the winter.

Problems of physical deterioration and economic stagnation in Pleasantville impact equally on blacks and whites. As the second largest municipality in Atlantic County, Pleasantville was formerly the major commercial and shopping center for the mainland. The opening of three nearby suburban shopping centers in the mid-1960s undermined the town's economic base, and the Main Street shopping district is now dilapidated with many vacant and rundown stores. A Main Street Merchants Association is attempting to upgrade the area, using Community Development Block Grant funds to improve street lighting and security. As a result of deterioration of the tax base, the city tax rate increased by nearly 40 percent between 1960 and 1972, causing further problems in the town's ability to provide municipal services.

General housing quality is commensurate with the age and low value of units. A code enforcement program and a housing rehabilitation loan program have been initiated, but these attempts suffered from initial mismanagement and an extremely limited number of loans have actually been made available.

Educational quality in the public schools is low, as is morale among administrators and staff. White parents generally send their children to parochial or private schools, and public school enrollment was 64.2 percent black in 1976. The public schools were completely segregated through the 1950s. The subsequent decline in white enrollment and the increase in black representation throughout the school system obviated the need for bussing, and a state-mandated desegregation plan was never implemented.

The advent of casino development in Atlantic City has generated both problems and benefits for Pleasantville. As the closest mainland community, the town has experienced development pressure and an increase in land values. This has been a boon to homeowners but low-income renters are being priced out of the market as some of the newer rental structures are being purchased and renovated for use by hotel and casino employees. New casino-related developments in Pleasantville include a laundry employing 200 that serves the casinos, a soft drink distribution warehouse, and a 224-unit condominium currently under construction. Possible future development includes a 140-acre shopping center being proposed by the Rouse Corporation and 400 units of rental apartments being planned by Holiday Inn. While these developments will undoubtedly benefit the municipality, they will also be accompanied by substantial gentrification and low-income households are likely to be displaced.

Current black and white residents of Pleasantville share a similarity in income, educational attainment, and occupational characteristics, and are influenced alike by social and economic developments affecting the town. The town nonetheless continues to be socially and residentially segregated, and there is little communication between the black and white communities. Blacks control the Board of Education, perhaps reflecting white abandonment of the public schools, but have little political influence elsewhere in municipal government. Most municipal personnel are white.[27] Social clubs and civic organizations are all white; blacks look to Atlantic City for participation in social, civic, and fraternal organizations. Neither the substantial problems confronting the community nor the potential benefits that may be derived from the resurgence of growth are likely to overcome the barriers of segregation that have been historically perpetuated in Pleasantville.

SUMMARY

The five communities represent the range of settings encompassing the growth of the suburban black population. Their differences accent the complexity of the problem while their similarities reflect basic commonalities in the suburban black experience.

Contrasts can be quickly summarized. An interracial coalition in Teaneck is publicly and proudly pursuing an activist model of integration maintenance. The large well-established affluent black community in Montclair is relatively isolated from and independent of the more affluent white population. In Franklin, high population turnover coupled with the instability of rapid growth have generated the greatest potential among the five towns for continuing overt conflict between whites and blacks. Relative stability has been achieved in Ewing through the relatively small size of the black population and the cessation of further growth, reflecting the stagnation of Trenton. Pleasantville remains caught between a bleak past and an uncertain future in which an investment boom would most likely mean displacement of poor blacks in the classic urban renewal solution of the 1960s.

The similarities among these towns are striking even given these contrasts. Each of the five communities represents one of the few opportunities within its region—if not the only opportunity—for blacks to find a suburban housing unit in a biracial community. A black family purchasing a home in most neighboring communities must be prepared for social isolation and potential harassment. Second, each of the five communities represents regional racial distributions in microcosm: each has a predominantly black area, extensive all-white areas, and various degrees of integration in between. However, most racial barriers to access to housing *within* each of these communities have been virtually eliminated, and units pass freely from white to black occupancy. This appears due in part to structural demographic shifts as well as to the peculiarities of local developments within each community. Structurally, recent black increases are occurring in a period in which the white population is decreasing or at best remaining stable. The result is that blacks must replace whites in housing units or the units will remain vacant. The lack of internal barriers is also attributable to local community idiosyncracies. In Teaneck, this has been the result of some thirty years of conflict, litigation, and ultimately, consensus building. It has been achieved in Montclair by a somewhat more covert process of interest group mobilization and internal political maneuvering. The likelihood of overt discrimination is perhaps greatest in Franklin, but here continued new housing construction and the virtually unlimited supply of developable land provide an escape valve for whites and defuse the potential for racial competition for available housing. The lack of further black population growth in Ewing may alleviate white fears of "tipping" given initial black entry. In Pleasantville black access is assured by the virtual absence of white housing demand. As a result, with the exception of units in the predominantly black neighborhoods, housing in each of the communities passes relatively freely between whites and blacks. This will prove to be significant in the discussion of housing prices in Chapter 8.

NOTES

1. U.S. Bureau of the Census, *1977 Population Estimates for Counties, Incorporated Places, and Minor Civil Divisions in New Jersey,* Current Population Reports, Population Estimates and Projections, Series P-25, No. 843, 1979; U.S. Bureau of the Census, *1977 Per Capita Income Estimates for States, Counties, Incorporated Places, and Select Minor Civil Divisions in the Northeast Region of the United States,* Current Population Reports, Population Estimates and Projections, Series P-25, No. 882, 1980.

2. New Jersey Department of Community Affairs, *U.S. Census Data for New Jersey Townships, 1970* (Trenton: New Jersey Department of Community Affairs, 1975).

3. U.S. Bureau of the Census, *General Population Characteristics,* Census of Population: 1970. Final Report PC(1)-B32 New Jersey, 1971.

4. Much of the history of black residence and white response in Teaneck is drawn from Reginald G. Damerell, *Triumph in a White Suburb* (New York: William Morrow, 1968).

5. The Code of the Township of Teaneck, N.J., *General Ordinances of the Township.* Section 26-22.1 contains the limitations on real estate canvassing. Further, Section 26-22.3 declares that it is unlawful to "attempt to induce directly or indirectly the sale or listing for sale of real property by representing that an adverse change has occurred or will or may occur with respect to the racial, religious or ethnic composition of the block, neighborhood or area in which the property is located" or to induce real estate listings by "representing that the presence or anticipated presence of persons of any

particular race, religion or national origin in the area will or may result in: (1) the lowering of property values. (2) an increase in the criminal or anti-social behavior in the area. (3) a decline in the quality of the schools serving the area."

6. "Council Urged to Enact Public Relations Plan Information Program to Attract Residents," *Teaneck Together,* Vol. 3, No. 1 (1976), p. 1.

7. Marc Duvoisin, "How Teaneck Overcame its Image Problems," *The Bergen Record,* January 14, 1980.

8. City of Montclair, *Master Plan Report 2, Demographic Characteristics, Town of Montclair, New Jersey,* 1977.

9. U.S. Bureau of the Census, *Detailed Housing Characteristics,* Census of Housing: 1970. Final Report HC(1)-B32 New Jersey, 1972.

10. Henry Whittemore, *History of Montclair Township* (Montclair, 1894).

11. New Jersey Conference of Social Work, "The Negro in Montclair," (Newark, 1935); also "The Colored Y.W.C.A." in New Jersey Council of Social Agencies, *Community Resources for Leisure Time Activities in Montclair* (Montclair, 1935).

12. Irwin Ross, "The Town That Took its Own Pulse," *Pageant Magazine,* (January 1950).

13. Montclair Young Women's Christian Association, "1964 Montclair Community Audit," mimeographed (Montclair, 1964).

14. New Jersey Department of Community Affairs, *U.S. Census Data for New Jersey Townships, 1970.*

15. *Franklin Township: Know Your Township* (Franklin Township: League of Women Voters, 1969).

16. "Industrial Parks Bring Jobs to Franklin Township," *New Jersey Business,* n.d.

17. Somerset County Planning Board, "Estimated Net Total Housing—Somerset County: Net Housing Units Added," February 1978.

18. U.S. Bureau of the Census, Census of Population: 1970. *General Population Characteristics,* New Jersey.

19. Dan Lazare, "Suburbia Agonizing Over Desegregation," *The New Brunswick Home News,* January 29, 1979.

20. *Franklin News Record,* September 12, 1974; "Brawls Spur School Officials," *Franklin (N.J.) News Record,* February 6, 1975.

21. New Jersey Department of Community Affairs, *U.S. Census Data for New Jersey Townships, 1970.*

22. "Ewing Township—First to 'Balance,' " (Ewing, N.J.) *School Board Notes,* November/December 1971.

23. "Ewing Township Reorganizes Their Schools," *Ewing Township Board of Education News,* Spring 1971.

24. "Busing Main Concern at Ewing Plan Hearing," *Trenton Evening Times,* September 15, 1970.

25. Community Housing and Planning Associates, Inc., *Updated Background Studies for the Master Plan, City of Pleasantville, New Jersey,* February 1970.

26. Atlantic County Division of Economic Development, *Atlantic County Growth Trends Report, Third Quarter,* 1979.

27. City of Pleasantville, "Memorandum of Understanding Between the City Council of Pleasantville, New Jersey and the Mainland Chapter of the National Association for the Advancement of Colored People," October 1976.

6

THE NEW SUBURBANITES:
THE RECENT BUYERS SURVEY

INTRODUCTION

What are the characteristics of black households buying homes in these five suburban communities? The discussion in Part I focusing on households residing in the suburbs indicates that on average suburban blacks live in lower-value housing units at lower socioeconomic levels. Differences between blacks moving to and away from the suburbs, however, suggest that continued black suburbanization may lead to convergence of socioeconomic characteristics of suburban blacks and whites. In this chapter, we use a unique source of survey data to establish a profile of recent suburban black homebuyers.

Data for this discussion are drawn from an extensive survey of 1,004 households who purchased homes in the five case study communities during the period July 1974 to June 1977. The Recent Buyers Survey, conducted between September and November 1978, contains detailed questions on respondents' previous residence and reasons for moving, housing search experiences, housing finances, ratings of neighborhood problems and services, preferences for neighborhood racial composition, and socioeconomic characteristics. Aggregating over the five communities, the survey yields a representative view of blacks and whites buying suburban homes in the mid-1970s.

The chapter begins with an overview of sample selection and survey methodology used in the Recent Buyers Survey. We then extend the discussion of racial transition introduced in Chapter 3 with a microscale analysis of the magnitude of white-to-black and black-to-white turnover at the level of the individual housing units sampled in the survey. Next, true suburbanization dynamics are assessed by comparing black homebuyers moving from central cities to suburbs with those moving within the New Jersey suburbs or from outside the region. This allows disaggregation of the suburban black homebuying population into its component migration streams and also permits comparison of black and white suburban households by origin. In the following section, we compare blacks buying in all-white versus integrated or all-black neighborhoods and consider the characteristics of whites buying in integrated versus all-white neighborhoods. The survey data yield profiles of white and black households buying homes in each of four neighborhood types defined by racial composition. Finally, white and black attitudes to integration are assessed using survey data and information from a follow-up series of group discussions held in the case study communities.

THE RECENT BUYERS SURVEY

Issues of sample selection, questionnaire design, and survey methodology for the Recent Buyers Survey were guided by the basic objective of this study: to compare the housing search and purchase experiences of black and white suburban homebuyers. The problem of locating black homebuyers in predominantly white suburbia was resolved by selection of the case study communities as sampling clusters. These communities ranged from approximately 10 to 30 percent black in 1970 and it was assumed that the racial distribution of homebuyers at mid-decade would be somewhat proportional. Segments of the suburban black population that have been excluded by restricting the survey to the five communities were identified in the preceding chapter. As indicated, these groups are not a substantial component of overall black suburbanization. We decided further to restrict sampling to *recent* homebuyers in order to maximize respondent recall of the purchase experience and to reflect conditions in the mid-1970s. The process of sample selection and survey methodology reflected these research objectives.

Sample Selection

In order to limit the survey to recent home purchases, sampling was restricted to single-family homes sold in the five communities during the period July 1974 to June 1977. The sampling frame represents a 100 percent record of all single-family homes sold in the study sites during this period. Records of every arms-length real estate transaction within the five municipalities were obtained on computer tape from the State of New Jersey Department of the Treasury, Division of Taxation.[1] These records identify the county and municipality of each sale, the month and year the deed was executed and recorded, the tax assessor's block and lot number of the parcel, the sale price, the assessed value of the land and of improvements, the assessment/sale price ratio, and a code indicating property type (e.g., single-family residential, commercial, farm, etc.).

Block and lot numbers for every single-family housing sale in the five communities were listed out for the specified three-year period, yielding a total sampling frame of 4,583 housing units (Exhibit 6-1). [2] Of these, 299 (6.5 percent) represented multiple sales of the same parcel within the three-year period; these were deleted and only the most recent sale was retained in the sample. The highest frequency of resales was found in Franklin (11 percent) and Pleasantville (9.6 percent), reflecting the high turnover rate in the former and the effects of casino-related speculation in the latter. The remaining 4,284 housing units, representing a 100 percent sample of single-family home sales, were matched by block and lot number with records in the local tax assessor's office in each municipality to identify the name and address of the buyer (the current owner) and the address of the property. Based on this matching procedure, an additional 302 units were deleted when the tax assessor's records indicated a discrepancy between the address of the owner and that of the property, i.e., a nonresident owner. The highest proportion of absentee owners (23.8 percent) was again found in Pleasantville, yet further evidence of speculative land holding generated by developments in Atlantic City. Corresponding percentages in the other communities were substantially lower.

Deletion of multiple sales and absentee-owned units yielded a total sample of 3,982 single-family housing units. Working telephone numbers could be obtained for 2,566 units, resulting in a total usable sample representing 65 percent of all arms-length sales of single-family units in the five communities. This proportion ranged between 62 and 72 percent of single-family sales in each community with the exception of Pleasantville, which reached only 45 percent.

Telephone interviews averaging from thirty to forty minutes in length were completed with a total of 1,004 recent homebuyers. Because of the preponderance of white households among suburban homebuyers, a racial screen question was employed and an additional 781 white interviews were terminated.[3] The total of 1,785 successful contacts represents 44.8 percent of single-family sales in the five municipalities during the three-year period, and 69.6 percent of the total usable sample. Only 6.1 percent of the total usable sample could not be reached after numerous call-backs, another 6.2 percent of interviews were in-

EXHIBIT 6-1

RECENT BUYERS SURVEY SAMPLE DISTRIBUTION

	MONTCLAIR		TEANECK		FRANKLIN		EWING		PLEASANTVILLE		TOTAL	
	Number	Percent	Number	Percent	Number	Percent	Number	Percent	Number	Percent	Number	Percent
Total sales	1215	100.0	1283	100.0	943	100.0	903	100.0	239	100.0	4583	100.0
Resales	60	4.9	45	3.5	104	11.0	67	7.4	23	9.6	299	6.5
Absentees	68	5.6	24	1.9	129	13.7	24	2.7	57	23.8	302	6.6
Total sample	1087	100.0	1214	100.0	710	100.0	812	100.0	159	100.0	3982	100.0
Unpublished or nonworking number	306	28.2	457	37.6	263	37.0	302	37.2	88	55.3	1416	35.6
Total usable sample	781	100.0	757	100.0	447	100.0	510	100.0	71	100.0	2566	100.0
Ineligible												
Business phone	1	0.1	2	0.3	1	0.2	2	0.4	–	0.0	6	0.2
Ineligible respondent	70	9.0	45	5.9	14	3.1	23	4.5	9	12.7	161	6.3
Respondent not available	13	1.7	4	0.5	2	0.4	3	0.6	1	1.4	23	0.9
Line busy	3	0.4	–	0.0	1	0.2	1	0.2	–	0.0	5	0.2
No answer	32	4.1	91	12.0	12	2.7	13	2.5	8	11.3	156	6.1
Incomplete	29	3.7	89	11.8	18	4.0	21	4.1	2	2.8	159	6.2
Refused	72	9.2	106	14.0	38	8.5	46	9.0	9	12.7	271	10.6
Terminated-over quota	317	40.6	141	18.6	134	30.0	184	36.1	5	7.0	781	30.4
Completions												
Black	47	6.0	88	11.6	61	13.6	25	4.9	13	18.3	234	9.1
White	197	25.2	191	25.2	166	37.1	192	37.6	24	33.8	770	30.0
Total	244	31.2	279	36.9	227	50.8	217	42.5	37	52.1	1004	39.1

complete, and just 10.6 percent refused to interviewed (Exhibit 6-1). Completed interviews are relatively evenly divided among the five communities with the exception of Pleasantville; the small initial sample size and large number of deletions result in only 37 completed interviews in the latter community. Of the 1,004 completed interviews, 234 or 23.3 percent were black and 770 or 76.7 percent were white.

Survey Questionnaire

The survey instrument incorporates a broad range of questions pertaining to the suburban housing search and purchase experience (the questionnaire is reproduced in the Appendix). For each housing unit, data on sales price, assessed value, month and year of sale, and block/lot number were transcribed from the computer tape records obtained from the Division of Taxation. The first question, identifying length of residence, provides a validity check on the month and year of sale and confirms that the respondent is part of the household involved in the home purchase recorded in the state records.[4]

The interview obtained data on the size of the housing unit, number of rooms, bedrooms, and baths, age of the house, and presence of a garage. Information about the respondent's previous residence includes location, tenure, and size; respondents also indicated the extent of housing improvement represented by the new compared to the previous unit. The respondent's reason for moving away from the previous unit was obtained next, followed by a detailed series of questions regarding the process of searching for a new residence. Questions pertaining to housing search address the amount of time spent in search, the information sources used, experiences with real estate agents, the race of the real estate agent, and the respondent's satisfaction with the services provided by the agent. Respondents were asked if they felt they had been discriminated against in any way in their search for housing, and indicated the race of the household from whom they bought their house. Additional questions on housing search indicated the number of housing units examined, the number of communities considered, and the reason for selecting the community.

A further set of questions addressed the issue of mortgage financing: this included information on type of mortgage, source of downpayment, mortgage terms, and experiences with financial institutions.

Respondents were next asked to evaluate their housing unit and their community and to provide ratings for a detailed list of municipal services and neighborhood problems. A further question identified the respondent's preferred neighborhood racial composition. The final set of questions elicited information on family size and composition, the age, educational attainment, and occupation of the household head, travel time to work, and total family income.

Approximately one year after completion of the structured telephone survey, respondents in three communities (Teaneck, Montclair, and Franklin) were invited to participate in follow-up group discussions of the issues introduced in the initial survey. These open-ended group discussions were designed to provide a subjective, qualitative complement to the more structured telephone surveys. The discussion format is a powerful technique in which interaction within the group stimulates individual responses in a cumulative, comparative, and interactive group dynamic. Prompted by descriptions of the purchase experience offered by group members, other members of the group recognize and articulate subtle and subjective differences in their own experiences. Eight sessions were organized involving a total of 122 participants, ranging from eight to twenty-two people per session. Separate discussions were arranged with all-black, all-white, and interracial panels of participants. The sessions were videotaped and were led by trained group discussion leaders. The discussions provide a rich source of insight and illustrations that clarify and complement the structured survey data.

RACIAL TRANSITION BY UNIT AND NEIGHBORHOOD

The neighborhoods selected and the housing units purchased by black and white survey respondents reveal the exceedingly strong influence of race in the suburban housing market. The national data discussed in Chapter 3 indicated that suburban housing units overwhelmingly transfer within racial submarkets. These findings are confirmed and extended by the survey data. Black homebuyers disproportionately purchase black-owned units in black or integrated neighborhoods, while whites are concentrated almost exclusively in all-white neighborhoods within the five communities.

Neighborhood Racial Composition

The four categories of neighborhood racial composition defined in Chapter 5 were based on the census block population percent black in 1970 and the race of in-movers between 1974 and 1977 identified by the survey. To recapitulate, blocks in All-White and Black-Entry neighborhoods were less than 5 percent black in 1970, with only white in-movers in the former and black in-movers in the latter. This distinction allows us to identify blocks into which black households are moving and will prove important in Chapter 8's discussion of housing price effects of black entry. All-Black neighborhoods were census blocks with more than 80 percent black population in 1970, and Inter-Racial neighborhoods comprised all intermediate blocks.[5] All-White neighborhoods clearly predominate in these suburban communities: over half of the entire homebuyer sample (56.3 percent) moved into units in this neighborhood category. Nearly equal proportions of the total sample bought homes in Black-Entry (21.8 percent) and Inter-Racial (18.7 percent) neighborhoods, and only 3.2 percent moved into All-Black neighborhoods.

Disaggregating these total figures by race, however, reveals very different patterns for whites and blacks (Exhibit 6-2). Just over half of all black house-

EXHIBIT 6-2

DISTRIBUTION OF SURVEY RESPONDENTS BY COMMUNITY, RACE, AND NEIGHBORHOOD TYPE

(percents)

Neighborhood Type	MONTCLAIR		TEANECK		FRANKLIN		EWING		PLEASANTVILLE		TOTAL	
	Black	White	Black	White	Black	White	Black	White	Black	White	Black	White
All-White	—	64.0	—	79.7	—	60.1	—	90.2	—	70.8	—	73.5
Black-Entry	40.4	12.7	57.0	10.2	55.9	29.7	47.6	2.3	30.8	0.0	50.9	12.8
Inter-Racial	42.6	21.8	32.6	9.1	32.2	10.1	42.9	7.5	69.2	29.2	37.6	13.0
All-Black	17.0	1.5	10.5	1.1	11.9	0.0	9.5	0.0	0.0	0.0	11.5	0.7
Total	100.0	100.0	100.0	100.0	100.0	100.0	100.0	100.0	100.0	100.0	100.0	100.0
Number of cases	47	197	86	187	59	158	21	174	13	24	226	740

Note: 1970 Census block data were unavailable for blocks on which 38 survey respondents were located; neighborhood types could therefore not be defined for these cases. See Chapter 5 for neighborhood definitions.

holds (50.9 percent) bought homes in Black-Entry neighborhoods, while 11.5 percent moved to units in All-Black areas. These data for blacks indicate the recency of access to white areas within the suburbs, the low turnover within predominantly black areas, and the relative paucity of intermediate black concentrations. Within individual towns, the lowest proportions of blacks buying in Black-Entry neighborhoods are in Montclair (40.4 percent) and Pleasantville (30.8 percent), suggesting that black population growth in these communities is contributing to consolidation of black residential areas rather than outward expansion into white neighborhoods. Black households moving into Inter-Racial areas comprise between 22 and 29 percent of black homebuyers in Montclair and Pleasantville and only 8 to 10 percent in the remaining communities. The far longer period of black residence in these two communities may explain this trend to consolidation. The highest proportions of black homebuyers in Black-Entry neighborhoods are found in Teaneck (57 percent) and Franklin (55.9 percent), indicating the relative recency of black expansion in these communities.

In contrast to the pattern for black households, the overwhelming majority of whites (86.3 percent) moved to blocks that were less than 5 percent black in 1970. Two-thirds of white homebuyers (65.8 percent) but only 36.7 percent of blacks moved to blocks that had no black population in 1970, in communities that as indicated above were between one-tenth and one-third black in that year. Nearly three-fourths of whites (73.5 percent) purchased homes in neighborhoods that were still All-White in the mid-1970s (i.e., less than 5 percent black with no black in-movers). Equal proportions of whites moved to Black-Entry (12.8 percent) and Inter-Racial (13.0 percent) neighborhoods, in both cases a far lower frequency than among blacks. Almost no whites (0.7 percent) bought homes in All-Black areas. Within these biracial suburban communities, whites move predominantly into all-white areas while blacks are evenly divided between expansion into white neighborhoods and consolidation of black residential areas.

Housing Unit Transition

Residential resegregation occurs when white households avoid units in integrated neighborhoods and units that become vacant under normal turnover are bought solely by blacks. Comparison of the race of buyers and sellers of individual housing units indicates the extent to which whites or blacks replace blacks in units that become vacant.

The greater propensity of blacks to move into black or integrated neighborhoods suggests a high probability that blacks will purchase black-owned units. Survey respondents indicated the race of the household from whom they had purchased their unit. As hypothesized, 25.9 percent of blacks but only 2.2 percent of whites purchased houses sold by blacks. This discrepancy exists within each neighborhood type. Even though by definition there are few black sellers in Black-Entry neighborhoods, blacks were twice as likely as whites in these neighborhoods (6.4 percent versus 3.3 percent) to purchase a black-owned unit. The disparity increases exponentially in Inter-Racial neighborhoods: here 41.5 percent of blacks but only 3.3 percent of whites purchased units sold by blacks. Fully 60 percent of black households bought units previously owned by blacks.

At the level of the individual housing unit, the frequency of black-to-white sales indicates the extent to which there exists a dual housing market in which whites do not bid for black-owned units. The absence of white demand for units sold by blacks severely affects the equity accumulation potential of those units. However, *not only are blacks more likely than whites to buy black-owned units, but the converse is also true: blacks are far more likely than whites to sell to a black buyer.* Among the 955 units purchased by survey respondents for which race of both buyer and seller are identified, 75 were sold by blacks. Fully 78.7 percent of these black-owned units were sold to black buyers, compared to only 18.9 percent of white-owned units.

In order to have no dual housing market and no resegregation, whites should purchase both black- and white-occupied units in equal proportions, corresponding to their representation within the total homebuyer sample. Whites purchased 76.4 percent of the 955 housing units with known race of both buyer and seller. In a color-blind housing market, then, whites should account for this proportion of units sold by whites and blacks. Instead, whites overpurchased white units (81.1 percent), and accounted for only 21.3 percent of units sold by blacks. Similarly, blacks should account for 23.6 percent of sales by both whites and blacks but instead they underpurchased white units and accounted for 78.7 percent of units sold by blacks. In short, black homebuyers in these communities disproportionately purchase black units in black neighborhoods. Blacks selling a house access a disproportionately small share of the white homebuying market.

The greater likelihood of blacks selling to blacks rather than to whites is not limited to the survey communities. Respondents who owned their previous unit identified the race of the household to whom they sold that unit. Among the 280 previous owners who furnished this information, 49 were black and 231 were white. Of these, 55 percent of black-owned units were sold to black buyers, compared to only 7.4 percent of white-owned units. Considering these previous sales, recent purchases within the suburbs, and the national data discussed in Chapter 3, the weight of the evidence indicates that transactions involving whites are confined largely to a white housing market, while blacks tend to buy from and sell to other blacks.

Unit Transition by Neighborhood Type

The underrepresentation of white buyers of black-owned units and of black buyers of white-owned units suggests substantial spatial differentiation in the location of white and black homebuyers within the communities. Racial tran-

EXHIBIT 6-3

HOUSING UNIT TRANSITION PROBABILITIES BY NEIGHBORHOOD RACIAL COMPOSITION

Housing Unit Racial Transition	NEIGHBORHOOD RACIAL COMPOSITION			
	All-White	Black-Entry	Inter-Racial	All-Black
White seller- white buyer	.983	.441	.506	na
Black seller- white buyer	.017	.015	.017	na
White seller- black buyer	na	.510	.279	.400
Black seller- black buyer	na	.035	.198	.600
Total	1.000	1.000	1.000	1.000
Number of cases	516	202	172	25

Note: na = not applicable due to neighborhood definitions.

$X^2 = 537.52$ p $< .001$

sition in individual housing units is closely associated with the racial composition of the neighborhoods in which they are located.

A transfer between a white seller and a white buyer clearly has the highest probability of occurrence in All-White neighborhoods (Exhibit 6-3). White buyers are attracted to these neighborhoods and the pool of white-owned units is proportionately the largest. Even in Inter-Racial neighborhoods, however, which may range up to 80 percent black, there is an even probability that housing units will transfer between white owners. White preference for a white-owned unit appears to extend into substantially integrated neighborhoods. The probability of transition from black to white is uniformly low in all neighborhood types: white buyers appear to avoid black-owned units, even in predominantly white neighborhoods.

Transition from white to black has the highest probability of occurrence in Black-Entry neighborhoods, followed closely by All-Black neighborhoods. These appear to represent two ends of a continuum, where white-to-black transfers accompany both initial black entry as well as final white withdrawal. Finally, the transfer of housing between two black households is most likely to occur in All-Black neighborhoods, with few white sellers remaining and no white buyers moving in.

The housing unit and neighborhood destinations of white and black home-buyers provide evidence of a housing market differentiated by race. Black-occupied units are more often sold to blacks than to whites, and whites are far less likely than blacks to move to integrated neighborhoods. Continuation of these patterns will clearly lead to resegregation within the suburbs. Whether this is due to individual preferences or institutional practices or a combination of the two is an issue addressed in subsequent chapters.

HOMEBUYER CHARACTERISTICS BY LOCATION OF PREVIOUS RESIDENCE

The housing unit and neighborhood destinations of homebuyers may be related to the origin of the mover. True suburbanization, involving a move from a central city, is likely to differ from moves within suburbia and between regions, and the characteristics of these migration streams may lead to different destinations within suburbia.

The relative recency of black suburbanization is evidenced by the proportions of black homebuyers moving from central cities (Exhibit 6-4). More than half (55.6 percent) of black homebuyers lived in a central city immediately before their move, compared to less than one-third (31.5 percent) of whites. Blacks were somewhat more likely than whites to move from a central city within New Jersey (e.g., Newark or Trenton), and were twice as likely to move from an out-of-state central city (e.g., New York or Philadelphia). Whites proportionately exceeded blacks in all other mover categories, including moves within the same neighborhood or community, moves from another New Jersey suburb, and

EXHIBIT 6-4

LOCATION OF PREVIOUS RESIDENCE, BY RACE OF SUBURBAN HOMEBUYERS
(percents)

Location of Previous Residence	Black	White
Same neighborhood	5.4	9.3
Different neighborhood	11.7	14.9
Other N.J. suburb	21.5	33.8
N.J. central city	14.8	9.7
Out-of-state suburb	4.9	7.9
Out-of-state central city	40.8	21.8
Nonmetropolitan or foreign	0.9	2.5
Total	100.0	100.0
Number of cases	223	719

moves from a suburb in another state. The longer history of suburbanization among whites means that a higher proportion of white moves takes place within suburbia, while blacks are more likely to initiate the city-to-suburb move in this generation. Less than one percent of black homebuyers lived in a nonmetropolitan area or abroad prior to moving. This finding supports the data in Part I and suggests that black migrants from nonmetropolitan areas are moving to central cities rather than to suburbs. As will be seen below, both black and white homebuyers in this category are predominantly upper-income white-collar professionals whose jobs led to a temporary sojourn abroad before returning to a suburban residence.

Do the characteristics of suburban homebuyers differ by origin? To answer this question we compared households by race and previous residence in terms of four basic characteristics: occupation, income, reason for moving, and reason for selecting the new residence. Of interest is first, the variation in these characteristics among black homebuyers from different origins, and second, variations between whites and blacks from the same origin.

Occupation

Occupational patterns of suburban black homebuyers clearly differ by location of previous residence but parallel in many respects the occupational patterns of whites (Exhibit 6-5). The largest discrepancies among blacks are those between New Jersey central city and interstate suburban movers. Only 9.1 percent of blacks moving from a central city within the state are employed as professionals, compared to half of black homebuyers moving from an out-of-state suburb. Proportions employed in blue-collar jobs reflect the converse: nearly half of New Jersey black central city movers but only 10 percent from an out-of-state suburb are in this category. Black homebuyers moving from an out-of-state central city, however, have higher status jobs than those moving from a central city within the state. More than three-fourths of blacks in the former category have white collar occupations, a proportion exceeded only by blacks moving from a suburban area in another state or abroad. Nearly equal proportions of blacks in all mover categories, between 15 and 27 percent, are managers or administrators, and the proportions of sales and clerical workers show little variation by origin.

These occupational differences among blacks are similar in direction to those of whites but are different in degree. For instance, both blacks and whites moving from a central city in New Jersey have the highest proportions of blue-collar workers within their respective racial groups, but the proportion of blacks in this category (48.5 percent) is almost twice as high as the proportion of whites (26.1 percent). Blacks are more likely than whites to have blue-collar jobs in every category of previous residence with the exception of movers from nonmetropolitan areas or abroad. However, other patterns are more complex. Whites from a New Jersey central city exceed blacks in the proportion of professionals (34.8 percent versus 9.1 percent), but blacks exceed whites in the pro-

EXHIBIT 6-5

OCCUPATION OF SUBURBAN HOMEBUYERS, BY RACE AND LOCATION OF PREVIOUS RESIDENCE

(percents)

LOCATION OF PREVIOUS RESIDENCE

Occupation of Household Head	Same Neighborhood Black	White	Different Neighborhood Black	White	Other N.J. Suburb Black	White	N.J. Central City Black	White	Out-of-State Suburb Black	White	Out-of-State Central City Black	White	Nonmetropolitan or Foreign Black	White
Professional	30.8	36.4	28.6	52.9	30.8	48.2	9.1	34.8	50.0	54.4	34.9	48.4	100.0	61.1
Manager/Administrator	15.4	28.8	19.0	20.6	26.9	22.3	21.2	11.6	20.0	28.1	20.5	31.8	0.0	22.2
Sales/Clerical	0.0	12.1	9.5	11.8	13.5	9.7	12.1	15.9	20.0	14.0	16.9	8.9	0.0	5.6
Blue-collar	53.8	12.1	38.1	9.8	28.8	16.2	48.5	26.1	10.0	3.5	22.9	7.6	0.0	11.1
Other	0.0	10.6	4.8	4.9	0.0	3.6	9.1	11.6	0.0	0.0	4.8	3.2	0.0	0.0
Total	100.0	100.0	100.0	100.0	100.0	100.0	100.0	100.0	100.0	100.0	100.0	100.0	100.0	100.0
Number of cases	13	66	21	102	52	247	33	69	10	57	83	157	3	18
X^2	13.74**		11.74*		9.50*		10.68*		1.24		17.87**		1.75	

Note: Chi-square statistics indicate the significance of the difference between black and white distributions within each category of previous residence. Indicated significance levels are (***) $p < .001$; (**) $p < .01$; (*) $p < .05$.

portion of managers and administrators (21.2 percent of blacks versus 11.6 percent of whites). Whites moving within the same community are more likely than blacks to be professionals (52.9 percent versus 28.6 percent), but the proportions are nearly equal among blacks and whites moving within the same neighborhood. Blacks and whites moving from an out-of-state suburb reflect almost identical occupational distributions, with 50.0 percent of the former and 54.4 percent of the latter employed as professionals. With the exception of the somewhat higher proportions of blue-collar workers among black homebuyers, the occupational similarities among whites and blacks within categories of previous residence are striking.

Income

Income differences among black homebuyers generally reflect occupational patterns but are nonetheless substantially similar to those of whites (Exhibit 6-6). The income distributions of black and white homebuyers within each neighborhood category are not significantly different. Black homebuyers in the lowest income category, less than $20,000, tend to have moved either from a different neighborhood within the same community or from a central city within the state. Just over a fourth of black movers from these locations are in the lowest income category, compared to 15 percent or less among movers from other locations. As expected from occupational patterns, blacks moving from an out-of-state suburb tend to be in the highest income group, with 77.8 percent earning $30,000 or more.

Despite the greater likelihood among blacks to have blue-collar jobs, a *smaller* proportion of blacks than whites is in the lower income category. Among movers from a New Jersey central city, for instance, 40.4 percent of whites but only 27.6 percent of blacks earned less than $20,000. The proportion of whites in the lower-income category exceeds that of blacks in every case with the exception of movers from a different neighborhood within the same community. Significantly, the proportions of blacks and whites in the highest-income category are nearly identical in every mover group with the exception of movers from an out-of-state suburb. Black homebuyers appear to be clustered within a narrower income range than whites, with greater proportions of whites than blacks in the lower-income category, and the upper-income category extending higher for whites than for blacks.[6] As a result, black suburban movers tend to have somewhat higher incomes than blacks moving from a central city, while overall black incomes are on a par with those of whites.

Reasons for Moving

The reasons for moving from the previous residence are startlingly identical for black and white homebuyers (Exhibit 6-7). About a fifth of both racial groups moved for job-related reasons, predominately because of a job change or transfer and to a lesser extent to facilitate commuting or accessibility. Approximately 30 percent of both groups moved for housing unit reasons, primarily

EXHIBIT 6-6

TOTAL FAMILY INCOME OF SUBURBAN HOMEBUYERS, BY RACE AND LOCATION OF PREVIOUS RESIDENCE
(percents)

Total Family Income	Same Neighborhood Black	White	Different Neighborhood Black	White	Other N.J. Suburb Black	White	N.J. Central City Black	White	Out-of-State Suburb Black	White	Out-of-State Central City Black	White	Nonmetropolitan or Foreign Black	White
Less than $20,000	0.0	25.9	26.3	14.1	13.0	21.6	27.6	40.4	0.0	7.8	15.2	11.1	0.0	10.0
$20,000-29,999	54.5	24.1	26.3	43.5	54.3	38.7	41.4	33.3	22.2	49.0	27.8	32.6	33.3	30.0
$30,000 or more	45.5	50.0	47.4	42.4	32.6	39.6	31.0	26.3	77.8	43.1	57.0	56.3	66.7	60.0
Total	100.0	100.0	100.0	100.0	100.0	100.0	100.0	100.0	100.0	100.0	100.0	100.0	100.0	100.0
Number of cases	11	54	19	92	46	222	29	57	9	51	79	135	3	10
X^2	5.79		2.68		4.12		1.37		3.82		1.02		0.33	

Note: None of the chi-square statistics is significant at the .05 level.

EXHIBIT 6-7

REASON FOR MOVING FROM PREVIOUS UNIT, BY RACE OF
SUBURBAN HOMEBUYERS
(percents)

Reason for Moving	Black	White
Job-related move	18.1	22.8
Job change or transfer	15.5	19.0
Commuting/accessibility	2.6	3.8
Housing unit reason	28.3	31.4
Unit too small	21.0	22.5
Unit too big	0.4	1.9
Rent increase	2.6	1.1
Other housing unit reason	4.3	5.9
Life-cycle reason	32.2	30.9
Wanted to own	27.0	26.4
Newly married/to start own household	3.9	3.2
Widowed/separated/divorced	1.3	1.3
Dissatisfied with neighborhood	18.8	11.8
Dissatisfied with neighborhood	13.7	9.5
Dissatisfied with schools	3.0	1.1
Taxes too high	2.1	1.2
Other reasons	2.6	3.2
Location of family or relatives	0.4	1.3
Urban renewal (public displacement)	0.4	0.0
Eviction, etc. (private displacement)	0.9	1.2
Other reasons	0.9	0.7
Total	100.0	100.0
Number of cases	233	761

because their previous unit was too small. Another third moved because of a change in stage in the life-cycle. Most of this latter group, representing identical proportions of blacks and whites, moved to satisfy a desire for homeownership—the classic suburban move. The only evident difference between whites and blacks is a somewhat greater likelihood among the latter to move because of dissatisfaction with the previous neighborhood. This discrepancy, though slight, can be attributed to the larger share of blacks than whites who moved from a central city location, where neighborhood characteristics—especially for blacks—are likely to be dissatisfying.

Since blacks and whites differ little in their reasons for moving, variations by location of previous residence are similar for the two groups. As with income, the reasons for moving given by white and black homebuyers are not significantly different within each category of previous residence. The highest proportions of both blacks and whites moving for job-related reasons are those who previously lived in a suburb of a different state or abroad. Among interstate suburban movers, 78 percent of whites and 64 percent of blacks moved because of a job transfer. Housing unit factors were an important reason for both blacks and whites moving within the same community. These moves represent an adjustment of living space within either the same neighborhood or between neighborhoods in the same community. Interestingly, black homebuyers moving within the same neighborhood were more likely than other groups to move because of a change in the life-cycle, primarily involving a desire to own a home. Fully 54 percent of blacks making intraneighborhood moves were motivated by the desire for homeownership. A move within the same neighborhood, presumably based on personal knowledge of availability of the unit and free from the uncertainties of moving to a new and potentially hostile suburban neighborhood, apparently serves as an important avenue to homeownership for suburban black households.

As indicated above, both blacks and whites moving from a central city either within or outside the state have the highest probability of moving because of neighborhood dissatisfaction. Approximately one-fourth of blacks and whites from central cities moved for this reason, compared to 10 percent or less of all other mover groups.

Selecting the New Residence

Reasons for selecting the present community reflect the original reasons for moving, and again discrepancies among mover groups outweigh those between blacks and whites. Moves within the same neighborhood for both blacks and whites were most often motivated by satisfaction with social and environmental neighborhood quality: 54 percent of blacks and 65 percent of whites who moved within the same neighborhood gave this reason for selecting their new residence.

Location and accessibility to place of work were important attractions for both blacks and whites moving from an out-of-state suburb. The high incidence of job-related moves among this group explains the importance of accessibility to work as a criterion in selecting a new residence. Large corporations and relocation services often impose a maximum radius travel time to work for employees using their home-finding services. In addition, accessibility is likely to be a more important criterion than social or environmental concerns among employees knowing they will be frequently relocated. Among movers from a New Jersey central city, however, location is a more important attraction of the present residence for whites (47.9 percent) than for blacks (22.9 percent). Internal community characteristics predominate for blacks in this mover category while whites appear to be attracted not to the community per se but rather to an easy commute.

The quality of municipal services provides a more salient attraction for blacks than for whites among central city movers and for blacks moving from another suburb within the state. For instance, 23 percent of blacks but only 6 percent of whites moving from a New Jersey central city cited the quality of services as their most important reason for choosing the community. For black homebuyers, this is likely to be a combination of dissatisfaction with services in central city black neighborhoods and the positive attraction of the high-quality services, including public education, available in these communities.

In sum, suburban black homebuyers are more likely than whites to be moving from a central city. Black households making such a move are more likely than previous black suburbanites to have blue-collar occupations, to have incomes below $20,000, and to have moved because of dissatisfaction with their previous neighborhood. However, blacks moving from an out-of-state central city, including New York and Philadelphia, have higher-status occupations and higher incomes than those moving from a central city within the state. This may well represent socioeconomic differences between blacks moving to dormitory residential suburbs in the classic suburbanization process as compared to those for whom suburbanization represents a short-distance move to a central city spillover community. Finally, variations among black homebuyers associated with the location of their previous residence are mirrored in similar variations among white movers. What discrepancies exist appear to be due more to the recency of black suburbanization and the location of previous residence rather than to differences between the racial groups.

HOMEBUYER CHARACTERISTICS BY NEIGHBORHOOD TYPE

While blacks and whites from identical original locations share similar characteristics, a larger proportion of blacks than whites moved from central cities and more whites than blacks moved from the suburbs. As a result, white/black differences within destination neighborhoods may be due in part to the different origins of the two groups.

Overall differences in the origin of black and white homebuyers are reflected in variations among and within destination neighborhoods (Exhibit 6-8). Whites in All-White and Black-Entry neighborhoods moved from essentially identical previous locations, with the exception that whites in All-White neighborhoods were somewhat more likely to move from a New Jersey suburb while whites in Black-Entry neighborhoods were more likely to move from a suburb in another state. Within Black-Entry neighborhoods, blacks are clearly new arrivals: less than one percent moved within the same neighborhood, compared to 7.5 percent of whites. While equal proportions of whites and blacks in Black-Entry blocks moved from a New Jersey suburb, the central city-suburb split shows up strongly in the remaining categories. The proportion of whites from an out-of-state suburb (17.2 percent) exceeds that of blacks (6.1 percent). In contrast,

EXHIBIT 6-8

CHARACTERISTICS OF SUBURBAN HOMEBUYERS,
BY RACE AND NEIGHBORHOOD RACIAL COMPOSITION
(percents)

	NEIGHBORHOOD RACIAL COMPOSITION					
	All-White	*Black-Entry*		*Inter-Racial*		*All-Black*
	Whites	*Whites*	*Blacks*	*Whites*	*Blacks*	*Blacks*
LOCATION OF PREVIOUS RESIDENCE						
Same neighborhood	9.6	7.5	0.9	9.7	10.7	8.0
Different neighborhood	15.2	14.0	6.1	14.0	17.9	16.0
Other N.J. suburb	34.7	21.5	22.8	40.9	21.4	16.0
N.J. central city	10.7	8.6	13.2	5.4	15.5	20.0
Out-of-state suburb	6.9	17.2	6.1	4.3	3.6	4.0
Out-of-state central city	21.0	25.8	50.9	22.6	28.6	36.0
Nonmetropolitan or foreign	1.9	5.4	0.0	3.2	2.4	0.0
Total	100.0	100.0	100.0	100.0	100.0	100.0
Number of cases	533	93	114	93	84	25
X^2 =95.50 p<.001						
PREVIOUS TENURE						
Own	38.0	44.4	31.8	26.6	22.9	19.2
Rent	62.0	55.6	68.2	73.4	77.1	80.8
Total	100.0	100.0	100.0	100.0	100.0	100.0
Number of cases	527	90	110	94	83	26
X^2 =17.17 p<.01						
HOUSEHOLD COMPOSITION						
Single-parent	5.0	3.4	4.8	2.4	10.0	4.8
Husband/wife, no children	54.8	47.1	37.5	59.8	21.3	33.3
Husband/wife, with children	40.1	49.4	57.7	37.8	68.8	61.9
Total	100.0	100.0	100.0	100.0	100.0	100.0
Number of cases	496	87	104	82	80	21
X^2 =45.74 p<.001						
AGE OF HEAD						
Less than 30	17.7	18.7	8.7	12.2	7.4	8.7
30-34	33.1	30.8	29.1	34.4	21.0	26.1
35-39	17.5	15.4	28.2	23.3	24.7	21.7
40-49	17.5	18.7	24.3	18.9	37.0	21.7
50 and over	14.1	16.5	9.7	11.1	9.9	21.7
Total	100.0	100.0	100.0	100.0	100.0	100.0
Number of cases	519	91	103	90	81	23
X^2 =39.87 p<.01						

EXHIBIT 6-8 (Continued)

CHARACTERISTICS OF SUBURBAN HOMEBUYERS,
BY RACE AND NEIGHBORHOOD RACIAL COMPOSITION
(percents)

| | NEIGHBORHOOD RACIAL COMPOSITION | | | | | |
| | All-White | Black-Entry | | Inter-Racial | | All-Black |
	Whites	Whites	Blacks	Whites	Blacks	Blacks
OCCUPATION OF HEAD						
Professional	47.1	47.3	38.0	48.9	23.8	18.2
Manager/Administrator	23.8	25.3	21.3	22.2	17.5	22.7
Sales/Clerical	10.6	14.3	16.7	13.3	10.0	13.6
Bluecollar	13.5	11.0	20.4	10.0	45.0	36.4
Other	5.0	2.2	3.7	5.6	3.8	9.1
Total	100.0	100.0	100.0	100.0	100.0	100.0
Number of cases	520	91	108	90	80	22
X^2=72.48 p<.001						
EDUCATION OF HEAD						
High school grad or less	19.0	11.7	26.8	19.8	42.4	48.0
Some college	13.8	12.8	22.3	11.5	24.7	28.0
College grad	32.2	44.7	30.4	34.4	22.4	12.0
Professional or						
graduate school	35.0	30.9	20.5	34.4	10.6	12.0
Total	100.0	100.0	100.0	100.0	100.0	100.0
Number of cases	537	94	112	96	85	25
X^2=76.73 p<.001						

13.2 percent of blacks but only 8.6 percent of whites moved from a New Jersey central city and 50.9 percent of blacks but only 25.8 percent of whites moved from a central city in another state. White/black differences within Inter-Racial neighborhoods reflect a similar pattern, with moves primarily originating within the state.

Socioeconomic Differences

The characteristics of white and black homebuyers by neighborhood reflect these variations in the location of previous residence (Exhibit 6-8). As central city residents, blacks were generally less likely than whites to own their previous residence, although this difference is most significant within Black-Entry neighborhoods. Blacks buying units in All-Black neighborhoods had the lowest rate of prior ownership (19.2 percent).

White household heads are nearly twice as likely as their black neighborhood counterparts to be under 30, and are somewhat more likely to be 50 or over. Black household heads, in other words, are more likely than whites in each neighborhood type to be in the prime income-earning years (35-49). Perhaps as a function of age, husband-wife families with children are more common among black households than in white ones in all neighborhood categories. This holds true particularly in Inter-Racial neighborhoods, where 68.8 percent of black households but only 37.8 percent of white households are composed of a husband and wife with children. Black households, as a consequence, are larger on average than white households, ranging from 3.3 for whites in All-White neighborhoods to 4.0 for blacks in Inter-Racial neighborhoods. The proportions of female-headed households are not significantly different, however, either across neighborhoods or between blacks and whites within neighborhoods. The number of household members employed (1.8) is also invariant across racial and neighborhood groups.

Between 18 and 25 percent of all racial and neighborhood groups are employed as managers or administrators, and another 10 to 15 percent of all groups work in sales or clerical positions. Whites in each neighborhood type are somewhat more likely than blacks to be in professional occupations (e.g., 49 percent of whites and 24 percent of blacks in Inter-Racial neighborhoods), while the converse is true for blue-collar occupations (45 percent of blacks and 10 percent of whites in Inter-Racial neighborhoods). Whites have somewhat higher educational levels than blacks in each neighborhood type: 75 percent of whites and 50 percent of blacks in Black-Entry neighborhoods have a college degree or better, while the percentages in Inter-Racial neighborhoods are 69 percent for whites and 33 percent for blacks.

Despite these differences in occupation and education, the mean income of suburban homebuyers does not vary significantly across neighborhood categories. Black homebuyers in Black-Entry neighborhoods record the highest mean income level ($32,695), followed by whites in All-White neighborhoods ($30,884) and Black-Entry neighborhoods ($30,764) and blacks in All-Black neighborhoods ($30,487). Whites and blacks in Inter-Racial neighborhoods are nearly matched, with a mean income of $26,546 for whites and $27,257 for blacks. These differences are not statistically significant at the .05 level.

The amount of housing purchased by blacks and whites is constant across neighborhoods, as measured by the number of rooms (7.7) and the number of bedrooms (3.5).

From these survey data emerge generalized profiles of the white and black households buying homes in each of the neighborhood categories.

Whites in All-White Neighborhoods. These are young families without children who owned a home in another New Jersey suburb prior to moving. Fully one-third of household heads are between 30 and 34, and family size is the smallest among all racial and neighborhood groups. Household heads are well-educated, with the highest proportion among all groups (35 percent) who attended professional or graduate school. Most are employed in professional occupations. These households chose their units because of the social and environmental ambience of the neighborhood.

Whites in Black-Entry Neighborhoods. Households in this category are identical on average in most respects with those in All-White neighborhoods. Compared to the latter, these households are somewhat more likely to have moved from a suburb outside the state rather than a New Jersey suburb. They have the highest probability of prior ownership among all six groups. As in All-White neighborhoods, whites in Black-Entry neighborhoods are young: they have the highest proportion of household heads under 30 (18.7 percent) but also the highest proportion over 50 (16.5 percent). Educational attainment and occupation are essentially equivalent to those of whites in All-White neighborhoods. For whites in Black-Entry neighborhoods, social ambience and environmental aesthetics of the neighborhood were more important than the characteristics of the housing unit in selecting a new residence.

Blacks in Black-Entry Neighborhoods. The highest socioeconomic status characteristics among black homebuyers is reflected in this category. These households include the highest proportion of previous owners among blacks and were most likely to have moved from a central city outside the state, i.e., New York. They are younger than other black household heads but are somewhat older than whites: they include the highest proportion (28.2 percent) of household heads between 35 and 39, and are more likely than white households to have children. Blacks in Black-Entry neighborhoods exceed the other neighborhood categories of black homebuyers in the proportion of household heads with professional occupations (37.5 percent) and postgraduate education (20.5 percent), but these levels are lower than those attained by whites in all neighborhood categories. These households, however, have attained the highest mean income level among all race and neighborhood groups. The primary factor in selecting a residence was the quality of schools and municipal services, and the characteristics of the neighborhood were more important than those of the house.

Whites in Inter-Racial Neighborhoods. Members of this group are young (30-34) with small families (3.4) and few or no children. Households in this group have the highest proportion employed in professional occupations (48.9 percent) and have high levels of educational attainment, but their mean income ($26, 546) is the lowest among the six race and neighborhood categories. These are first-time homebuyers who rented their previous residence in a New Jersey suburb. The price and characteristics of the housing unit were more important considerations than the characteristics of the neighborhood in selecting a house. These households are at the beginning of their income-earning potential and can be expected to move out of the neighborhood as incomes increase.

Blacks in Inter-Racial Neighborhoods. In contrast to their white counterparts, these homebuyers are older (40-49), are more likely to have children, and have a larger average family size (4.0). These are predominantly blue-collar workers (45 percent) with a high school education (42.4 percent) commensurate with the educational opportunities available to blacks in the 1940s and 1950s. Prior to moving, homebuyers in this category lived in a New Jersey central city where they rented their previous residence. The qualities of the house and the neighborhood were equally important in selecting a new residence; these households chose their community because of a combination of the characteristics of the unit and the quality of municipal services.

Blacks in All-Black Neighborhoods. Household heads in this category have the highest mean age (41.7 years) and the highest proportion aged 50 or over (21.7 percent). These households include the highest average number of employed workers (2.1) but also have the highest proportion in the "other" occupational category, i.e., retired, student, housewife, or unemployed. In brief, these households have the highest frequency of multiple wage-earners, but it appears that a substantial segment of these may be in marginal employment categories. While the incidence of these characteristics is higher than in the other race/neighborhood categories, however, it is low in absolute terms: 54.5 percent of blacks in All-Black neighborhoods are employed in white-collar occupations. The characteristics of the house and of the neighborhood were equally important in looking for a new house, but 50 percent of households in this category indicated that the social characteristics of the neighborhood was the most important factor in choosing their present residence.

Discrimination

The range of household characteristics within the recent homebuyers sample suggests the potential for substantial differences in the home purchase experiences of blacks and whites. The relative importance of socioeconomic differences versus discrimination in explaining variations in purchase experiences is assessed in the following chapter. Initial indications of black/white differences in the homebuying process, however, are provided by data on perceived discriminatory treatment and the race of the real estate agent used in finding a house.

Survey respondents were asked a direct question regarding their perception of discriminatory treatment in buying a house: "In looking for a home, did you feel you were discriminated against in any way?" (Question 27). Responses to this general question clearly must be treated cautiously. The definition of discriminatory treatment was left to the respondent and is likely to vary among individuals. Lacking a framework for comparison, homebuyers may often be unaware that the treatment they are receiving differs in quality or quantity from that provided others. Black homebuyers may be unwilling to admit to receiving discriminatory treatment, since this would be a tacit confirmation of subordinate status. For all these reasons one may expect responses to this question to underestimate actual levels of discriminatory treatment.

Despite these caveats, a significant share of black homebuyers reported discriminatory treatment. For the sample as a whole, 20.3 percent of black homebuyers felt they had been discriminated against, and this proportion is fairly consistent across neighborhood categories (Exhibit 6-9). The corresponding proportion among whites was 5.6 percent, most of whom cited age or sex as the basis of their discriminatory treatment. As expected, this reported level of discrimination is somewhat below that anticipated on the basis of other studies. A recent HUD study of housing market practices in forty metropolitan areas estimated the probability of a black homebuyer experiencing discrimination as 28 percent if two sales agents are visited and 39 percent with visits to three agents.[7] Since respondents to the Recent Buyers survey used an average of 2.8 real estate agents regardless of race, reported instances of discrimination appear to underestimate actual levels, presumably due to the factors cited above. The data do provide an initial basis for expecting differences in the housing search and purchase experiences of black and whites.

A second element of the homebuying process suggesting differences in the experiences of blacks and whites is the race of the final real estate agent used in finding a house (Exhibit 6-9). Essentially no white homebuyers used a black real estate agent in their housing search. Among black homebuyers, the proportion using a black agent ranges from 4.3 to 12.9 percent, with the percentage increasing as the neighborhood percent black population increases. This suggests that black real estate agents serve only black homebuyers and have an increasing level of activity in black neighborhoods. Startlingly little information is available in the literature on the role of black agents and their niche within the white real estate establishment. It may be assumed, however, that the confinement of the activity of black agents to black neighborhoods greatly restricts the pool of housing options that a black agent can offer to prospective buyers and that, conversely, a buyer using a black agent can expect to be shown houses predominantly if not entirely within black neighborhoods.

ATTITUDES TO INTEGRATION

Stated preferences for residential integration are associated with the neighborhood racial composition of the respondent's housing unit. The gradual improvement over time in white attitudes toward integration has been documented in reviews of longitudinal survey evidence.[8] Pettigrew has qualified these trends by arguing that white acceptance of the principle of integration has not been accompanied by greater willingness to implement desegregation.[9] Taylor has urged similar restraint in interpreting trends in white attitudes on the grounds that expressed attitudes must be viewed in the context of market constraints in the supply of housing.[10] In a unique study, Farley, et al. assessed black and white preferences for a range of hypothetical neighborhood conditions defined by racial composition.[11] Substantiating earlier findings, they found strong preferences among blacks for integrated neighborhoods with even proportions of blacks and whites and strong opposition to either all-black or all-white neighborhoods. White preferences were strongest for all-white or predominantly white neighborhoods, and 40 percent of whites said they would move away from a neighborhood that was one-third black.

Our findings support those of Farley and his associates. They found that 82 percent of blacks identified an evenly mixed neighborhood as either their first or

EXHIBIT 6-9

EXPERIENCE OF DISCRIMINATION AND RACE OF REAL ESTATE AGENT, BY RACE OF SUBURBAN HOMEBUYERS AND NEIGHBORHOOD RACIAL COMPOSITION
(percents)

| | *NEIGHBORHOOD RACIAL COMPOSITION* | | | | | |
| | *All-White* | *Black-Entry* | | *Inter-Racial* | | *All-Black* |
	Whites	*Whites*	*Blacks*	*Whites*	*Blacks*	*Blacks*
Reported Discrimination in Home Purchase						
Yes	5.4	7.4	18.6	7.3	22.4	23.1
No	94.6	92.6	81.4	92.7	77.6	76.9
Total	100.0	100.0	100.0	100.0	100.0	100.0
Number of cases	540	95	113	96	85	26
$X^2 = 45.25$ p $< .001$						
Race of Real Estate Agent						
Black	0.6	0.0	4.3	0.0	12.9	11.5
White	99.4	100.0	95.7	100.0	87.1	88.5
Total	100.0	100.0	100.0	100.0	100.0	100.0
Number of cases	544	95	115	96	85	26
$X^2 = 67.06$ p $< .001$						

second preference among a range of neighborhood choices defined by racial composition. We asked respondents to the Recent Buyers Survey: "Assuming you could find the kind of house you wanted, what type of community would you most prefer to live in: mainly white, mainly black, or a mixture?" Among black homebuyers, 80.8 percent identified the mixed neighborhood as their first preference, 5.2 percent chose an all-black neighborhood, and 3.1 percent chose an all-white neighborhood. Among white respondents, 54.5 percent selected a mixed neighborhood, 35.5 percent chose a mainly white neighborhood, and only 0.1 percent opted for a mainly black neighborhood. Nearly equal proportions of blacks and whites (10.9 percent and 9.8 percent respectively) claimed no preference.

The proportion of whites expressing a preference for integration is likely to be higher in these biracial communities than among white suburbanites in general. In fact, stated preferences vary by the actual racial composition of the respondent's neighborhood (Exhibit 6-10). Whites in all neighborhoods far exceed the proportion of blacks favoring a mainly white neighborhood. Nonetheless, the percentage of whites expressing this preference decreases with increasing black concentrations, from 38 percent in All-White neighborhoods to 28.7 percent in Black-Entry neighborhoods to 22.8 percent in Inter-Racial neighborhoods. Similarly, the percentage of whites preferring an integrated neighborhood increases with increasing black neighborhood concentrations. The data do not reveal whether these interneighborhood differences reflect self-selection among whites or the liberalizing effect of interracial contact. Perhaps more significant is the finding that nearly one-fourth of whites in Inter-Racial neighborhoods would prefer to be in mainly white areas, which suggests the potential for white flight from these neighborhoods.

EXHIBIT 6-10
RACIAL PREFERENCES OF SUBURBAN HOMEBUYERS, BY RACE AND NEIGHBORHOOD RACIAL COMPOSITION
(percents)

Preferred Neighborhood Racial Composition	NEIGHBORHOOD RACIAL COMPOSITION					
	All-White Whites	Black-Entry Whites	Black-Entry Blacks	Inter-Racial Whites	Inter-Racial Blacks	All-Black Blacks
Mainly white	38.0	28.7	6.3	22.8	0.0	0.0
Integrated	51.7	64.9	83.0	66.3	83.1	57.7
Mainly black	0.2	0.0	4.5	0.0	6.0	7.7
No preference	10.1	6.4	6.3	10.9	10.8	34.6
Total	100.0	100.0	100.0	100.0	100.0	100.0
Number of cases	524	94	112	92	83	26

$X^2 = 148.42$ p $<$ .001

The stated preferences of blacks are more stable across neighborhood categories, reflecting the overwhelming preference for integrated neighborhoods. Significantly, the only category of blacks expressing any preference for mainly white areas is that in Black-Entry neighborhoods, presumably reflecting self-selection on the part of these households. However, equal proportions of blacks in Black-Entry and Inter-Racial neighborhoods prefer a mixed residential setting.

The greatest proportion of homebuyers (34.6 percent) claiming no preference in neighborhood racial composition is found among blacks in All-Black neighborhoods. The opportunity for homeownership and improved housing quality evidently outweighs considerations of neighborhood composition for this group. As two black homebuyers stated:

> "I wasn't so much concerned about who lived in the neighborhood. I wanted a home––wanted to own my own home."

> "I don't care where I live so long as the person next to me is not rowdy and damaging to my property. That's what I'm looking for––a nice home. If the people are decent, if they like to take care of what's theirs and not damage mine, I don't care what color they are."

White preferences for integration vary monotonically with income and education. The proportion of whites favoring a mainly white neighborhood decreases from 46.7 percent of those with a high school education or less to 34.7 percent of college graduates to 29.4 percent of whites with professional or graduate education. The proportions favoring integration are reversed: 36.3 percent of those with high school or less but 63.9 percent with postgraduate education preferred integration. The patterns are similar when disaggregating by income. The distribution of white preferences by age is bipolar. The proportion of whites favoring integration increases with age, from 41.8 percent of those under 30 to 65.9 percent of those between the ages of 40 and 49. Fewer whites aged 50 or over (46.3 percent), however, prefer a mixed neighborhood, which indicates that this neighborhood type is least favored among the oldest and youngest age categories.

The reasons offered by whites who preferred an integrated neighborhood focus on perceived savings in housing prices and cultural enrichment for children. Citing the lower prices available in his integrated neighborhood, a white respondent explained that in several all-white communities he had seen

> "houses identical to or less than the one that we bought selling for way more money, on busier streets. If somebody's willing to pay $30,000 more for a lesser house in a community without police and fire or sewers just because there are no black people around, I think that's crazy."

Several whites valued the experience of an integrated community for their children:

"I wanted an integrated community, a varied community. I never knew anyone that was different from me, so I kind of wanted to have an integrated community for my children."

"I think my children have a cultural advantage that I never had. I lived in a predominantly white neighborhood in Texas and grew up there. My children have a much easier time socially in a mixed atmosphere than I did as a child when we moved to California and I was confronted with it."

While some whites see advantages to integration, it is evident that the *extent* of integration is a paramount concern:

"When we bought the house, we knew it was an integrated area. We wanted it integrated. But we didn't want it all black. That's not integrated."

The perception of stability in racial balance is important to whites:

"We were concerned about whether it was a stable integrated community. We were concerned about shifting or tipping."

In fact, the proportion of blacks that whites will tolerate with equanimity is quite low. An important requirement for whites is evidence that whites continue to replace blacks in housing units that come up for sale:

"Before we moved in, the four other houses on our street were two white families and two black families. Now those houses are owned by four white families. As long as it's that sort of situation I think that that's healthy."

A primary criterion for whites is the perception that the neighborhood continues to be defined as part of white residential space.[12]

Black preferences for integration subsume an overarching concern to avoid situations of potential white hostility:

"I wanted to know what kind of a neighborhood I was moving in. I went down the block and looked who lives here, what color lives here, because I really wanted it to be a mixed neighborhood. I wanted to make sure I didn't have neighbors who would burn a cross on my lawn."

A strong element of black preference is to avoid the conspicuousness of being the only black family in an all-white community:

"I looked in B. for a while but I felt very uncomfortable there. It was just a sense that I didn't belong there. Nobody said anything, nobody did anything, but it was like being in a snowbank. I looked at any house I wanted to see but I could sense that that wasn't the place."

Black families with children particularly want to avoid the social isolation that would result from residence in an all-white community. This problem is particularly severe for adolescents for whom social activities take on connotations of interpersonal interaction that engender emotional fears among white parents. A black respondent explained:

> "Our oldest son is fourteen, our youngest son is twelve, and I just don't want them in a situation where they have no options. Or sitting in because somebody's father said he won't allow them in the house or they don't want their daughter seen with them. I would not want to subject my children to that."

Biracial communities not only avoid problems of social isolation for blacks but from a positive perspective also allow for maintenance of a black identity:

> "Aside from it being integrated, we wanted to be in a community that had a sizable black population. Because we felt that it was important for our children to grow up with a sense of identity and culture. We didn't want our children to grow up in an all-white town, apart from the culture and the total society."

The interaction of neighborhood and community may be crucial. Whites appear willing to accept a biracial community to the extent that they can maintain white dominance in their immediate neighborhood. Blacks appear relatively immune to concerns about neighborhood racial composition as long as a black peer group is available at the community level. A key issue then, may be to resolve these two perspectives in a way that does not lead to a racial bifurcation of municipal services and facilities and neighborhood quality.

SUMMARY

The Recent Buyers Survey permits a comparison of blacks and whites among recent entrants to suburbia. Black suburbanites are similar to whites moving from equivalent previous locations. The longer history of large-scale white suburbanization, however, means that recent arrivals from the central cities to the suburbs make up a larger proportion of black than white homebuyers. What may thus appear to be differences between suburban blacks and whites is rather a function of proportional differences in the origins of black and white homebuyers.

The residential sorting process inherent in the dynamics of home purchase generates distinctive patterns in the neighborhood distribution of black and white recent homebuyers. Blacks in predominantly white neighborhoods represent the highest-status segment of the suburban black population. The income of blacks in these neighborhoods exceeds that of their white neighbors, perhaps in part compensating for slightly lower levels of occupational status and educational attainment. Whites in integrated neighborhoods tend to be young first-time homebuyers for whom lower housing prices rather than a commitment to integration appears to be the dominant motivation for purchase. This tendency bears strong potential for instability and resegregation in integrated neighborhoods as whites moving out in search of improved housing are replaced by blacks.

Whether as a result of socioeconomic background differences or racial discrimination or both, black homebuyers are more likely than whites to purchase units in black or integrated neighborhoods, to purchase black-owned units regardless of neighborhood racial composition, to use a black real estate agent, and to experience discrimination in the housing search and home purchase process. The relative importance of socioeconomic differences versus racial discrimination in explaining these patterns is assessed in the following chapters. The survey data, nonetheless, provide strong initial evidence of the substantial significance of race as a factor influencing a household's experience in the suburban housing market.

NOTES

1. The New Jersey Department of the Treasury, Division of Taxation, maintains centralized records of real property sales based on the Realty Transfer tax stamps affixed to the deed. These data have been compiled annually by the Treasury Department since 1965. Arms-length transfers refer to sales between unrelated parties in which the sale price is a valid representation of market value. The "Usable Sales" records used for sampling for the Recent Buyers Survey, therefore omit property transfers between members of the same immediate family, foreclosure, bankruptcy, or sheriff's sales, transfers in which "love and affection" or a nominal payment are a part of the consideration, and similar nonstandard title transfers. The three-year period ending in June 1977 was the most recent period for which sales data were available at the initiation of sampling in September 1978.

2. Property sales were relatively evenly distributed over the three-year period, with 30.1 percent in 1974/75, 32.4 percent in 1975/76, and 37.4 percent in 1976/77. The slight increase in the proportion of sales in the latter year may reflect the effects of the national recession in 1974/75.

3. Interviews were terminated on a quota basis within each community. All interviews were completed until 100 successful white interviews were obtained; white interviews were subsequently terminated until at least 25 black interviews were obtained, whereupon all further interviews were completed. Note that the termination of white interviews obviates analysis of the *magnitude* of white home purchases but has no effect on relative proportions within the white group.

4. A response to Question 1 of less than fifteen months indicated that the unit had been purchased in the time interval between the end of the sampling

period (June 1977) and the beginning of interviewing (September 1978). In these cases, updated sales price and assessment data corresponding to the date of the most recent sale were obtained from the local tax assessor's office.

5. The distribution of survey respondents across neighborhood categories is fairly uniform for each of the five communities. This uniformity assures that interneighborhood differences can be ascribed to neighborhood racial categories and not to differences among the study sites. Montclair respondents, for instance, comprise between 21 and 36 percent of each neighborhood type, Teaneck respondents between 25 and 36 percent, and so on. The primary exception is in Ewing Township, which is slightly overrepresented in the All-White neighborhood category: Ewing respondents comprise 28.9 percent of this category but only between 7 and 12 percent of the remaining three categories. The low proportion black population and narrow geographic extent of integrated neighborhoods in Ewing accounts for this discrepancy.

6. The standard deviation of income is $17,890 for whites and $13,610 for blacks.

7. Ronald E. Wienk, et al., *Measuring Racial Discrimination in American Housing Markets: The Housing Market Practices Survey* (Washington, D.C.: Department of Housing and Urban Development, 1979).

8. Thomas F. Pettigrew, "Attitudes on Race and Housing: A Social-Psychological View," in *Segregation in Residential Areas,* ed. Amos H. Hawley and Vincent P. Rock (Washington, D.C.: National Academy of Sciences, 1973), pp. 21-84; Angus Campbell, *White Attitudes Toward Black People* (Ann Arbor, Mich.: Institute for Social Research, The University of Michigan, 1971).

9. Thomas F. Pettigrew, "Racial Change and Social Policy," *Annals of the American Academy of Political and Social Science* 441 (January 1979): 114-31.

10. D. Garth Taylor, "Housing, Neighborhoods, and Race Relations: Recent Survey Evidence," *Annals of the American Academy of Political and Social Science* 441 (January 1979): 26-40.

11. Reynolds Farley, et al., " 'Chocolate City-Vanilla Suburbs': Will the Trend Toward Racially Separate Communities Continue?" *Social Science Research* 7 (December 1978): 319-44.

12. Brian J.L. Berry, Carole A. Goodwin, Robert W. Lake, and Katherine B. Smith, "Attitudes Toward Integration: The Role of Status in Community Response to Racial Change," in *The Changing Face of the Suburbs,* ed. by Barry Schwartz (Chicago: University of Chicago Press, 1976), pp. 221-64.

7

HOUSING SEARCH
AND DISCRIMINATION

INTRODUCTION

Differences between white and black homebuyers in socioeconomic characteristics, in the location of previous residence, in housing unit and neighborhood destinations, and in reported discrimination all suggest that housing search experiences may also differ in crucial ways. The search for housing involves a multi-stage process of establishing criteria, identifying and evaluating alternatives, and selecting a unit, and extracts costs measured in monetary, psychic, time, and effort terms. Disparities in the search costs incurred by whites and blacks may have consequences for the housing units obtained by black homebuyers and for the proportion of potential black buyers who successfully find and buy a home.

For blacks who successfully locate and purchase a suburban unit, time, satisfaction, or housing quality may be sacrificed in a tradeoff with rising search costs. Black households in this context may often settle for a less-desirable unit if the commitment of further time and search effort is thought unlikely to produce access to a more satisfactory unit. Greater costs or difficulties in search would likewise contribute to a higher attrition rate among potential black home-buyers. According to this argument, if the search costs for a new residence exceed the costs of remaining in place, then search may be terminated, accompanied by either a downward readjustment of aspirations or increasing dissatisfaction.[1] Systematically greater search costs confronting black potential homebuyers would thus bar substantial numbers of otherwise qualified black households from seeking and/or finding a suburban residence. If this is the case, a growing number of black households are living in suboptimal housing (i.e., less housing than they need or can afford) amid mounting dissatisfaction.

At least three models of racial differences in housing search can be posited. First, lack of previous experience in the housing market, relatively lower levels of prior ownership, and lower educational attainment may result in greater inefficiency and therefore higher costs of black search as opposed to white. Second, overt discrimination by gatekeeper institutions such as real-estate brokers and mortgage lenders may curtail the flow of information on housing vacancies and borrowing opportunities, thereby increasing search costs for blacks. Third, the expectation of discriminatory treatment may cause black potential homebuyers to approach and use these institutional gatekeepers differently and less efficiently than their white counterparts. In this final model, search costs are increased for blacks by the necessity of adapting search behavior to the constraints imposed by having to work with discriminatory institutions.

This chapter assesses the relative importance of each of these models for explaining differences in the housing search experiences of black and white respondents to the Recent Buyers Survey. The analysis asks whether the search experience of black buyers was more protracted, costly, or inefficient than was the housing search of white buyers, and if so, whether background differences, overt discrimination, or black adaptation better explains observed differences in housing search.

The chapter is divided into seven further sections. The first two sections summarize a basic framework for conceptualizing residential mobility and the housing search process, and present the three models of racial differences in housing search. In the next section, we document these racial differences as measured by the length and extensiveness of search, the number and type of information sources used, and the like. The discussion uses regression analysis in the following three sections to assess the extent to which racial differences in search remain after controlling for background differences in socioeconomic characteristics, previous residence, and similar factors affecting the search process. We consider whether these background factors affect black and white search behavior similarly, and we estimate the extent to which eliminating background differences would decrease discrepancies between white and black search experiences. The next section describes experiences of racial steering reported by both black and white homebuyers, and the final section presents a summary of findings.

CONCEPTUALIZING SEARCH BEHAVIOR

The congruence between a household and its housing unit is embodied in the concept of place utility.[2] A utility threshold, unique for each household, can be defined as a level below which the household's present unit is unsatisfactory. This lack of congruence causes stress, and a negative utility threshold is reached when stress (the cost of staying) exceeds the cost of moving.[3] Search costs, measured in monetary, psychic, time, and effort terms, are a component of total moving costs. Stress, or disequilibrium, results from a change in either the household (changes in life cycle, job opportunity, aspirations) or the housing unit (changes in condition, maintenance costs, neighborhood conditions).

Three options are available to households confronting rising dissatisfaction with their housing unit. The first is to adjust needs, expectations, or aspirations to bring them back into line with the existing unit. The second is to restructure the unit (e.g., add on rooms, close off rooms, etc.) so as to better fit the household's needs. The third option is to exchange the existing unit for a more satisfactory one. Relative costs determine which option is chosen. Stress caused by deteriorating neighborhood conditions, for instance, may constitute a psychic cost that outweighs any costs of search and moving.[4] Conversely, a household that has initiated search may exhaust its resources of time and effort, discontinue search, and readjust its aspirations downward in order to stay in the existing unit. Most residential moves that are completed tend to be relatively short-distance moves involving an adjustment of housing needs within the same social area.[5]

The functions of housing search, once initiated, are to locate acceptable alternatives and to develop criteria for evaluating those alternatives.[6] The efficiency of a household's search process depends on the amount and quality of information possessed initially (i.e., prior experience), the information channels available to and utilized by the searcher, and the way in which this information is used by the searcher.[7] Thus, the first-time homebuyer may require additional time (and therefore costs) to develop criteria for evaluation, to identify and learn to use potential sources of information and to synthesize the information obtained.

Information about housing vacancies is typically disseminated through at least one of four channels: mass media (e.g., newspaper listings), specialized agencies (e.g., real estate brokers), public information displays (e.g., "For Sale" signs), and the seller's personal contact network.[8] A seller or agent controlling a vacancy will use one or another of these dissemination channels depending on the relative cost/effort required and the anticipated or desired audience to be reached. Thus, each channel contains information biases, and utilization by the searcher of one channel over another will yield a spatially and qualitatively biased subset of information regarding housing vacancies. For instance, word-of-mouth channels are typically used to disseminate information about either extremely exclusive or extremely deteriorated units. In the former case, audience restriction is of concern, while for deteriorated units cost minimization predominates. Risa Palm has shown that real estate agents tend to be very localized in their recommendations to buyers, so that choice of a particular broker may limit search to that area encompassed by the broker's information field.[9]

To summarize the perspective outlined here, the effort in time, money, and other considerations a household will spend in search for a new unit is relative to the costs extracted by staying in place. The search process involves acquiring new information, evaluating it in the light of existing knowledge, and measuring the relative costs of moving to the new unit, continuing the search for further alternatives, or terminating search without moving. The efficiency of a household's search behavior depends on the amount and quality of prior knowledge, the content of information channels available to the household, and the household's ability to utilize those information channels. Systematic differences between black and white homebuyers along any of these dimensions would generate different search costs by race, effectively reducing access to housing opportunities for the disadvantaged group.

MODELS OF DISCRIMINATION AND
HOUSING SEARCH

Three models are proposed that account for less efficiency and greater costs of search behavior for potential black homebuyers. These models ascribe greater black search costs to either direct or indirect racial discrimination (Exhibit 7-1).

The *contextual model,* implying indirect effects of historical discriminatory patterns, proposes the existence of significant differences between whites and blacks in background or contextual factors that influence residential location and mobility. Thus, lower educational attainment, lower income-earning ability, greater concentration in central cities, a low probability of prior ownership, and concentration in rental housing—all legacies of a historical tradition of discrimination—generate disproportionately greater obstacles in the search process of potential black homebuyers. These contextual differences between blacks and whites result in inadequate prior knowledge of the workings of the housing market, an inability to obtain information about housing unit vacancies, and an inability to evaluate and use information effectively.

The contextual model thus suggests that racial differences in search *experience* are due to racial differences in search *behavior.* Less sophisticated than white buyers, blacks use less efficient information sources (e.g., personal networks rather than formal sources), require more time to obtain and process information, and constrain their search to only a small fraction of available vacancies.

EXHIBIT 7-1

MODELS OF SUBURBAN HOUSING SEARCH DISCRIMINATION

Model	Operant	Discriminatory Impact	Policy Response
(1) CONTEXTUAL (Indirect Discrimination)	Searchers differ due to past discrimination: lower education, income, previous ownership; concentration in central cities, etc.	Inexperience in search; lack of knowledge of information sources; use of inefficient sources.	Compensatory affirmative action.
(2) DIRECT DISCRIMINATION (2a) Overt Discrimination	Searchers treated differently by intermediaries on account of race: noncooperation, racial steering, etc.	Unavailability of information on vacancies.	Strengthen and enforce open housing legislation.
(2b) Black Adaptation to Discriminatory Institutions	Searchers behave differently vis-à-vis intermediaries: differential utilization of search mechanisms.	Inefficiency in search; more effort, longer time required to obtain equivalent information.	Develop alternative unbiased information sources.

Two additional models contend that racial differences in search experience arise from direct discrimination. The first of these points to *overt discrimination* practiced by institutional gatekeepers such as real estate brokers and mortgage lenders. Such institutional actors can effectively limit the flow of information to black buyers by denying that a particular unit is on the market, by canceling appointments, by failing to appear or claiming to be out of the office, by steering black buyers to particular neighborhoods, and so on. The overt discrimination model therefore argues that blacks are no less adept in search than are whites but that they are treated differently by key intermediaries in the search process.

Instances of overt discrimination may in fact be relatively infrequent. As indicated in Chapter 6, one-fifth of black survey respondents reported experiencing discrimination, and a national study by HUD estimates the probability of discrimination at 39 percent for the black homebuyer who contacts three real estate agents.[10] It has been argued that changing mores and Federal fair housing legislation have led to less overt and increasingly subtle forms of racial discrimination.

A low incidence of flagrant discrimination, however, is not necessarily an indication of unbiased broker behavior or the efficacy of open housing legislation. Rather, the third model suggests that black homebuyers, sophisticated enough to avoid situations of outright discrimination, adapt their search behavior to account for constraints imposed by a discriminatory market. The *black adaptation model* therefore proposes that racial differences in search experience arise from the way potential black buyers approach and use institutional intermediaries given the expectation of discriminatory treatment. For example, a white buyer might use a real estate agent to obtain information about housing vacancies. An equivalent black buyer, in contrast, expecting minimal cooperation from the agent, might first learn of the vacancy through another source (e.g., a "For Sale" sign) and only then approach the agent to inquire about the unit.

To recapitulate (see Exhibit 7-1), the *contextual model,* based on indirect discrimination, posits the use of different search strategies by whites and blacks due to contextual or background differences in socioeconomic characteristics and experiences of the two groups. Direct discriminatory effects underlie both the *overt discrimination model* and the *black adaptation model;* in the former case blacks are seen as treated differently by institutional intermediaries, while the latter model sees blacks using these intermediaries differently given the expectation of discriminatory treatment.

The extent to which differences between black and white search experiences are accounted for by each of these models has significant policy implications. Discrepancies in search due to contextual factors require a policy aimed to compensate for these background differences, which is the principle behind affirmative action-type programs. Further support for this sort of response might be generated by a finding that blacks are more subject than whites to the negative effects of contextual factors, i.e., if differences are race-based and not simply founded on class/economic distinctions.

In contrast, a finding of a 'pure' race effect persisting after controlling for contextual factors requires a different policy response. Evidence of outright discrimination against qualified black homebuyers would justify further strengthening and enforcement of open housing legislation. For example, proposed amendments to Title VIII of the Civil Rights Act of 1968 would broaden the definition of discriminatory acts, increase maximum penalties, and widen HUD's role in initiating action against discriminatory sellers or agents. [11]

Finally, evidence of black adaptation to existing institutions in order to minimize the experience of outright discrimination requires the introduction of alternative unbiased sources of information. Penalties of black adaptation to a discriminatory market include poorer quality information, the requirement of extra time, and a less efficient search process. The availability of alternative information sources, such as a public multiple listing service, would allow blacks to bypass or lessen their dependence on potentially discriminatory institutions.

RACIAL DIFFERENCES IN SEARCH BEHAVIOR

The search for housing encompasses a range of dimensions including the variety of information sources used, time spent in preparation for search and time in active search, the number of units looked at and the number internally inspected, the geographic extent of search, and contact with lending institutions to obtain financing.

Information Sources

Startlingly little difference is discernable in either the information sources used or found helpful by black and white homebuyers in the sample (Exhibit 7-2). Well over 90 percent of both blacks and whites used a real estate agent and comparable proportions rated the broker as somewhat or very helpful. Nearly identical proportions of both blacks and whites used the remaining sources listed. Although not shown in the Exhibit, there is also no significant difference in the reasons given for selecting the real estate broker: 44 percent of both blacks and whites selected their agent through a personal recommendation. This initial finding yields little support for the contextual model that claims that blacks are less experienced or knowledgeable than whites in the housing search process.

Two significant differences do emerge from the data, however. First, blacks place somewhat more importance on information obtained from friends: 33.2 percent of blacks but only 25.5 percent of whites say this was 'very helpful.' Evidently, personal networks are an important information source for black suburban homebuyers who may require assurance that a particular community is hospitable to black entry.

EXHIBIT 7-2
SOURCES OF INFORMATION USED AND FOUND HELPFUL,
BY RACE OF BUYER
(percents)

Information Source[a]	SOURCE USED AND FOUND					Source Not Used	Number of Cases
	Very Helpful	Somewhat Helpful	Total Helpful	Not Helpful	Can't Say		
Talk to friends[b]							
Black	33.2	23.1	56.3	8.7	0.9	34.1	229
White	25.5	34.2	59.7	6.0	1.3	32.9	765
Talk to relatives							
Black	20.8	16.9	37.7	5.6	0.0	56.7	231
White	14.5	20.3	34.8	7.4	0.9	56.8	767
Talk to fellow employees							
Black	17.2	19.3	36.5	4.7	1.7	57.1	233
White	14.4	21.4	35.8	6.4	0.5	57.3	763
Check newspaper listings							
Black	23.1	34.1	57.2	10.9	1.7	30.1	229
White	26.9	33.9	60.8	12.5	0.9	25.9	762
Walk around							
Black	13.4	17.2	30.6	3.9	0.0	65.5	232
White	14.3	13.1	27.4	4.3	0.5	67.7	761
Drive around							
Black	42.2	27.6	69.8	4.7	0.9	24.6	232
White	35.7	32.7	68.4	6.2	1.1	24.4	759
"For Sale" signs[c]							
Black	17.5	21.8	39.3	7.4	0.4	52.8	229
White	10.6	14.1	24.7	8.7	1.3	65.3	758
Real estate agent							
Black	76.4	15.9	92.3	2.1	1.3	4.3	233
White	71.6	16.1	87.7	3.1	1.6	7.6	765

Notes: a. "Other" sources including community groups, bank personnel, and builders or contractors, were used by fewer than 15 percent of the sample, with no significant differences found between blacks and whites.

b. $X^2 = 12.99 \, p < .01$

c. $X^2 = 19.45 \, p < .001$

Second, black homebuyers reveal a greater dependence than whites on "For Sale" signs as a source of information on vacancies: nearly 40 percent of blacks but only 25 percent of whites said this was very or somewhat helpful. Ironically, municipal ordinances banning "For Sale" signs to forestall panic selling may have the unintended consequence of removing a vital information source for black buyers. A pattern emerging from the interviews is that black buyers often first identify an available unit through a "For Sale" sign and only then approach a real estate broker for information on the asking price and on gaining access to the unit. This initial evidence may suggest that while both black and white buyers nominally use the same sources, black buyers approach these sources differently and with a different set of expectations for the type of information that will be forthcoming.

Length and Extent of Search

Further evidence for the similarity in white and black search experience is found in a comparison of the duration and extensiveness of search (Exhibit 7-3). Raw-score comparisons of search activity reveal almost no racial difference in the number of housing units seriously considered (2.2), the number of brokers contacted (2.8), the number of information sources used (5.0), and the number found helpful (4.3).

The parity in sources utilized, however, appears to bear less of a payoff for blacks than for whites: black search appears restricted to fewer housing units and fewer communities while extending over a longer time period. A measure of this discrepancy is obtained by dividing the number of housing units looked at by the number of months in active search, yielding an indication of efficiency of access to potential units. Whites gained access to an average of 4.1 units per month compared to 3.2 for blacks, and this discrepancy increases among home-buyers who ultimately purchased in Inter-Racial or All-Black neighborhoods. Whites who eventually bought in an Inter-Racial neighborhood looked at an average of 6.0 units per month compared to 2.7 for blacks, and blacks in All-Black neighborhoods looked at only 1.8 units per month. The lesser efficiency of housing search among blacks despite the use of equivalent information sources provides yet further indication of different treatment of blacks and whites by mediators of housing market information.

The relatively low ratio of housing units inspected per unit of time for both blacks and whites results from a number of cases in which housing search extends over a considerable period. To mitigate potential distortions introduced by unusually long search periods, racial differences on a smaller set of search measures are reported in log form (Exhibit 7-4). The log transformation is useful for both analytical and substantive reasons. Analytically, the log transformation reduces error introduced by extreme values and, in a later section of the analysis, will facilitate interpretation of regression coefficients. Substantively, the difference between, for example, search periods of twenty-four and thirty-six months is less important than the difference between searches of one and six months.

Percent differences in mean log search activities of whites and blacks are reported in Exhibit 7-4. Blacks spend on average half again as much time as whites thinking about looking for a new unit. This is time spent prior to active

EXHIBIT 7-3

HOUSING SEARCH ACTIVITY OF SUBURBAN HOMEBUYERS, BY RACE AND NEIGHBORHOOD RACIAL COMPOSITION

(means)[a]

Race of Buyer and Neighborhood[b]	Months Thinking of Looking	Months in Active Search	Number of Units Looked At	Number of Units Internally Inspected	Number of Units Seriously Considered	Number of Communities Searched	Number of Brokers Contacted	Number of Banks Contacted	Number of Information Sources Used	Number of Information Sources Found Helpful
All whites	6.5 (742)	5.6 (761)	22.8 (751)	17.0 (756)	2.2 (769)	3.5 (759)	2.8 (708)	1.9 (671)	4.9 (735)	4.2 (735)
All blacks	10.2 (213)	5.7 (229)	18.1 (221)	13.9 (225)	2.2 (233)	3.3 (231)	2.8 (223)	1.4 (194)	5.1 (226)	4.5 (226)
All-White neighborhoods										
Whites	6.1 (522)	6.1 (538)	22.8 (531)	17.3 (534)	2.2 (543)	3.5 (538)	2.8 (503)	1.9 (475)	5.0 (544)	4.3 (544)
Black-Entry neighborhoods										
Whites	6.1 (92)	4.7 (94)	22.8 (93)	18.1 (94)	2.3 (95)	3.9 (93)	2.6 (89)	2.4 (79)	4.7 (95)	4.0 (95)
Blacks	9.6 (105)	4.7 (114)	21.2 (110)	16.4 (110)	2.3 (115)	3.7 (115)	3.0 (112)	1.4 (99)	5.2 (115)	4.4 (115)
Inter-Racial neighborhoods										
Whites	8.0 (94)	3.7 (95)	22.2 (93)	13.9 (94)	2.1 (96)	2.8 (95)	3.4 (86)	1.9 (82)	4.8 (96)	4.1 (96)
Blacks	10.9 (79)	6.2 (82)	16.5 (79)	12.9 (82)	2.2 (84)	3.1 (82)	2.5 (82)	1.5 (66)	5.1 (85)	4.6 (85)
All-Black neighborhoods										
Blacks	11.5 (22)	7.4 (25)	13.2 (24)	9.2 (25)	2.1 (26)	2.3 (26)	2.6 (21)	1.4 (19)	4.8 (26)	4.2 (26)

Notes: a. Number of cases indicated in parentheses.
b. Neighborhood racial categories do not sum to the total number of whites and blacks because missing racial data for some blocks in the 1970 census prevented assignment of these cases to neighborhood categories.

search in assessing options, identifying potential destination communities, evaluating financial resources, obtaining recommendations from personal networks, and similarly learning about market operations. Comparing blacks and whites moving into the same neighborhood category, the greatest discrepancy is found in Inter-Racial neighborhoods. Whites moving into these neighborhoods appear to be making the most precipitous moves. Compared to whites moving into All-White neighborhoods, whites in other neighborhoods show no difference in time thinking prior to active search. Blacks, in contrast, spend up to 62 percent more time in premove deliberations. These findings may in part be due to the greater likelihood among whites to move because of a job transfer, while blacks are more likely to move because of dissatisfaction with the neighborhood. An additional reason for the discrepancy may also be a greater reluctance among blacks to move from a familiar setting to a potentially inhospitable one.

Black households also spend substantially more time in active search than do their white counterparts. Black search time is 28 percent higher than that of whites in Black-Entry neighborhoods and 50 percent higher in Inter-Racial areas. Compared to whites in All-White neighborhoods, whites moving into other neighborhood types actually spend on the order of 20 percent *less* time in active search, while blacks spend between 20 and 30 percent *more* time.

Though black housing search extends over a longer period of time, there is little difference in the log number of units looked at or internally inspected. The housing search experience of blacks again appears to be less efficient in this regard, since the same number of units is examined but in a longer time period. If anything, blacks actually gain access to *fewer* units though they spend more time in search: compared to whites in All-White neighborhoods, blacks in Inter-Racial neighborhoods look at 10 percent fewer units, and blacks in All-Black areas inspect 12 percent fewer units.

The geographic extent of search is also more constrained for blacks than for whites. Again using whites in All-White neighborhoods as the norm, blacks in Inter-Racial and All-Black areas confine their search to between 10 and 20 percent fewer communities (the difference for blacks in Inter-Racial areas is not statistically significant).

Contact with Lenders

Black homebuyers are substantially more confined than whites in the number of lending institutions they contact for a mortgage. Evident here is that black homebuyers do substantially less "shopping around" for a bank with favorable mortgage terms than do white buyers. Several factors contribute to this difference including the type of mortgage obtained, use of a mortgage company, and reliance on the real estate agent to arrange financing.

Considering type of financing, black homebuyers are significantly more likely than whites to have an FHA or VA mortgage. Among blacks, 14 percent used an FHA and 28.7 percent a VA mortgage. Comparable figures for whites were 3.8

EXHIBIT 7-4

DIFFERENCES IN MEAN LOG SEARCH ACTIVITIES OF SUBURBAN HOMEBUYERS, BY RACE AND NEIGHBORHOOD RACIAL COMPOSITION
(percents)

Race of Buyer and Neighborhood	Months Thinking of Moving (ln)	Months in Active Search (ln)	Number of Units Looked At (ln)	Number of Units Internally Inspected (ln)	Number of Communities Searched (ln)	Number of Banks Contacted (ln)
All blacks vs. all whites	47.3*	22.6*	−1.5	−0.2	0.3	−31.5*
Blacks vs. whites in Black-Entry neighborhoods	37.2*	27.8*	−0.2	−1.0	−1.1	−41.6*
Blacks vs. whites in Inter-Racial neighborhoods	58.6*	50.4*	−6.6	−2.7	5.9	−31.9*
Compared to whites in All-White neighborhoods:						
Whites in Black-Entry neighborhoods	−6.9	−22.3*	4.4	6.6	12.5	10.0
Blacks in Black-Entry neighborhoods	27.8*	−0.7	4.2	5.5	11.3	−35.7*
Whites in Inter-Racial neighborhoods	2.0	−19.1*	−3.1	−8.2	−16.9*	−9.2
Blacks in Inter-Racial neighborhoods	61.8*	21.7*	−9.6*	−10.7	−11.9	−38.2*
Blacks in All-Black neighborhoods	55.3*	29.8*	−4.7	−12.4*	−19.2*	−39.8*

Note: * = differences between means are significantly different from zero at the .05 level (two-tailed test).

percent and 7.6 percent, respectively. These differences hold within neighborhood types as well. Eight percent of blacks, but no whites, in Black-Entry neighborhoods obtained FHA mortgages. The proportions in Inter-Racial neighborhoods were 19 percent of blacks and 6.6 percent of whites. The proportion of blacks with FHA mortgages increases as the neighborhood percent black increases, reaching 22.7 percent in All-Black neighborhoods. Similar white/black differences within neighborhoods apply to the frequency of VA mortgages: in Black-Entry neighborhoods, 28.7 percent of blacks but only 7.3 percent of whites obtained VA mortgages, and the proportions in Inter-Racial neighborhoods were 27.8 percent of blacks and 12.1 percent of whites. The greater black frequency of FHA and VA mortgages persists at all levels of income, age, education, family composition, and previous tenure.

In part as a consequence of this pattern, blacks in all neighborhood types are more likely than whites to arrange financing through a mortgage company. Many banks are unwilling to negotiate the additional inspections and approvals required for FHA or VA mortgages and mortgage companies are the primary lending source for buyers choosing this form of financing. Consequently, 22 percent of black homebuyers but only 6.4 percent of whites obtained financing from a mortgage company. Once again, this difference is consistent within each neighborhood type: 18.8 percent of blacks but only 2.7 percent of whites in Black-Entry neighborhoods used a mortgage company and in Inter-Racial neighborhoods the black/white ratio was nearly three-to-one.

Finally, black homebuyers were far more reliant on the real estate agent to arrange financing than were white buyers: 40 percent of blacks but 24 percent of whites had their mortgage arranged by the agent. Yet again this difference persists across all neighborhood types and at all levels of income, age, and education.

The combined effect of black dependence on nonconventional mortgages, mortgage companies, and real estate agent recommendations of lenders is that black homebuyers are less able to select among alternative financial institutions to obtain the most advantageous mortgage terms. Black dependence on the real estate agent's recommendation is perhaps the crucial issue here, since the agent will in most cases direct the buyer to a single lender rather than suggest a range of options from which to choose. Further, such recommendations are likely to be based on the agent's guess as to which lender is most likely to approve the loan. In many cases, this may lead automatically to a mortgage company, completely bypassing conventional lenders. As a consequence, blacks are less likely than whites to select a financial institution on the basis of favorable mortgage terms.

In sum, black housing search appears to be significantly less efficient than that of whites, with the same number or fewer units examined—in fewer communities—over a longer time span. The previous chapter documented the extent of background differences between whites and blacks that might account for observed differences in search experience. The next section examines this relationship in light of the models described above.

DETERMINANTS OF SEARCH BEHAVIOR

Factors likely to influence housing search are suggested by the conceptualization of search behavior outlined above. These fall into seven general categories of variables. *Housing needs* are measured by unit size, age, neighborhood location, and value. Purchase of a larger or higher-value unit would justify a longer and more extensive search since the costs of search can be amortized over the higher purchase price. *Buyer characteristics* include age, education/occupation, and previous tenure. Older homebuyers and those with lower education and occupational attainment are likely to limit search to relatively few units in few communities. First-time homebuyers, lacking experience in the market, should be less efficient than previous owners and require more time to identify and evaluate potential units.

The *location of previous residence* encompasses both type of area and distance moved. Movers from a central city may require more search time but inspect fewer units than buyers moving within the suburbs, again on grounds of familiarity. *Reasons for moving* dictate the time available for search. A job-related move, for instance, is likely to be more sudden than a move motivated by dissatisfaction with the neighborhood. The household's *selection criteria* should influence the extensiveness of search. Movers for whom the characteristics of the unit are most important can be expected to inspect more units, while those for whom the community social environment is paramount may examine fewer units but more communities. *Prior knowledge* of the community should result in a more constrained search pattern, often restricted to only that community. Finally, the *information sources used* determine the amount of information obtained: use of a real estate agent as the primary information source should yield access to the largest number of potential units.

These expectations are tested in a series of regression models relating six measures of housing search to the above set of background factors and the race and neighborhood of the homebuyer (Exhibit 7-5). The dependent variables include two measures of the length of search—months thinking of moving and months in active search—and four measures of the extensiveness of search—the number of units looked at and internally inspected, the number of communities searched, and the number of lending institutions contacted to arrange financing.

The functional form used throughout is log-linear, in which the dependent variable is the natural log of the search measure and the independent variables are in linear form. The only exceptions are for the assessed value of the land and the sale price of the unit, which are both in log form. The explanatory power of the equations is modest at best: the models account for between 12 and 24 percent of the variation in the six search measures. These relatively low R^2 values suggest that additional factors, probably including personal idiosyncrasies, also contribute to variations in housing search but are not accounted for in the equations. This might be a substantial drawback if the analysis aimed to predict housing search behavior from a set of known background characteristics. Of more importance for our immediate purposes, however, is the significance of individual variables, including race of the homebuyer, when controlling for background variables selected on theoretical and substantive grounds.

Unit and Buyer Characteristics

The characteristics of the buyer comprise the most significant block of factors influencing the length of time spent in preparation for search (Exhibit 7-5). As will be seen below, active search time is affected most directly by the reason for moving.

Purchase price of the unit, which is a summation of housing size and quality and a proxy for resources available to the buyer, is directly and significantly related to the extensiveness of search. A higher sale price is associated with a longer period of active search that covers more units in more communities. As expected, a longer and more extensive search is warranted since the costs attendant on this activity can be amortized over a larger purchase price. Interestingly, higher purchase price leads to search in more communities while purchase of a larger unit (with more bedrooms) constrains search to fewer communities. The need for an exceptionally large unit appears to limit buyers to a few communities with an appropriate housing stock. Similarly, a high assessed value of the lot, signifying large lot size and high capitalized value of neighborhood amenities, is also associated with search in a limited number of communities. In short, while high purchase price is related to a longer and more extensive search process, purchase of a large unit on a high-value lot limits search to a few communities with a housing stock and neighborhood amenities that can meet these criteria.

Age of household head has a constraining impact on search behavior: older homebuyers spend more time in pre-search deliberation, examine fewer units, and confine their search to fewer communities. Blue-collar occupation and a high school education (simple r = .513) lengthens search time by more than one-third compared to white-collar homebuyers but restrict search to fewer units. In contrast, previous ownership allows for a more efficient search process. Households with previous market experience reduce their search time by some 15 to 20 percent, compared to first-time homebuyers. A move from rental occupancy seems to require greater deliberation and a longer search process in which options are discovered and evaluated.

Previous Residence and Mobility

As indicated above, the household's reason for moving strongly influences the length and extensiveness of its housing search. A job-related move allows little time for deliberation or search: households moving for this reason spent 35.7 percent less time in active search than did otherwise equivalent households (regression coefficient of −.4414 on log scale). The search process for these households is nonetheless quite efficient, since they inspect on average 25.6 percent more units than other households despite the limited time available to them. In contrast, families moving for housing unit or neighborhood reasons engage in proportionally longer search. Moves of this type are less pressing than a job transfer and allow for a more extended review of alternatives. Since these

EXHIBIT 7-5

FACTORS INFLUENCING SEARCH BEHAVIOR OF SUBURBAN HOMEBUYERS

Independent Variables	Months Thinking of Moving	Months in Active Search	Number of Units Looked At	Number of Units Internally Inspected	Number of Communities Searched	Number of Banks Contacted
			DEPENDENT VARIABLES (ln)			
UNIT CHARACTERISTICS						
Number of bedrooms	.0473	.0424	.0328	.0657**	-.0657***	-.0149
Age of house	-.0007	-.0001	.0017	.0008	.0009	.0001
Land assessed value (ln)		.0313			-.6670***	
Community type (Montclair or Teaneck=1)	.0396		.0080	.0743		.0366
Sale price (ln)	.0818	.2859**	.9051***	.9370***	.4925***	-.0231
BUYER CHARACTERISTICS						
Age of head	.0129***	-.0024	-.0169***	-.0149***	-.0089***	-.0058**
Previous tenure (Own=1)	-.1947*	-.1614**	-.0048	-.1204	-.0785	-.1042**
Blue-collar occupation (Yes=1)	.3098***	.1339*	-.1845**	-.1635**	-.0863*	-.0742*
High school grad or less (Yes=1)						
PREVIOUS RESIDENCE						
Same neighborhood (Yes=1)	.1945*	-.0564	-.2204*	-.2422**	-.2681***	.0794
Out-of-state central city (Yes=1)	.0358	.0616	-.0042	.0234	-.0251	.0034
Job-related move (Yes=1)	-.4492***	-.4414***	.1309	.2281**	.1038	.0611
Housing unit reason (Yes=1)	-.0070	.1411**	.0396	.0605	-.0280	.0448
Neighborhood reason (Yes=1)	.1641	.1887**	.2406**	.2426**	.0608	.0262

MOBILITY BEHAVIOR

	(1)	(2)	(3)	(4)	(5)	(6)
Chose unit for financial reason (Yes=1)	-.0022	-.0402	.0293	.0140	.3001***	.0680
Chose unit for social reason (Yes=1)	-.1257*	-.0858	-.1467**	-.0822	-.0501	.0235
Chose unit for housing unit reason (Yes=1)	-.0155	-.0683	.1811*	.2261**	.3925***	-.0494
Prior knowledge of community (Yes=1)	-.0461	.1345**	-.1249*	-.1362**	-.2622***	-.0341
Real estate agent as most important source (Yes=1)	.0445	-.0253	.2495***	.2662***	.0111	-.0145
FINANCING FACTORS						
Chose bank for terms (Yes=1)	.4312***	.2142***				.5604***
Chose bank for convenience (Yes=1)						.3923***
FHA/VA mortgage (Yes=1)						-.2281***
RACE (Black=1)			.0779	.0887	.0218	.0528
Constant	-.1731	-2.1510	-6.8019	-7.6576	-3.1509	.7023
F	5.5002	5.5536	7.9749	10.4947	9.9708	10.0575
R^2	.112	.110	.150	.188	.179	.239
Sample Size	805	831	830	836	841	694

RACE AND NEIGHBORHOOD

Compared to whites in All-white neighborhoods:

	(1)	(2)	(3)	(4)	(5)	(6)
Whites in Black-Entry neigh.	.0248	-.2343**	.0349	.0666	.0577	-.0118
Blacks in Black-Entry neigh.	.3316***	.0139	.0639	.0673	.0343	.0419
Whites in Inter-Racial neigh.	.0713	-.2319**	-.0249	-.0554	-.0783	-.0085
Blacks in Inter-Racial neigh.	.5930***	.3324***	.1114	.1432	.0218	.0907
Blacks in All-Black neigh.	.6099***	.3969***	.3399	.1796	.0141	.1144
R^2	.117	.131	.153	.189	.184	.243

Notes: Significance levels show one-tailed test that coefficient is significantly different from zero: (***) $p < .01$; (**) $p < .05$; (*) $p < .10$.

In interpreting the regression coefficients (b), note that in the log-linear model b (100) approximates the percent change in the dependent variable Y only when b is small. Otherwise use (e^b-1) 100.

moves are motivated by dissatisfaction with the present unit, households continue searching until the desired improvement is realized.

A move within the same neighborhood appears to be anticipated over a relatively long time period but involves the purchase of a fortuitous vacancy in the neighborhood. Such movers spend a longer period thinking of moving prior to search, but inspect fewer units than other movers and confine their search to essentially a single community. Households in this category may resolve a long-standing dissatisfaction with their housing unit by purchasing a better unit that is put on the market in the same neighborhood; these households improve their housing quality while maintaining social ties and activities within the neighborhood.

The household's selection criteria principally influence the extensiveness rather than the length of housing search. Families for whom the price or characteristics of the unit per se are the primary criteria extend their search over a broader geographic area encompassing more communities. Also as would be expected, households choosing their unit because of its characteristics have inspected a larger number of units. Conversely, families for whom "social criteria" are the most important (to some extent a euphemism for racial composition) restrict their housing search to fewer units. Prior knowledge of the community also curtails the extent of search, especially as measured by the number of communities. Time in active search, however, is longer, perhaps the converse of the brief search period engaged in by job transferees from outside the area. Finally, the use of a real estate broker as the most important information source results in 28 percent more units looked at and 31 percent more units internally inspected as compared to other sources of information.

Financing Factors

A separate set of financing factors pertains specifically to the number of banks contacted to obtain a mortgage. Choosing a bank because of advantageous terms results in a 75 percent increase in the number of banks contacted, as compared to other reasons for selection (e.g., real estate agent recommendation). In contrast, obtaining an FHA or VA mortgage results in a 20.4 percent decrease in the number of banks contacted, presumably reflecting the importance of broker assistance in obtaining the mortgage in these cases.

Race

All other things equal, black homebuyers spend substantially more time in search of housing than otherwise comparable white buyers. Comparing all blacks with all whites in the sample, the coefficient on a dummy variable for race indicates that black households spent 54 percent more time thinking about moving and 24 percent more time in active search than did white households equivalent in unit and buyer characteristics, previous residence, and mobility behavior. *Thus, the search process of black homebuyers extends over a longer period than that of whites even when differences in background contextual factors are controlled.*

Despite the longer duration of black housing search, there is no difference in the number of units looked at or examined or the number of communities searched by whites and blacks when controlling for background differences. This is in accord with the comparison of log search values reported above. However, the finding of racial parity in the number of units examined when controlling for intervening factors refutes the null hypothesis that contextual variables may have concealed racial differences in the extensiveness of search. Finally, differences between whites and blacks in the number of banks contacted disappear when controlling for the reason for selecting the bank and for the type of mortgage obtained.

Further insights into the effect of race on search behavior are obtained by considering neighborhood racial composition as well as the race of the buyer (Exhibit 7-5). Identical regression equations were run with the single race dummy replaced by separate dummies for each of the race/neighborhood combinations. With the variable for whites in All-White neighborhoods left out of the equation, the independent effect of each of the remaining categories is expressed relative to this norm.

Focusing first on decision time prior to search, neither whites in Black-Entry nor whites in Inter-Racial neighborhoods are appreciably different from whites in All-White neighborhoods. The difference for each black group, however, is significant, with the difference increasing appreciably with increasing black neighborhood concentration. Compared to whites in All-White neighborhoods, otherwise comparable blacks in Black-Entry neighborhoods spend 39 percent more time in deliberation prior to active search, blacks in Inter-Racial areas spend 81 percent more time, and blacks in All-Black neighborhoods spend 84 percent more time, all other things being equal.

A similar pattern is evident in time in active search. Here, whites in Black-Entry neighborhoods and Inter-Racial neighborhoods spend some 21 percent *less* time in active search than whites in All-White neighborhoods, controlling for background factors. Each black group, in contrast, averages longer search time relative to whites in All-White neighborhoods.

These comparisons against the norm in All-White neighborhoods suggest a significant divergence of black and white search experience *within* biracial neighborhoods. If whites in these neighborhoods spend less time in search than whites on All-White blocks but blacks spend more, then we can interpret these differences as a longer time spent by blacks than whites within the same neighborhood. Summing the coefficients for blacks and and whites within Black-Entry neighborhoods reveals that blacks spend 35.9 percent more time thinking of moving and 28.2 percent more time in active search than whites moving into the same neighborhoods with the same background characteristics. Blacks in Inter-Racial neighborhoods spend 69 percent more time thinking of moving and 76 percent more time in active search than their otherwise comparable white neighbors.[12]

In sum, the analysis lends considerable support to the direct discrimination models of racial differences in housing search, since significant impediments to search by blacks remain after controlling for a broad array of background characteristics. Regression analysis with a unified sample and dummy race variables reveals that the housing search experience of black homebuyers is significantly less efficient than that of whites with identical background characteristics. While comparable blacks and whites examine equal numbers of housing units, the process for blacks extends over a considerably longer time period, with greater implied costs of time and effort expended and benefits foregone.

These racial differences in search behavior cannot be ascribed to socioeconomic or demographic factors or differences in previous tenure, since disparities in search remain after controlling for these characteristics. It is possible, however, that variations in these characteristics affect blacks and whites differently and that pooling the two groups in a single equation obscures these differential effects. We turn to this issue in the next section.

THE DIFFERENTIAL IMPACT OF BACKGROUND FACTORS ON WHITES AND BLACKS

Do variations in socioeconomic and mobility characteristics affect blacks and whites differently? For example, the age of the buyer was seen in the unified search equations to constrain housing search to fewer housing units in a restricted area. This effect may be more pronounced for whites than for blacks but this difference would be obscured in the pooled estimates. To consider this question, the pooled search equations have been reestimated separately for the white (Exhibit 7-6) and black (Exhibit 7-7) subsamples with the race dummies omitted. These stratified equations permit comparative analysis of factors influencing the search experiences of black and white homebuyers. The analysis indeed reveals substantial differences in the pattern of influences on white and black housing search.

Time Prior to Search

Age of the household head extends time in pre-search deliberations for whites but not for blacks. The age distribution among white homebuyers covers a broader span of years than is the case among blacks and thus encompasses greater variation. In addition, the mean age of black homebuyers is higher than that of whites, and older black households may be in the best position to move as measured by income and assets.

Conversely, previous ownership reduces pre-search preparations for white buyers but has no impact on black deliberations. The longer time required for black homebuyers to begin active search is evidently not a function of lack of ownership experience since blacks who owned and who rented their previous unit spend an equal amount of time thinking of looking for a house (the coefficient is not statistically significant at the 10 percent level). Instead, the expectation of discriminatory treatment and wariness of entering a potentially

EXHIBIT 7-6

FACTORS INFLUENCING SEARCH BEHAVIOR OF WHITE HOMEOWNERS

Independent Variables	Months Thinking of Looking	DEPENDENT VARIABLES (ln)				
		Months in Active Search	Number of Units Looked At	Number of Units Internally Inspected	Number of Communities Searched	Number of Banks Contacted
UNIT CHARACTERISTICS						
Number of bedrooms	.0417	.0390	.0508	.0706*	-.0675**	-.0216
Age of house	-.0016	-.0015	.0015	.0012	.0005	.0004
Land assessed value (ln)		.0357			-.0682**	
Community type (Montclair or Teaneck=1)	.0724		-.0638	-.0034		.0456
Sale price (ln)	-.0011	.2813**	.9419***	1.0211***	.4246***	-.0414
BUYER CHARACTERISTICS						
Age of head	.0137***	-.0038	-.0176***	-.0147***	-.0072***	-.0060**
Previous tenure (Own=1)	-.2829***	-.1816**	-.0842	-.2205**	-.1469**	-.1138**
Blue-collar occupation (Yes=1)	.1364	.0210				
High school grad or less (Yes=1)			-.1863*	-.1802*	-.0609	-.0837
PREVIOUS RESIDENCE						
Same neighborhood (Yes=1)	.1771	.0400	-.1753	-.1732	-.1602*	.0852
Out-of-state central city (Yes=1)	-.0994	-.0136	-.0250	-.0043	-.0605	.0452
Job-related move (Yes=1)	-.3243**	-.4259***	.1622	.2724**	.1578**	.0638

EXHIBIT 7-6 (Continued)

Housing unit reason (Yes=1)	.1002	.1618**	.0388	.0365	-.0259	.0572
Neighborhood reason (Yes=1)	.3228**	.1986*	.3284**	.3043**	.1323*	-.0269
MOBILITY BEHAVIOR						
Chose unit for financial reason (Yes=1)	.0507	-.0046	.0711	.0756	.3339***	.0701
Chose unit for social reason (Yes=1)	-.0982	-.0681	-.1317*	-.0680	-.1395**	.0027
Chose unit for housing unit reason (Yes=1)	-.0311	-.1023	.1724	.2800**	.3998***	-.0844
Prior knowledge of community (Yes=1)	-.0839	.1178*	-.1506*	-.1351*	-.2654***	-.0300
Real estate agent as most important source (Yes=1)	.1281*	-.0138	.3322***	.3228***	.0311	-.0057
FINANCING FACTORS						
Chose bank for terms (Yes=1)						.5600***
Chose bank for convenience (Yes=1)						.4077***
FHA/VA mortgage (Yes=1)						-.2319***
Constant	.6709	-1.9808	-7.2301	-8.5904	-2.4355	.9116
F	2.5291	3.9768	6.8151	8.9107	9.1943	8.2307
R^2	.065	.097	.154	.192	.197	.237
Sample size	632	651	653	656	656	552

Note: Significance levels show one-tailed test that coefficient is significantly different from zero: (***) $p < .01$; (**) $p < .05$; (*) $p < .10$.

EXHIBIT 7-7

FACTORS INFLUENCING SEARCH BEHAVIOR OF BLACK HOMEBUYERS

Independent Variables	Months Thinking of Moving	Months in Active Search	DEPENDENT VARIABLES (ln) Number of Units Looked At	Number of Units Internally Inspected	Number of Communities Searched	Number of Banks Contacted
UNIT CHARACTERISTICS						
Number of bedrooms	.0708	.1028*	-.0585	.0631	.0129	.0145
Age of house	.0049	.0078**	.0042	-.0032	.0024	-.0005
Land assessed value (ln)		.0446			-.0414	
Community type (Montclair or Teaneck=1)	-.1678		.2058	.3522**	.6830***	-.0218
Sale price (ln)	.3827	.2669	.8367***	.5769**		.0954
BUYER CHARACTERISTICS						
Age of head	.0042	.0015	-.0099	-.0122	-.0160*	.0003
Previous tenure (Own=1)	.2338	-.0514	.3545**	.3749**	.1237	-.0815
Blue collar occupation (Yes=1)	.6318***	.3632***				
High school grad or less (Yes=1)			-.2439*	-.1742	-.0833	-.0760
PREVIOUS RESIDENCE						
Same neighborhood (Yes=1)	.4001	-.6409***	-.2701	-.3482	-.5981***	-.0211
Out-of-state central city (Yes=1)	.4573**	.1484	.0452	.1769	.0208	-.1700*
Job-related move (Yes=1)	-1.1239***	-.5084**	-.1528	-.1138	-.1711	.0878
Housing unit reason (Yes=1)	-.3203*	-.0020	-.0272	.1409	-.0525	-.0033
Neighborhood reason (Yes=1)	-.3344	.1423	-.0279	.0428	-.1268	.1644

EXHIBIT 7-7 (Continued)

MOBILITY BEHAVIOR

Chose unit for financial reason (Yes=1)	-.1909	-.2674	-.1331	-.1566	.1759	-.0082
Chose unit for social reason (Yes=1)	-.2799*	-.2051*	-.2423*	-.1604	.1963**	.0852
Chose unit for housing unit reason (Yes=1)	.1556	.0693	.3196*	.0539	.3967***	.0392
Prior knowledge of community (Yes=1)	.0177	.1781	-.0940	-.1994	-.2959***	-.0809
Real estate agent as most important source (Yes=1)	-.2433*	-.0180	-.0085	.1128	-.0130	-.0496
FINANCING FACTORS						
Chose bank for terms (Yes=1)						.4790***
Chose bank for convenience (Yes=1)						.2752**
FHA/VA mortgage (Yes=1)						-.1747**
Constant	-2.6056	-2.4475	-5.9184	-3.7825	-5.6195	-.7192
F	2.2835	2.5794	2.5680	3.0917	3.2670	2.4463
R^2	.200	.213	.215	.245	.250	.288
Sample Size	173	180	177	180	185	142

Note: Significance levels show one-tailed test that coefficient is significantly different from zero: (***) $p < .01$; (**) $p < .05$; (*) $p < .10$.

inhospitable environment require an equal amount of prepartion by both owners and renters. Stated otherwise, the advantages of previous ownership in reducing preparation time for whites are not enjoyed by black homebuyers.

Blue-collar occupation extends preparation time among black homebuyers but not among whites. Lower occupational achievement seems to present whites with no obstacle to moving while increasing time spent in deliberation by blacks by 88.1 percent. Similarly, a move from an out-of-state central city impacts uniquely on time spent by blacks in planning prior to search. This initial sub-urbanizing move requires 58 percent more time in preparation by blacks while it has no significant impact on whites. In contrast, a job-related move accelerates pre-search decision making far more precipituously for blacks (−67.5 percent) than for whites (−27.7 percent). Black households moving because of a job transfer may be more secure in their status than other blacks and therefore less hesitant about moving. Assistance provided by a relocation service would also help assuage black fears of a hostile welcome and curtail the longer time required by other black households to obtain such information from friends and relatives and similar personal contacts.

Blacks moving for a housing unit reason spend less time in pre-search deliberation than other black households, while this factor has no impact on white behavior. Conversely, whites moving for a neighborhood-related reason spend more time thinking prior to search, while the coefficient for this variable is not significant in the black subsample. Housing unit inadequacy appears to be a more pressing problem for blacks, with active search following quickly on the decision to move. Neighborhood inadequacy appears to be a less pressing problem for whites, allowing a longer period of deliberation prior to actual search. In yet another racial disparity, black homebuyers who choose their new unit for social reasons reduced the time before search by 24 percent compared to other blacks, while this factor has no influence on white search. Choosing a unit for social reasons suggests the neighborhood presence of friends or relatives or other information sources that would resolve black concerns of white hostility.

Finally, black homebuyers who used a real estate agent as their most important information source *reduced* their pre-search preparation by 22 percent relative to other blacks. White homebuyers who used a real estate agent as their primary source spent 14 percent *more* time than other whites in thinking about moving. Among blacks, use of a real estate agent may represent relative sophistication in the housing market, facility with white institutions, and consequently a reduced period of pre-search deliberation. Blacks who do not use an agent but search for housing outside the mainstream of information spend a longer period in discussion and decision making prior to search. In contrast, whites who do not use an agent appear to be making relatively abrupt moves, spending less time in deliberation prior to search. Whites do not use an agent when they have already obtained information about an available unit from another source, while blacks not using an agent conduct their search outside the mainstream of housing market information.

Time in Active Search

The comparative determinants of active search time for whites and blacks mirror in many respects the pattern of time spent prior to search. Housing unit characteristics are a stronger influence on the length of search than on time in preparation but again the pattern is different for blacks and whites. Blacks buying older and larger homes spend more time in search than other blacks, while these particular housing needs pose no additional burden on the housing search of whites. The ability to amortize costs of a larger search over a higher sales price, however, is restricted to whites; the coefficient for log sale price is significant only in the white equation.

As with time spent prior to search, previous ownership yields a savings in search time only for whites. Blacks who owned their previous unit spend as long in the search for housing as do black first-time homebuyers. This provides yet further evidence that black/white differences in search experiences cannot be ascribed to the greater proportion of first-time homebuyers among blacks and their lack of familiarity with the housing market. Also in parallel with the findings above, blue-collar occupation lengthens search time only for blacks. Whites with blue-collar occupations spend no more time in search than do other whites.

Moving within the same neighborhood decreases black search time by nearly half (-47.3 percent) compared to other black buyers, and has an insignificant effect on white search. Trading up within the same neighborhood appears to be a significant means for blacks to improve their housing without incurring substantial search costs. Again reflecting the data on pre-search decision time, choosing the housing unit because of neighborhood social characteristics substantially reduces search time for black homebuyers but has no effect on the housing search of whites. The desire to ensure social compatability and avoid white hostility appears to be a dominant theme in the suburban housing search of black homebuyers.

Extensiveness of Search

Purchase of a higher-value unit results in a more extensive housing search for both blacks and whites as measured by the number of units and communities examined. Both blacks and whites with a high school education or less look at fewer housing units than do homebuyers with a higher educational level. Significant differences in the extensiveness of black and white housing search emerge despite these similarities. Among white homebuyers, search becomes more restricted with age and older household heads look at and inspect fewer units. Age is not a significant factor in the number of units examined by black homebuyers. As suggested above, older black homebuyers may be in the best income and asset position to allow for an extensive housing search, in part offsetting the potentially constricting influence of age.

Previous ownership influences the number of units inspected, but the direction of influence is opposite for blacks and whites. Previous owners among white homebuyers inspect 20 percent *fewer* units than other whites; among blacks, previous owners inspect 45.5 percent *more* units. Ownership of a previous unit seems to allow whites to be more discerning in their selection of units to inspect internally. Among black homebuyers, in contrast, previous ownership seems to impart an appreciation of housing quality that requires the rejection of the inadequate units that are often shown to black prospects. First-time black homebuyers, in other words, may quickly accept the less adequate units made available to the black submarket that more experienced black homebuyers reject.

The most significant racial difference in the extensiveness of housing search pertains to the use of a real estate agent as the primary information source. *Use of an agent increases the number of housing units looked at or inspected by whites by nearly 40 percent over whites using other primary information sources but has no impact on facilitating the housing search process of blacks.* Black homebuyers using a real estate agent gain access to no more and no fewer units than blacks using newspaper listings, personal contacts or other sources as their primary information source. Evidence from the followup interviews provides an explanation of this finding. Black homebuyers who use a real estate agent are typically given information on relatively few available units, often no more than the one or two units that the agent has advertised in the newspaper. While whites are shown a range of additional units, black homebuyers are told that nothing else is available at the moment. The experience reported by a black respondent is instructive:

> "There was a house in the paper that was advertised in a price range that we could afford, and the realtor took us to the house and we said, you know, did she have any others that we would be interested in. She didn't have anything else, and she would call us if she did, and she never called."

In the aggregate, blacks using an agent effectively obtain information about no more units than are advertised in other sources.

Number of Lenders Contacted

The factors influencing contact with lenders appear to be identical for black and white homebuyers. The ability to "shop" for favorable mortgage terms or the tendency to select a bank because of a convenient location influence black and white search patterns equally. Use of FHA or VA financing reduces the number of banks contacted by blacks and whites to a similar extent. The data do not permit an assessment of the reasons for greater black dependence on FHA or VA mortgages or the greater frequency among whites to shop for advantageous terms. An explanation of these patterns is beyond the scope of this analysis, although it is clearly crucial for an understanding of black and white experiences in obtaining financing.

REMOVING BACKGROUND DIFFERENCES

Analysis of the unified sample revealed that racial differences in search remain even after background differences between whites and blacks have been controlled. Stratifying by race revealed in turn that background variables affect the housing search experiences of blacks and whites differently. The remaining question, then, is what proportion of the racial difference in search experience would be eliminated by removing these unique effects of background characteristics?

This analysis utilizes the stratified equations for black and white housing search reported above, with the black subsample means entered into the white equations and white means applied to the black equations (Exhibits 7-6 and 7-7). In this method, the unique black impact of background characteristics is applied to the sample of white homebuyers, and the particular dynamics of white search are applied to the black sample. Two estimates are obtained for each search measure: (1) the difference between the mean black score on that measure and the black score estimated with the white equation; and (2) the difference between the mean white score and the white score estimated with the black equation. The weighted average of these two estimates yields the difference between white and black search controlling for the unique impact of background characteristics on the two racial subsamples. The method is extended to differences between neighborhood racial categories using the stratified equations reported in Appendix Exhibit 7A-1.[13]

The result of eliminating unique background effects on white and black search in this fashion is limited at best. For time spent thinking prior to search, fully 75 percent of the original difference between blacks and whites remains after controlling (Exhibit 7-8). A somewhat better effect is achieved for blacks versus whites in Black-Entry neighborhoods, yet 64 percent of the original difference still remains. Controlling for unique background influences removes less than 20 percent of the difference between whites and blacks in other neighborhood categories.

The effect on time in active search is even less impressive (Exhibit 7-9). As in the case of pre-search time, some 72 percent of the original difference between whites and blacks remains. Within particular neighborhood categories, controlling for background influence has no appreciable effect on black-white disparities in search time.

Only in the case of number of banks contacted does an original significant difference disappear (Exhibit 7-10). The implication here, however, is that the number of banks contacted by whites and blacks would no longer be different if

EXHIBIT 7-8

RESULT OF CONTROLLING FOR CONTEXTUAL FACTORS INFLUENCING MONTHS THINKING OF LOOKING FOR A HOUSE

Race of Buyer and Neighborhood	DIFFERENCE IN MEAN SEARCH		
	Raw Effect (Before Controlling)	Estimated Effect (Controlling For Context)[a]	Estimated Effect as Percent of Raw Effect
All blacks vs. all whites	.5702*	.4296*	75.3
Blacks vs. whites in Black-Entry neighborhoods	.4226*	.2709*	64.1
Blacks vs. whites in Inter-Racial neighborhoods	.7297*	.6337*	86.8
Compared to whites in All-White neighborhoods:			
Whites in Black-Entry neighborhoods	−.0836	.0328	b
Blacks in Black-Entry neighborhoods	.3390*	.2796*	82.5
Whites in Inter-Racial neighborhoods	.0245	.0109	b
Blacks in Inter-Racial neighborhoods	.7542*	.6180*	81.9
Blacks in All-Black neighborhoods	.6750*	1.3319*	197.3

Notes: * Indicates differences between means are significantly different from zero at the .05 level (two-tailed test).

a. Weighted average of the differences obtained when white means are entered into the black equation, and vice versa, where the weights correspond to the number of whites and the number of blacks, respectively.

b. Neither difference is significantly different from zero at the .05 level.

the latter were as able as the former to select a bank because of advantageous credit terms.

Initial differences in the search experiences of white and black homebuyers remain after controlling for both shared and unique effects of background socio-economic and mobility differences. The data provide no support for the contextual model of racial differences in search behavior and suggest instead that such differences are due to overt discrimination and black adaptation to a discriminatory market. Evidence of racial steering would provide one indication that blacks and whites are treated differently by market intermediaries and would confirm black perceptions of the need for adaptive behavior.

EVIDENCE OF RACIAL STEERING

In numerous cases, black respondents reported that real estate agents provided full and complete access to available units throughout the case study communities. Yet it must be recalled that these are identified as integrated communities in their respective regions, and adjoining communities are less open to blacks. Black homebuyers are often steered to these communities while white buyers are steered away. The issue of steering cannot be divorced from the

EXHIBIT 7-9

RESULT OF CONTROLLING FOR CONTEXTUAL FACTORS INFLUENCING MONTHS IN ACTIVE SEARCH

Race of Buyer and Neighborhood	DIFFERENCE IN MEAN SEARCH		
	Raw Effect (Before Controlling)	Estimated Effect (Controlling for Context)[a]	Estimated Effect as Percent of Raw Effect
All blacks vs. all whites	.2632*	.1886*	71.7
Blacks vs. whites in Black-Entry neighborhoods	.2711*	.2575*	95.0
Blacks vs. whites in Inter-Racial neighborhoods	.5122*	.4875*	95.2
Compared to whites in All-White neighborhoods:			
Whites in Black-Entry neighborhoods	−.2799*	−.2816*	100.6
Blacks in Black-Entry neighborhoods	−.0088	−.0888	b
Whites in Inter-Racial neighborhoods	−.2393*	−.2099*	87.7
Blacks in Inter-Racial neighborhoods	.2727*	.2486*	91.2
Blacks in All-Black neighborhoods	.3745*	.4250*	113.5

Notes: * Indicates differences between means are significantly different from zero at the .05 level (two-tailed test).

a. Weighted average of the differences obtained when white means are entered into the black equation, and vice versa, where the weights correspond to the number of whites and the number of blacks, respectively.

b. Neither difference is significantly different from zero at the .05 level.

question of scale, with steering occurring at the level of the individual housing unit, the neighborhood, and entire communities.

Black homebuyers reported numerous instances of real estate agents showing housing units only in predominantly black neighborhoods:

> "She showed us some homes and I thought she was wasting my time. We told them what we didn't want, and we still were being steered to areas where there was a good mix of blacks."

The result of such treatment is for some black homebuyers to terminate or postpone search or to use alternative information sources. The former course

EXHIBIT 7-10

RESULT OF CONTROLLING FOR CONTEXTUAL FACTORS INFLUENCING NUMBER OF BANKS CONTACTED

Race of Buyer and Neighborhood	*DIFFERENCE IN MEAN SEARCH*		
	Raw Effect (Before Controlling)	*Estimated Effect (Controlling for Context)*[a]	*Estimated Effect as Percent of Raw Effect*
All blacks vs. all whites	−.1254*	.0387	0.0
Blacks vs. whites in Black-Entry neighborhoods	−.1909*	−.0043	2.3
Blacks vs. whites in Inter-Racial neighborhoods	−.1211*	.0211	0.0
Compared to whites in All-White neighborhoods:			
Whites in Black-Entry neighborhoods	.0416	−.0068	b
Blacks in Black-Entry neighborhoods	−.1493*	−.0352	23.6
Whites in Inter-Racial neighborhoods	−.0386	−.0453	b
Blacks in Inter-Racial neighborhoods	−.1597*	−.0064	4.0
Blacks in All-Black neighborhoods	−.1661*	.1720*	NA

Notes: * Indicates differences between means are significantly different from zero at the .05 level (two-tailed test).

a. Weighted average of the differences obtained when white means are entered into the black equation, and vice versa, where the weights correspond to the number of whites and the number of blacks, respectively.

b. Neither difference is significantly different from zero at the .05 level.

results in the lengthier search process described above; the latter, though impersonal and thus objective, is relatively inefficient.

"Before we bought our house, we had gone to P. We went to two people, and they seemed to take us to black run-down areas. And I didn't want a black run-down house in a black run-down area, *so we just stopped looking altogether.* My husband just happened to see this particular home, he liked it, and we bought it. How did I find it? It was on the placard they put out front."

Steering of this sort limits the housing options available to blacks to the housing stock in predominantly black neighborhoods. This often leads to extreme dissatisfaction with the units being shown and a sense of frustration at the service provided by the agent:

"They would try to sell us homes that they wanted to sell us rather than ones that we really wanted to look at. They were trying to make us stick to a certain area." [Interviewer: "By a certain area, what do you mean?"] "Well, basically a black area. Or those areas that had blacks in them."

Several black homebuyers reported a sense of frustration upon being steered to black neighborhoods by black real estate agents:

"We also called a black realtor because, being from the area, I thought maybe they would give us a fair shake. But they did the same thing, they showed us black homes in black areas, but probably because those were the only listings that they had."

As noted earlier, almost no information is available regarding the role of the black real estate agent in the housing market. It appears, however, that black agents obtain most if not all of their listings from black sellers, so by implication their listings are primarily located in predominantly black areas.[14] A broker obtains the full commission when he sells one of his own listings, whereas the sale of a unit listed by another broker (e.g., through a multiple listing service) requires the commission to be split. As a consequence, and because black brokers are often barred from access to multiple listing services, it is not unusual for black homebuyers using a black real estate agent to be shown homes only in predominantly black neighborhoods.

In addition to steering blacks to black neighborhoods, real estate agents contribute to reinforcing white prejudice by steering blacks away from white neighborhoods. This is the strongest sense of the gatekeeper role played by the real estate agent.

"I found a real estate fellow in S. He took me all around the area and he cautioned me that I didn't want to live in M." [Interviewer: "Did he say why?"] "Because blacks weren't allowed in M. The real estate agent, he would not sell me a house in M."

An interracial couple reported a similar experience:

> "There was a house we were interested in on _____Avenue and she said, 'Oh, you wouldn't want to live there. There's too many Italians.' And we went home and we put it off for a few months because we thought this was a reflection of the town."

This same couple reported the steering they experienced when trying to sell their previous house:

> "When we had our house on the market, there were people taken aback when they saw my wife was black. In the beginning, I think they deliberately brought just black (buyers). I called and asked them a few questions about it once: 'Weren't there any whites with money too?' you know, and it stopped."

Steering occurs not only at the level of the individual housing unit and the neighborhood but on the community-wide level as well. Residents and real estate agents within the case study communities report the high frequency with which black homebuyers from other areas are steered to these communities. An agent explains:

> "You get a call from a broker up in D. who says 'Oh, I have this lovely couple here. They'd like to spend $100,000, $80,000' whatever it is. 'What do you have to offer?' A hundred times out of a hundred, it's a minority family."

At the same time, white homebuyers report numerous experiences of being steered away from these communities:

> "We went to a broker in N. before we looked in Teaneck. We asked him about Teaneck because we had many friends who had moved to Teaneck before us and had raved about it. And the broker said, 'Oh no, you don't want to go to Teaneck.' We came to Teaneck through the newspaper, just an open listing, not going through a broker. We had been steered away."

> "We ran into a real estate agent in O. where we also looked and we mentioned to her that we were looking in Montclair, and she said, 'Oh, I wouldn't go to Montclair because of the racial problem.' "

The classification of real estate agents of neighborhoods and communities on the basis of racial and ethnic identity is a common practice reported by several white respondents.[15]

> "The realtor was very careful about showing us white neighborhoods and black neighborhoods. He was very, very set on this point about where we could live and where we couldn't, and it really turned us off."

"Every neighborhood we entered she classified it either by major ethnic background or religious classification. She would tell us we didn't want to live in a particular area and we would say 'Why?' and she would say 'It's a Jewish neighborhood.' There was more prejudicial pressure coming from the agent than I would have expected."

In volunteering such information, the agent assumes that this is an important consideration for the client, perpetuates racial and ethnic stereotyping, and artificially reinforces neighborhood barriers that might otherwise be less salient.

Racial steering directs black homebuyers to black housing units and black areas, and away from white areas. It directs white homebuyers away from black and integrated areas. In artificially maintaining these distinctions, it contributes directly to the operation of a housing market based on explicit recognition of race. The incentives for maintaining such distinctions are discussed in Chapter 9. The result is to contribute to the qualitative and quantitative difference in the housing search experiences of black and white homebuyers.

SUMMARY

Little difference is discernable between the housing search experiences of suburban black and white homebuyers when measured on the number of information sources used, the number of real estate brokers contacted, and the number of housing units seriously considered. Evidently, certain basic requirements of search must be met by all homebuyers, on the average, in order to successfully purchase a dwelling unit.

The evidence is strong, however, that black housing search is considerably less efficient — and therefore more costly — than white search. Black homebuyers required substantially more time prior to active search to assess options, consider alternatives, collect information, and overcome hesitations. Black households in the sample similarly spent significantly more time in active search, again accumulating greater costs of time and effort and foregone benefits. Despite the longer time required, however, black housing search is at best equivalent in extent to white search and in many cases encompasses fewer units in fewer communities.

The analysis yields little support for the contextual model of racial differences in housing search experience. Regardless of differences in the background characteristics of white and black suburban homebuyers, both groups utilize the same information sources with the same frequency and evaluate these sources equally. Existing differences between black and white search behavior are virtually undiminished when the effects of background differences are controlled. Thus, blacks matched in background characteristics with whites still spend substantially more time in search to find an acceptable suburban housing unit. Further, these differences remain even when the unique influences of background characteristics on black and white search experience are removed.

The protracted nature of black housing search thus appears to be due to some combination of overt discrimination and black adaptation to avoid discrimination. Evidence of differential treatment of whites and blacks is strong. Use of a real estate agent as the primary information source yields access to a greater array of units for whites but not for blacks. Black searchers, in other words, examine no more units through a broker than they would if they relied solely on newspaper listings or personal networks. Racial steering persists despite federal legislation, affecting black housing search at the housing unit, neighborhood, and community levels.[16] Prior ownership among whites facilitates the search process by allowing the searcher to better specify what is desired. Among blacks, prior ownership extends search time by educating the searcher to reject inadequate units offered in the black submarket. In short, the findings suggest that the information and options made available to black home seekers are inadequate in both quantity and quality relative to the white experience, requiring a greater expenditure of time and effort to obtain the same end.

In addition to evidence of overt discriminatory treatment, the data suggest the equally important effect of black adaptation to discriminatory institutions. Avoidance of a hostile white reception is a deep-seated concern and adds substantially to time spent in preparation as well as in active search. Personal networks are an important source of reassurance regarding the likelihood of a peaceful reception in a given community. Selection of a unit because of neighborhood social characteristics facilitates black housing search by assuring social compatability. The expectation of discrimination also leads blacks to approach real estate agents cautiously, expecting less information than is anticipated by white homebuyers. Indeed, the finding that equal proportions of blacks and whites use a real estate broker may be misleading. Relatively few black homebuyers walk into a real estate office and ask to be shown homes. Rather, blacks are more likely to contact a broker for information on a particular unit that they have identified through a newspaper or a "For Sale" sign.

The implications for policy point to a combination of strengthening antidiscrimination legislation and the development of an unbiased source of information on vacancies. For example, a publicly supported multiple listing service, established on a county-wide basis and available to all home seekers for a small fee, would equalize the availability of information. These policy implications are discussed in detail in Chapter 10. The effects on housing search of racial bias in the dissemination of housing information are also felt in the economics of the market, and these effects are discussed in the following chapter.

APPENDIX EXHIBIT 7A-1

FACTORS INFLUENCING SEARCH BEHAVIOR AMONG SIX RACE AND NEIGHBORHOOD GROUPS

	Whites in All-White Neighborhoods	Whites in Black-Entry Neighborhoods	RACE OF BUYER AND NEIGHBORHOOD Blacks in Black-Entry Neighborhoods	Whites in Inter-Racial Neighborhoods	Blacks in Inter-Racial Neighborhoods	Blacks in All-Black Neighborhoods
MONTHS THINKING ABOUT LOOKING:						
Sale price (ln)	-.1043	.1182	.5179*	-.0471	.1637	2.4210*
Age of head	.0066*	.0088	-.0109	.0223*	.0287*	.0155
Job-related move (Yes=1)	-.4619*	-.5549*	-.3997*	-.2598	-1.1634*	-1.4131*
Neighborhood reason (Yes=1)	.3402*	.7858*	.7092*	-.3423	-.3594*	-.5084
Chose unit for housing unit reason (Yes=1)	.0980	-.0035	.1815	-.7031*	.3843*	.5565
Constant	2.1415	.3190	-3.6828	1.0780	-.7520	-23.7016
F	6.1246	1.7827	1.7533	1.0895	2.6481	1.5838
R^2	.059	.100	.089	.063	.163	.361
N	491	86	96	87	74	20
MONTHS IN ACTIVE SEARCH:						
Sale price (ln)	.2039*	.6223*	.2770	.1785	.2494	.7271*
Number of bedrooms	.0526*	-.0487	.1195*	-.1477*	.1915*	.0446
Previous residence in same neighborhood (Yes=1)	.0406	.6294*	-1.3661*	.0079	-.4992*	-1.3049*
Job-related move (Yes=1)	-.7340*	-.5716*	-.4833*	-.2433*	-1.0249*	-1.4586*
Chose unit for financial reason (Yes=1)	-.0365	.5964*	-.3132	.2780	.2942	.0646
Constant	-.9653	-5.5613	-1.9809	-.3359	-1.6094	-5.8595
F	10.3755	4.0415	2.7863	1.2108	2.7514	3.3799
R^2	.092	.196	.116	.066	.157	.471
N	5??	?0	11?	?1	?0	?5

NUMBER OF UNITS LOOKED AT:

Sale price (ln)	.8272*	.3222	.3081	1.2381*	1.4658*	.4616
Number of bedrooms	.0802*	.2581*	.0316	-.0407	.0351	.2041*
Age of head	-.0211*	-.0016	.0190*	.0032	-.0289*	-.0148
Previous residence in same neighborhood (Yes=1)	-.4752*	.7233*	-1.5571*	-.7673*	-.0828	.6936*
Job-related move (Yes=1)	.1116	.2670	.1188	.1889	-.1056	.2322
Chose unit for social reasons (Yes=1)	-.1380*	-.6751*	-.0649	-.0933	-.1747	-.4823*
Constant	-5.7312	-1.5809	-1.4592	-10.5834	-12.0678	-2.3611
F	12.2299	2.7190	1.1167	3.9106	6.1274	1.4005
R^2	.132	.175	.069	.231	.358	.393
N	491	84	97	85	73	20

NUMBER OF UNITS INTERNALLY INSPECTED:

Sale price (ln)	.8388*	-.2017	.1008	1.3206*	1.4785*	.0679
Number of bedrooms	.1032*	.3268*	-.0981	-.0894	.0014	.1731
Age of head	-.0244*	.0007	.0206*	.0071	-.0251*	-.0329*
Prior knowledge of community (Yes=1)	-.2856*	-.6130*	-.4254*	.1124	-.1243	-.1279
High school grad or less (Yes=1)	-.1895*	-.6574*	-.1959	-.3916*	.1866	-.5839*
Community ambience (Montclair or Teaneck=1)	.0486	-.0898	.3743*	-.0597	.0271	.2324
Constant	-6.0525	3.7600	.1169	-11.8248	12.6510	2.2846
F	16.1702	3.6925	2.4142	4.6199	4.9341	2.5235
R^2	.162	.213	.139	.253	.294	.502
N	508	89	97	89	78	22

EXHIBIT 7A-1 (Continued)

NUMBER OF COMMUNITIES SEARCHED:

Sale price (ln)	.1665*	.2687	.3229*	.2254	.7564*	.3933
Age of head	-.0113*	-.0011	-.0139*	-.0029	-.0085	-.0128
Previous residence in same neighborhood (Yes=1)	-.3715*	-.2530	-1.0224*	-.2858	-.5117*	-.9682*
Job-related move (Yes=1)	-.1459*	.4376*	.1699	-.0174	-.1219	-.4782*
Chose unit for social reasons (Yes=1)	-.2511*	-.2949*	.0687	-.4087*	.2171*	-.0674
Chose unit for housing reasons (Yes=1)	.1905*	.4898*	.4265*	.2220	.5289*	.0500
Constant	-.3170	-1.8678	-1.9753	-1.3287	-6.9022	-2.6381
F	10.5178	4.3639	1.3057	2.1474	4.6686	1.2551
R^2	.114	.254	.077	.140	.289	.334
N	497	84	101	86	76	22

NUMBER OF BANKS CONTACTED:

Sale price (ln)	.0614	-.1928	.1089	-.2513*	.1350	-.6356
Previous tenure (Own=1)	-.2206*	-.0856	.0776	-.2705*	-.1487	-.4732*
Chose bank for terms (Yes=1)	.6192*	.6396*	.5847*	.7340*	.3904*	.0834
Chose bank for convenience (Yes=1)	.4561*	.4120*	.4813*	.2898*	.1462	.3951*
FHA or VA mortgage (Yes=1)	-.2528*	-.2254	.0078	-.2344*	-.2339*	-.7921*
Constant	-.4049	2.2771	-1.0836	2.9224	-1.1076	7.5815
F	28.9724	2.6874	7.8235	7.6530	1.2330	4.9625
R^2	.256	.171	.340	.350	.112	.693
N	428	71	82	77	55	17

Note: *Indicates a coefficient significant at the .10 level or better.

NOTES

1. W.A.V. Clark and T.R. Smith, "Modelling Information Use in a Spatial Context,"*Annals of the Association of American Geographers* 69 (December 1979): 275-88; Kevin F. McCarthy, *Housing Search and Consumption Adjustment* (Santa Monica, California: Rand Corporation, 1980); Kevin F. McCarthy, *Housing Search and Mobility* (Santa Monica, California: Rand Corporation, 1979).

2. Julian Wolpert, "Behavioral Aspects of the Decision to Migrate,"*Papers of the Regional Science Association* 15 (1965): 159-72; William Michelson, *Man and His Urban Environment,* rev. ed. (Reading, Mass.: Addison-Wesley, 1976).

3. Julian Wolpert, "Migration as an Adjustment to Environmental Stress," *Journal of Social Issues* 22 (October 1966): 92-102.

4. William Michelson, *Environmental Choice, Human Behavior and Residential Satisfaction* (New York: Oxford University Press, 1977).

5. James W. Simmons, "Changing Residence in the City, A Review of Intra-Urban Mobility," *Geographical Review* 58 (October 1968): 622-51.

6. Donald J. Hempel, *Search Behavior and Information Utilization in the Home Buying Process* (Storrs, Conn.: Center for Real Estate and Urban Economics Studies, University of Connecticut, 1969).

7. Lawrence A. Brown and Eric G. Moore, 'The Intra-Urban Migration Process: A Perspective," in Larry S. Bourne, ed. *Internal Structure of the City* (New York: Oxford University Press, 1971), pp. 200-209.

8. Eric G. Moore, *Residential Mobility in the City*, Commission on College Geography Resource Paper No. 13 (Washington, D.C.: Association of American Geographers, 1972).

9. Risa Palm, "Real Estate Agents and Geographical Information," *Geographical Review* 66 (July 1976): 266-80; Risa Palm, *Urban Social Geography from the Perspective of the Real Estate Salesman* (Berkeley, Calif.: Center for Real Estate and Urban Economics, University of California, 1976).

10. Ronald E. Wienk, et al., *Measuring Racial Discrimination in American Housing Markets: The Housing Market Practices Survey* (Washington, D.C.: U.S. Department of Housing and Urban Development, 1979).

11. Title VIII of the Civil Rights Act of 1968, the Fair Housing Title, provides the basic federal legislation prohibiting racial discrimination in housing (Pub. L. 90-284, Civil Rights Act of 1968, Title VII — Fair Housing, 82 Stat. 81-90). The Fair Housing Amendments Act of 1979 was debated as H.R. 5200 in the House and S. 506 in the Senate. The proposed amendments would broaden the coverage of Title VIII and extend HUD's role beyond conciliation to administrative enforcement. See Chapter 10.

12. These intraneighborhood differences are computed from the dummy variable coefficients for race and neighborhood in Exhibit 7-5. For example, within Black-Entry neighborhoods, the black-white difference in months thinking of moving is:

$.3316 - .0248 = .3068$ and $(e^{.3068}-1)$ $100 = 35.9$ percent.

The difference in months in active search is:

$.0139 - (-.2343) = .2482$ and $(e^{.2482}-1)$ $100 = 28.2$ percent.

Similar calculations apply in Inter-Racial neighborhoods.

13. The reduced-form estimating equations in Appendix Exhibit 7A-1 were developed to accommodate the reduced sample size in the neighborhood strata. For each search measure, variables were entered in stepwise fashion until the maximum adjusted R^2 value was reached. A smaller subset of variables significant across all strata was then selected from among those entered prior to termination.

14. Hearings by the U.S. Commission on Civil Rights documented the difficulties faced by black real estate agents in the white-dominated housing market. A white broker testified, however, that "one of the ways to do black business is to have black salespeople." U.S. Commission on Civil Rights, *Equal Opportunity in Suburbia* (Washington, D.C.: U.S. Commission on Civil Rights, 1974), p. 20.

15. The National Association of Realtors has adopted a "Code of Equal Opportunity in Housing" that states in part that "members . . . have no right or responsibility to volunteer information regarding the racial, creedal or ethnic composition of any neighborhood or any part thereof." This code is adopted by NAR-affiliated local real estate boards or state associations that voluntarily adopt an Affirmative Marketing Agreement. See National Association of Realtors, *Affirmative Marketing Handbook* (Chicago: National Association of Realtors, 1975) and Chapter 9 below.

16. T. Alexander Aleinikoff, "Racial Steering: The Real Estate Broker and Title VIII," *Yale Law Journal* 85 (1976): 808-25.

8

HOUSING PRICES,
EQUITY, AND RACE

INTRODUCTION

Higher black entry costs extracted in housing search are only preliminary to racial differences in actual purchase price and a differential rate of equity accumulation. The debate on the extent of price discrimination against blacks is largely unresolved: a sizable and contradictory literature finds evidence of racial premiums in some cases and racial discounts in others.[1] Popular conceptions of falling property values associated with black entry are persistent and strong. At least one suburban community has initiated a foundation-supported program to insure participating homeowners against loss of property value thought to accompany residential integration, hoping thereby to "eliminate irrational fears of racial change."[2]

179

This chapter draws on data from the Recent Buyers Survey to consider four interlocking issues:

(1) *The influence of white buyer prejudice on housing market weakness in integrated communities.* Comparing across neighborhoods, are housing prices in predominantly black neighborhoods lower than prices for comparable housing in white neighborhoods?

(2) *The extent of purchase price discrimination against blacks.* Do blacks pay more than whites for comparable housing within the same neighborhood?

(3) *Resale value of black-owned units.* Do units sold by blacks bring a lower price than comparable units sold by whites?

(4) *Equity accumulation and return on investment.* Do black-owned units appreciate at a faster or slower rate than comparable units owned by whites?

Most analyses of the race/price relationship have been hindered by data limitations from considering all of these issues. Studies focusing on neighborhood racial composition often lack data on the race of the buyer, and few studies have been able to consider the race of the seller. Consequently, such studies have been unable to extend models based on white prejudice against black neighborhoods to consider the effect of white prejudice against black-owned units within particular neighborhoods. This is significant, however, for assessing both the implications of black/white purchase price differentials as well as the equity accumulation potential of black homeownership. Similarly, few students have been able to extend a cross-sectional comparison to also consider longitudinal change in housing prices over time. This chapter incorporates each of these factors in an extension of general models of the race/price relationship.

Our analysis reveals that, in this set of suburban communities, sales prices for comparable units are lower in black than in white neighborhoods, and that blacks pay less than whites within the same neighborhood. These discrepancies are traced to the low prices obtained by black sellers and are in turn traced to the weakness of white demand for units sold by blacks or for units in black neighborhoods. Such market weakness is usually attributed to white buyer prejudice but prejudice must be broadly conceived. Institutional practices including steering of whites away from black units contribute to the weakness of demand, generating a self-fulfilling prophesy that in turn reinforces white prejudice.

MODELS OF RACE AND HOUSING PRICES

Systematic analyses of the relationship between race and selling price show some variation in trends over the postwar period. While contradictory findings exist, studies based on data from the 1950s and early 1960s generally found that blacks paid more than whites for comparable housing.[3] Studies based on more recent data, however, suggest that earlier black premiums have been replaced by discounts or at least parity in prices paid for comparable housing.[4] Using Annual Housing Survey data for 1973-74 for thirty-nine metropolitan areas, Follain and Malpezzi found that in owner-occupied units blacks paid less than whites in thirty-four SMSAs, and in rental units blacks paid less in twenty-six SMSAs. The average black discount was 15 percent for owners and 6 percent for renters.[5]

Explanations of such price differentials generally rest on *models of white buyer prejudice* against residence in a predominantly black or integrated area, and *models of price discrimination* or premiums charged black buyers for housing in predominantly white areas. The recent evidence of a temporal shift in the direction of the race effect, however, has introduced the issue of *market constraints* in the supply and demand for housing for whites and blacks respectively, as factors mediating the potential influence of prejudice and discrimination.

Market Constraints

The thrust of this argument is that prejudice and discrimination are market externalities mediated through short run constraints of supply and demand and the ease with which units are transferred from white to black occupancy. To examine this hypothesis, Schnare and Struyk analyzed comparable data on black/white price differences in Boston and Pittsburgh for both 1960 and 1970.[6] They found that in Pittsburgh a 20 percent markup in all-black census tracts in 1960 was reduced to 7 percent in 1970, and in Boston a 12 percent black premium was replaced by a 5 percent discount. Based on changing patterns of supply and demand for housing in Boston and Pittsburgh over the twenty-year period, Schnare and Struyk argue convincingly that the black premiums observed in 1960 resulted from a shortage in the supply of quality housing available in black areas through the 1950s. Continued white suburbanization, adoption of fair housing legislation, and a slowdown in the black growth rate during the sixties alleviated this shortage and resulted in the virtual disappearance of racial markups by 1970.

If these conclusions are correct, one implication is that the quest for a definitive response to the "Do blacks pay more?" question is illusory, and instead must be verified empirically for each setting at a particular time period. A complication inherent in these studies, however, concerns specification of the racial variable. The Schnare/Struyk results were obtained by introducing a measure of the proportion black population in census tracts into a housing price model. Follain and Malpezzi used race of household head in a similar model. Neither of these specifications allows one to determine whether an observed race effect is due to differences in prices paid by black and white households or to differences between housing prices in predominantly black and predominantly white areas. This distinction is crucial, however, for separating out the effects of buyer prejudice from those of seller discrimination within the context of market constraints.[7]

Prejudice Models

Models based on the racial prejudice of white buyers posit interneighborhood price differences: white preference for segregation causes prices in black neighborhoods to fall as white demand shifts away from such areas and whites pay a premium to live in predominantly white areas.[8] Two variations of prejudice models have evolved. In *border models* of prejudice, the strength of white racial preferences is measured by the white household's distance from the border between the white and black areas.[9] Border models assume that blacks and whites are completely segregated (i.e., there are no interracial areas), that all blacks are located in a single ghetto area in the city center, that whites prefer to live away from blacks, and that blacks prefer to live near whites.[10] If these assumptions hold, then white demand will be highest (and whites will pay a premium) in white areas further from the white/black border, black demand will be higher near the border than in the black interior, and consequently prices will be highest in all-white areas, lowest in the ghetto, and intermediate at the border.

Yinger has introduced a variation on this approach based on more realistic assumptions.[11] Rather than assuming complete segregation, *amenity models* measure white prejudice not by distance from the black-white border but by the percent concentration of blacks in and around the white household's residential area. Here, racial composition is viewed as an amenity, and white demand increases as the proportion black of the population decreases. If the residential preferences of whites and blacks are the same as those assumed in border models, then the effect on prices will be the same except that neighborhoods are defined on the basis of racial composition rather than distance from black concentrations.

Discrimination Models

Discrimination models compare black/white prices *within* neighborhoods and test whether price discrimination by sellers and/or market intermediaries imposes a "race tax" or racial premium that blacks must pay to buy into integrated or mostly white neighborhoods. While prejudice models focus on racial influences on demand for housing in different neighborhoods, discrimination models focus on the relative supply of housing available to whites and blacks within a given neighborhood. Overt discrimination by sellers against black buyers imposes a dual market in which units available to whites are unavailable to blacks at an equivalent price. The result is that blacks pay a premium relative to whites for equivalent housing in the same neighborhood. For instance, Schafer has reestimated Schnare's 1970 data for Boston to measure black/white differences for various housing bundles within neighborhoods defined by metropolitan location and racial composition; though sample size limitations suggest the need for caution, Schafer's findings point to substantial intraneighborhood premiums paid by blacks, with higher-quality housing commanding a higher premium.[12]

The issue of reconciling models of prejudice (interneighborhood black discounts) with models of discrimination (intraneighborhood black premiums) has been aptly summarized by Mieszkowski:[13]

> The difference in the predictions of the prejudice model and the discrimination or market-segregation models turns on differences in the predictions regarding the ease at which neighborhoods are converted from white to black occupancy . . . . [The] prediction of the prejudice model that prices will be lower in all black neighborhoods will be overturned by the existence of discrimination only if discrimination is a significant barrier to the conversion of white housing to black housing.

In short, market constraints of overall supply and demand again mediate the effects of racial externalities. In a tight market, supply shortages will curtail the ability of prejudiced whites to bypass available housing in integrated neighborhoods, at the same time increasing the profitability of seller discrimination against blacks. Under such conditions, we can expect interneighborhood black discounts to disappear while intraneighborhood black markups increase. In contrast, alleviation of white housing shortages allows the effects of prejudice to be manifested through weaker demand—and lower prices—for integrated housing, while price discrimination is unlikely as units pass easily from white to black ownership.

Model Shortcomings

Neither prejudice nor discrimination models have been extended in the literature to consider the market for black-owned units. Focusing on white avoidance of black neighborhoods, prejudice models fail to incorporate intraneighborhood implications of white avoidance of black-owned units. Discrimination models that assume that blacks buy from whites similarly ignore the transfer of units from black-to-white or from black-to-black. The simple extension of these models, however, suggests the possibility of *intraneighborhood discounts* in units bought *from* blacks, if white antipathy for black areas is echoed in white antipathy for black-owned units. Further, such intraneighborhood discounts would accrue disproportionately to black buyers if blacks purchase black-owned units and whites do not. Such price discounts for blacks buying black-owned units might result from market weakness generated by numerous sources. These include overt white avoidance of such units, white real estate agents steering whites away from such units, and black sellers listing their house with a black real estate agent who lacks access to a pool of white buyers. All of these forces are likely to coexist within a biracial suburban housing market.

A further issue not adequately addressed in the literature is that of resale value and equity recapture. Lower initial prices paid by blacks may be an illusory savings if resale values of black-owned units are correspondingly lower as well.[14] A simple extension of this analysis compares relative rates of price appreciation for units owned by blacks and whites. The outcome is largely dependent on the racial composition of the neighborhood, the race of the buyer and seller, and the impact of these factors as predicted by the models described above. The role of institutional intermediaries that mediate the effective demand for particular housing units through marketing and brokerage practices is likely to be an important component.[15] Steering of white buyers away from black-owned units would result in lower effective demand and, consequently, lower sales prices for such units.

In contrast to the debate on racial influences on price *levels*, very little evidence is available on relative price *changes* for white- and black-owned units. Berry's analysis of price movements in Chicago for the 1968-1972 period produced findings consistent with the prejudice model. Relative to units in outlying white areas, housing prices increased less rapidly in white neighborhoods closer to the ghetto, increased at a faster rate in areas of black expansion, and changed the least rapidly in the ghetto.[16] These findings, however, apply to neighborhood price movements and leave unresolved the issue of relative equity accumulation in units owned by blacks and whites.

Data on the race of the buyer, the seller, and the neighborhood for a sample of suburban housing units are available from the Recent Buyers Survey and permit testing and extension of these models of the effect of race on purchase price, resale value, and equity accumulation.

ESTIMATING HOUSING PRICES

Systematic analysis of the race/price relationship views housing as a composite bundle of attributes including unit size and improvements, location, and neighborhood amenities. Each of these attributes contributes independently to value and must be controlled to isolate the effect of race on otherwise comparable units. The method commonly employed is to construct an additive index of implicit prices of housing bundle attributes and then to test for the additional independent effect of race in the determination of housing prices.[17]

Data

The sales price data employed here are the actual sales prices recorded in the New Jersey State Treasury Department tax files used in sampling for the Recent Buyers Survey (see Chapter 6). All other data were obtained from survey respondents (Exhibit 8-1).

Sale Price Data. Use of actual transaction prices has advantages over alternatives employed in other studies. Analyses based on census data, as well as Kain and Quigley's St. Louis study and other studies using their data set (e.g. Yinger) all utilize the owner's estimate of current market value.[18] The bias in such estimates is unclear, although Mieszkowski summarizes a number of sources suggesting that owners undervalue their homes substantially.[19] If this tendency

EXHIBIT 8-1

SUMMARY MEASURES FOR VARIABLES USED IN
SALE PRICE ANALYSIS

Variable	Expected Sign	Mean	Standard Deviation	Minimum	Maximum	Simple Correlation with Log Sale Price
HOUSING UNIT CHARACTERISTICS						
Number of rooms	+	7.749	1.958	2	17	.475*
Number of bedrooms	+	3.509	1.061	1	9	.423*
Number of bathrooms	+	1.968	0.742	1	3	.546*
Age of house (years)	–	35.422	21.101	2	100+	–.048
Garage (Yes=1)	+	0.839	0.367	0	1	.429*
NEIGHBORHOOD CHARACTERISTICS						
Land assessed value (ln)	+	8.400	1.173	5.278	10.712	.400*
Community type (Montclair or Teaneck=1)	+	0.547	0.498	0	1	.345*
Journey to work (≤ 10 min=1)	–	0.180	0.385	0	1	–.068*
Journey to work (≥ 1 hr. = 1)	+	0.162	0.368	0	1	.122*
Rating of municipal services	+	2.902	0.528	1	4	.142*
Rating of neighborhood problems	+	3.109	0.566	1	4	.074*
Presence of rundown houses	–	0.103	0.304	0	1	–.139*
Presence of heavy street traffic	–	0.267	0.442	0	1	–.038
Presence of street crime	–	0.166	0.372	0	1	–.044
HOUSEHOLD CHARACTERISTICS						
Length of residence (months)	–	31.094	12.284	1	72	–.179*
Blue-collar occupation (Yes=1)	–	0.167	0.374	0	1	–.353*
Total family income ($1,000's)	+	30.656	15.437	1.500	240.000	.517*
Previous tenure (Own=1)	+	0.319	0.466	0	1	.248*
Age of head (years)	+	36.964	8.469	21	80	.175*
Total family size	+	3.480	1.267	1	12	.070*
Log sale price		10.729	0.328	8.631	12.113	

Note: (*) indicates coefficient significant at $p \leq .05$.

is unequally distributed among whites and blacks (due, for instance, to differences in length of residence), price comparisons are likely to be artificially biased. Similarly, several studies utilize aggregate (census tract or block) sale price values rather than actual sales prices for individual units, again introducing an unknown source of bias into the analysis.

Housing Unit Characteristics. Housing unit attributes include the size of the unit and its improvements. Size is measured by both the number of rooms and the number of bedrooms. The bedroom count indicates the general capacity of the unit, while the number of rooms indicates the presence of additional floor area devoted to family and recreational pursuits beyond basic shelter requirements. Housing quality and improvements are measured by the number of bathrooms, the age of the house, and the presence of a garage. All housing unit characteristics are expected to bear a positive relationship with selling price with the exception of age of the unit. Older units may be more likely to show signs of wear and thus be of lower value. Alternatively, older housing may possess architectural amenities and construction quality that are prized and therefore more highly valued. A third consideration, however, is that new units typically come on the market at a higher square-foot cost than existing units. The weight of these factors leads us to expect a negative sign for the correlation between age of the unit and selling price.

Neighborhood Characteristics. Relevant neighborhood attributes include location and the quality of neighborhood amenities. Assessed value of the lot is included under neighborhood rather than unit characteristics since it reflects the value of both location and neighborhood amenities capitalized into land value. As such, we expect land assessed value to be positively related to sale price.

Most housing price studies using a metropolitan-wide focus measure neighborhood location relative to a unifocal central business district, following traditional Alonso-type urban land-use models.[20] An appropriate locational measure in the purely suburban context incorporating a number of sampling locations, each oriented to a different center, is less easily identifiable. Two measures of the household head's actual travel time to work are employed. Both are dummy variables, the first taking a value of "1" for travel time of ten minutes or less, and the second for travel time of an hour or more. The shorter travel time is most likely associated with local blue-collar, clerical, or service employment and, accordingly, lower housing prices, while travel time of an hour or more reflects upper-status professional employment in New York City or Philadelphia, and therefore higher housing prices.

Numerous housing price studies have stressed the importance of controlling for neighborhood amenities, municipal services, and neighborhood problems. Several neighborhood quality measures were accordingly employed in this analysis, although not all proved to be equally significant. The "community type" measure is a dummy variable differentiating the sampling sites according to the suburban community typology outlined in Chapter 4. Units were coded "1" if located in Montclair or Teaneck, both higher-value dormitory residential communities, and were coded "0" if located in the remaining (central city spillover) communities.

The "neighborhood services rating" is the respondent's mean score on evaluations of seven municipal services and facilities along a four-point scale from poor (1) to excellent (4). The items rated include police protection, public education, public transportation, neighborhood shopping, day care facilities, teenage recreation facilities, and facilities for the elderly.

The "neighborhood problems rating" is the respondent's mean score on evaluations of the severity of six commonly occurring problems. Street crime, burglary of homes and apartments, heavy street traffic, noise, rundown houses, and discipline in the schools were rated by respondents on a four-point scale ranging from very serious (1) to no problem (4), and the six scores were averaged. A high mean score indicates the absence of perceived neighborhood problems. The community type, neighborhood services, and neighborhood problems variables are all expected to be positively related to sale price.

Finally, three separate dummy variables were created to indicate the presence of individual, potentially deleterious, neighborhood problems. A "rundown houses" variable was coded "1" if the respondent felt this to be a very serious or fairly serious neighborhood problem, and "0" otherwise. "Heavy street traffic" and "street crime" variables were computed similarly.

In practice, the most consistently significant neighborhood quality measure proved to be the "community type" variable. This simple community-level dichotomy appears to capture the principal source of variation in neighborhood quality among the sample units, most likely encompassing development density and the level of environmental/scenic amenities. Both of these neighborhood quality attributes differ more between than within the five sampling sites and are adequately measured at the community level. The "community type" variable might therefore be termed an "environmental quality" measure.

The additional neighborhood quality measures ultimately proved to be insignificant in the overall sale price model.[21] Neither the municipal services nor the neighborhood problems ratings, nor the dummy variables indicating a problem with rundown houses, heavy traffic, or crime ever attained statistical significance. Further, their inclusion in the model has no effect on the performance of any of the racial variables (see Appendix Exhibit 8A-1), suggesting that observed racial differences cannot be attributed to the variations in neighborhood quality measured by these variables.[22] This finding holds regardless of whether the neighborhood measures used are the general ratings of services and problems or the identification of specific problems.[23]

The suburban setting may account for the poor performance of neighborhood quality measures that have proved important in central-city or metropolitan-wide analyses. For example, the distribution of serious crime is likely to exhibit less spatial variation within and among the case study sites than across a metropolitan area encompassing both city and suburban locations. Similarly, expected variations in the quality of educational services are likely to be diminished, given uniformly high per pupil expenditures in the case study sites and the prevalence of district-wide busing for school integration. As a consequence, the cross-sectional sale price regressions retain the community-type (scenic/environmental quality) variable but omit the remaining measures of neighborhood services and problems. The longitudinal price appreciation models, however, include the municipal services rating that appears to contribute to the explanation of price changes over time (see below).

Buyer Characteristics. Several characteristics of buyer households are included in the model in order to permit identification of the independent effect of race: i.e., the effect of race on selling price for otherwise comparable households buying comparable housing units. The length of residence variable, measured in months, controls for housing price inflation over the sampling period (July 1974-June 1977). Households who purchased their units earlier in this period would have paid less because of inflation. Total family income is expected to be positively related to sale price, while occupation, measured by a dummy variable identifying blue-collar workers, would be negatively related. (An education variable proved to be synonymous with occupation and was dropped from the analysis at an early stage). The household's asset position, as or more important than current income in influencing home purchase, is measured by tenure in the previous unit. The downpayment and equity available to previous owners should be translated into a higher purchase price in the new unit.

Age of household head and total family size serve as indicators of the household's stage in the life cycle. Older household heads and larger family size suggest households in higher income-earning years with greater demand for housing services and a greater likelihood of previous ownership—all indicative of greater housing consumption at a consequently higher price level. Smaller, younger families, in contrast, are likely to be more constrained in the amount of housing they can purchase.

Model Estimation

Estimation of the basic selling price model is summarized in Appendix Exhibit 8A-2 (column 1). The functional form used throughout the cross-sectional analysis is semi-log, where the natural log of selling price is the dependent variable and the independent variables are linear. The only exception is that land assessed value is in logarithmic form. This form was found to have higher explanatory power than the linear model and has the added advantage of simplifying interpretation of the regression coefficients.

The basic model accounts for 63.4 percent of the variation in log selling price, and almost all of the variables are significant and in the expected direction. The only exceptions are the journey-to-work and the age of head measures that have the expected sign but are weakly significant only in the expanded versions of the model. Total family size is negative but insignificant in all versions. The five housing unit characteristics together contribute more than 60 percent of the model's explanatory power, with the neighborhood and buyer variables contributing 19 and 18 percent, respectively.

RACIAL DIFFERENCES IN PURCHASE PRICE

The various race/price theories described above can be tested by introducing appropriate racial variables into the housing price model (Exhibit 8-2). A single dummy variable identifying the race of the buyer indicates that black households pay 7.3 percent less than otherwise comparable white households for comparable housing units. This is consistent with other findings of black discounts in the 1970s. The issue remains to disaggregate this overall effect and specify the separate influence of prejudice and discrimination.

Effects of White Buyer Prejudice

The first test of the effects of white buyer prejudice is to compare prices for equivalent units in neighborhoods defined by racial composition. Neighborhood delineations are those used in previous chapters (see Chapter 6): All-White and Black-Entry neighborhoods are blocks less than 5 percent black in 1970 differentiated only by the race of in-movers during the survey period. All-Black neighborhoods were more than 80 percent black in 1970, and the remaining blocks are Inter-Racial.

Prices in Black-Entry neighborhoods are equal to those in All-White neighborhoods (the difference of 1.4 percent is not statistically significant). Compared to All-White neighborhoods, however, prices are 10.9 percent lower in Inter-Racial neighborhoods and 16.6 percent lower in All-Black neighborhoods. These findings lend support to the amenity model of white prejudice: prices decrease as the neighborhood percent black increases, reflecting the progressive weakening of white demand with increasing black concentrations.

Following Yinger, we can retest this model with a single variable measuring the percent black population by block in 1970.[24] The coefficient for this variable, significant at the .01 level, indicates that for the entire suburban area, sale price goes down 2.4 percent for every 10 percent increase in black population. Since All-Black neighborhoods were on average 86 percent black in 1970, the racial discount based on black concentration (86/10 x 2.4 = 20.6 percent) is

EXHIBIT 8-2

SALE PRICE DIFFERENCES IN STANDARDIZED
SUBURBAN HOMES PURCHASED BY BLACKS AND WHITES[a]

	Regression Coefficient	t-Value[b]	Percent Difference in Sale Price[c]
Relative to white buyers:			
Black buyers	−.0758**	−4.086	−7.3
Relative to All-White neighborhoods:			
Black-Entry neighborhoods	−.0145	−0.759	−1.4
Inter-Racial neighborhoods	−.1158**	−5.745	−10.9
All-Black neighborhoods	−.1811**	−3.755	−16.6
Relative to whites in All-White neighborhoods:			
Whites in Black-Entry neighborhoods	.0159	0.587	1.6
Blacks in Black-Entry neighborhoods	−.0370*	−1.574	−3.6
Whites in Inter-Racial neighborhoods	−.1052**	−4.251	−10.0
Blacks in Inter-Racial neighborhoods	−.1331**	−4.426	−12.5
Blacks in All-Black neighborhoods	−.1839**	−3.814	−16.8

Notes: a. Housing units standardized in regression of log sale price on five housing unit characteristics, four neighborhood characteristics, and six buyer characteristics. See Appendix Exhibit 8A-2.

b. Test that coefficient is significantly different from zero. The one-tailed .01 significance level (**) is 2.326 and the .10 significance level (*) is 1.282.

c. In the log-linear model b(100) approximates the percent change in Y only when b is small. Otherwise, use $(e^b - 1)$ 100.

slightly higher than the discount indicated by the All-Black neighborhood dummy (16.6 percent).

In fact, there is evidence of interaction between the percent black concentration and neighborhood type. The coefficients for 1970 percent black population by block assume different values in sale price regressions stratified by neighborhood type (Exhibit 8-3). Sale prices in All-White and Black-Entry neighborhoods are unaffected by mean 1970 black concentrations of less than one percent. In Inter-Racial neighborhoods, prices drop 1.7 percent for every 10 percent increase in black population between 5 and 80 percent. Beyond 80 percent black, in All-Black neighborhoods, the effect is accelerated, with prices decreasing 4.8 percent with every 10 percent increase in percent black. These data provide substantial support for amenity-based prejudice models, with progressively higher black concentrations generating a progressive weakening of white demand—and consequent drop in sale price—for housing.

EXHIBIT 8-3

EFFECT OF NEIGHBORHOOD RACIAL COMPOSITION IN FOUR HOUSING PRICE MODELS STRATIFIED BY NEIGHBORHOOD TYPE

	Regression Coefficient[a]	t-Value	Percent Effect
Percent black in All-White neighborhoods	.00043	0.045	none
Percent black in Black-Entry neighborhoods	.00955	0.705	none
Percent black in Inter-Racial neighborhoods	−.00168	−2.158	−0.168
Percent black in All-Black neighborhoods	−.00483	−5.762	−0.482

Note: a. Based on the full purchase price model. See Appendix Exhibit 8A-2.

Several authors have suggested that estimating the race effect with a single regression model assumes a unified housing market, whereas housing attributes may be valued differently in different racial submarkets.[25] If such disparities exist, price discounts or premiums observed in the unified market model may be reduced or even reversed for different-quality housing bundles in individual submarkets. Accordingly, separate sale price regressions were estimated for each neighborhood type by using a reduced form equation employing the unit and neighborhood variables and length of residence (Appendix Exhibit 8A-3). Buyer characteristics were omitted from the new stratified neighborhood equations since the issue is whether housing bundle attributes (e.g., number of rooms, a garage, etc.) are valued differently in different submarkets.[26] The assumption of homogeneity of the four sets of neighborhood coefficients can be rejected at the .01 level ($F_{27,905} = 4.47$).

Do the black price discounts observed in the unified market model apply equally to all housing bundles in all neighborhoods? Following Schafer, we used the four neighborhood equations to estimate prices for the average housing bundles in each of the neighborhood types. Prices paid in All-White neighborhoods for each of the four average housing bundles serve as the benchmark to compare prices that apply in each of the other neighborhood types (Exhibit 8-4). Comparisons across neighborhoods are almost identical to results from the unified housing market model. Prices for all four housing bundles are essentially the same in All-White and Black-Entry neighborhoods, from 11 to 15 percent lower in Inter-Racial neighborhoods, and are 25 percent lower in All-Black neighborhoods. Further, these differences are almost invariant across all four housing bundles. Schafer found that in the central city ghetto areas of Boston, lower-quality units commanded a premium.[27] The uniformity of our findings suggests that although there may be differences in implicit values of housing bundle components across neighborhood types, the actual bundles available in these suburban neighborhoods are relatively homogeneous.

In sum, evidence of interneighborhood suburban housing price differences is strong and consistent, with prices in All-Black neighborhoods from 16 to 25 percent lower than in All-White neighborhoods. The price discount appears to accelerate as the proportion black in the population increases. Discounts apply equally to the full range of housing quality bundles. These results provide strong support to models based on white buyer prejudice in which lower prices reflect weak white demand for housing in all-black or integrated neighborhoods.

EXHIBIT 8-4

PRICES PAID FOR VARIOUS HOUSING BUNDLES IN THREE NEIGHBORHOOD TYPES, RELATIVE TO PRICES PAID IN ALL-WHITE NEIGHBORHOODS[a]
(percents)

	PRICES PAID IN:		
Average Housing Bundle in:	Black-Entry Neighborhoods	Inter-Racial Neighborhoods	All-Black Neighborhoods
All-White neighborhoods	−1.78	−12.49*	−26.99*
Black-Entry neighborhoods	−1.07	−11.28*	−25.97*
Inter-Racial neighborhoods	−1.80*	−13.54*	−26.88*
All-Black neighborhoods	−1.68	−15.03*	−21.30*

Notes: a. Based on neighborhood equations (not stratified by race) in Appendix Exhibit 8A-3.
*Indicates that the difference in estimated prices between the indicated neighborhood and All-White neighborhoods is significantly different from zero at the .05 level (two-tailed test).

Evidence of Seller Discrimination

The price discrimination theory proposes black markups within neighborhoods when supply shortages induce strong barriers to the transfer of units from white to black occupancy. Descriptions of the case study sites provide little evidence of such barriers during the interview period, when the black proportion of the population was increasing while the total population remained fairly constant (see Chapter 5). Appearance of a racial premium under these conditions would require reconsideration of the theory.

To test for intraneighborhood racial price differences, the unified market regression was reestimated with separate dummy variables to distinguish prices paid by blacks and whites within each neighborhood type (Exhibit 8-2). Relevant comparisons are confined to Black-Entry and Inter-Racial neighborhoods, since by definition all buyers in All-White neighborhoods were white and there were no white buyers in All-Black neighborhoods. As evident in Exhibit 8-2, both whites and blacks in all neighborhood types purchased houses at a discount relative to whites in All-White neighborhoods. There is clearly no evidence of a black premium within neighborhoods; if anything, the discount for blacks is greater than for whites by a small margin. Whites in Black-Entry neighborhoods pay the same prices as whites in All-White neighborhoods, while blacks receive a slight discount (−3.6 percent, significant at the .10 level). In Inter-Racial neighborhoods, the white discount of 10 percent is again slightly exceeded by a black discount of 12.5 percent, both significant at .01. While these black/white differences within neighborhoods are hardly substantial, the more important finding is the absence of intraneighborhood price barriers affecting suburban black buyers.

The unanticipated possibility of a black *discount* within neighborhood submarkets prompts further analysis. Given the potential shortcomings of the unified market model, the regression was again stratified by neighborhood type with a dummy variable indicating race of the buyer. In Black-Entry neighborhoods the coefficient of the race dummy indicates that blacks pay 5.1 percent less than whites for the equivalent housing unit, significant at .05. This is identical with results from the unified model, where a 1.6 percent white markup and a 3.6 percent black discount amount to a black/white difference of 5.2 percent. In Inter-Racial neighborhoods, the race dummy reveals an 8.2 percent markdown for black homebuyers, also significant at the .05 level.

As in the analysis of interneighborhood differentials above, the possibility remains that blacks and whites within neighborhood types constitute separate submarkets with different implicit prices of housing attributes. The reduced form eight-variable price model was therefore reestimated yet again, this time stratifying by race of the buyer within each neighborhood type (Appendix Exhibit 8A-3). This yielded six separate price estimations of six average housing bundles. Prices paid for each bundle by blacks and whites in each neighborhood were then compared to prices paid by whites in All-White neighborhoods.[28]

The results are again consistent with earlier evidence of an intraneighborhood black discount (Exhibit 8-5). Within Black-Entry neighborhoods, white prices are the same or slightly higher than prices paid in All-White neighborhoods, while black prices are some 4 percent lower. Whites in Inter-Racial neighborhoods reveal a 6 to 11 percent discount relative to All-White neighborhoods, but black discounts are approximately double this amount. Once again, these results are relatively invariant across all six housing quality bundles. The consistency of results obtained with various estimating techniques is encouraging. In the stratified market model, Black-Entry white premiums combined with black discounts result in a net black discount of 5.7 to 8.6 percent, depending on the housing bundle. This is clearly comparable to the 5.1 percent black discount revealed by the racial dummy variable aggregating over all housing bundles. Similarly, the difference between black and white markdowns in Inter-Racial neighborhoods yields a net black discount of between 7 and 11 percent, again equivalent to the 8.2 percent figure obtained in the dummy variable analysis.

EXHIBIT 8-5

PRICES PAID BY BLACKS AND WHITES FOR VARIOUS
HOUSING BUNDLES IN THREE NEIGHBORHOOD TYPES,
RELATIVE TO PRICES PAID BY WHITES IN ALL-WHITE
NEIGHBORHOODS
(percents)

| | PRICES PAID BY: | | | | |
| Average Housing Bundles Bought by | Black-Entry Neighborhoods | | Inter-Racial Neighborhoods | | All-Black Neighborhoods |
	Whites[a]	Blacks[b]	Whites[a]	Blacks[b]	Blacks[b]
Whites in All-White neighborhoods	1.75	−4.26*	−8.12*	−18.13*	−26.99*
Whites in Black-Entry neighborhoods	1.73	−4.00*	−6.53*	−17.57*	−26.93*
Blacks in Black-Entry neighborhoods	3.51*	−3.30*	−6.22*	−16.99*	−25.18*
Whites in Inter-Racial neighborhoods	1.76	−4.17*	−10.33*	−19.68*	−29.55*
Blacks in Inter-Racial neighborhoods	3.76*	−3.96*	−7.20*	−17.46*	−23.32*
Blacks in All-Black neighborhoods	4.18	−4.39*	−11.43*	−18.36*	−21.30*

Notes: a. Based on white equations in Appendix Exhibit 8A-3.
         b. Based on black equations in Appendix Exhibit 8A-3.

   * Indicates that the difference in estimated prices paid by indicated group and whites in All-White neighborhoods is significantly different from zero at the .05 level (two-tailed test).

To summarize the results thus far, we have found, *ceteris paribus,* that housing prices are lower in black neighborhoods than in white neighborhoods, and
that blacks pay less than whites within the same neighborhood. These findings
are consistent with the interneighborhood expectations of prejudice models but
contradict the intraneighborhood hypothesis of the discrimination model. The
apparent strength of white buyer prejudice prompts us to extend the argument
of the prejudice model to assess the weakness of the market not only for units in
black neighborhoods but also for black-owned units within neighborhoods.
According to this argument, a negative black/white intraneighborhood difference
could result if blacks buy disproportionately from blacks and in effect "profit"
from the weakness of white demand for black-owned units. By implication,
however, this extension of the prejudice model to consider race of the seller in
addition to neighborhood racial composition also suggests the negative impact of
white prejudice on black resale value and equity accumulation.

RESALE VALUE OF BLACK-OWNED UNITS

Respondents to the Recent Buyers Survey identified the race of the household *from whom* they had purchased their house.[29] We can therefore ascertain,
first, whether units sold by blacks bring a lower price than comparable units sold
by whites, and second, whether lower black purchase prices can be linked to
blacks buying black-owned units at a discount.

Sale Price of Black-Owned Units

Using the housing price model to standardize for unit, neighborhood, and
buyer characteristics, it is apparent that units sold by blacks throughout the
suburban area command an average of 10.4 percent less than units sold by
whites (Exhibit 8-6). Does this difference apply within neighborhoods?

At the neighborhood level, as we have seen above, prices decline with increasing black concentrations. Within this framework, however, *the discount
applied to black-owned units is greater than that for white-owned units in every
neighborhood type* (Exhibit 8-6). For instance, using sales by whites in All-White
neighborhoods as the norm, equivalent white-owned homes in Black-Entry
blocks sell for equivalent prices; black-owned homes in these neighborhoods sell
for 11.1 percent less. Within Inter-Racial neighborhoods, the 10.3 percent discount applied to units sold by whites is exceeded slightly by the 12.1 percent
discount in units sold by blacks. The respective price differences in All-Black
neighborhoods are −12.3 percent for white-owned units and −18.6 percent for
black-owned units. In short, although prices obtained by both blacks and whites
are lower with increasing black concentrations, the discrepancy is consistently
greater for blacks than for whites.

Buyer/Seller Interaction

Not only do obtained prices decrease with increasing black concentrations, but in general the greatest average loss of resale value is recorded in units that transfer from one black household to another (Exhibit 8-6). This reflects and supports the national data on equity accumulation reported in Chapter 3. Within Black-Entry neighborhoods, for instance, whites gain 2.9 percent when they sell to other whites, and lose only 3.1 percent when they sell to blacks. In contrast, blacks lose 7.1 percent selling to whites and 13.9 percent selling to blacks. (The coefficient for black-to-white transactions is not significant at the .10 level, due most likely to too few cases of black sellers in this neighborhood type.) White units in Inter-Racial neighborhoods sell for discounts of 9.3 percent to whites and 12.8 percent to blacks, while black units are discounted from 11.5 to 19.3 percent. Here, however, the greatest markdown occurs in black-owned units purchased by whites, reflecting the weakness of white demand for black-owned units in Inter-Racial neighborhoods. In All-Black neighborhoods, disaggregation by race of buyer is moot since only blacks are buying in, and the results are as reported above: whites selling to blacks lose 12.6 percent while blacks selling to blacks lose 18.8 percent.

Thus, in both Black-Entry and All-Black neighborhoods, lower prices paid by black buyers are largely the converse of lower prices obtained by black sellers. Black purchase prices are lower in Inter-Racial neighborhoods as well since the relatively high discount in black-to-white transfers is offset by the low discount in white-to-white sales. The negative black/white differential in purchase prices shown above is indeed largely a product of the low prices paid by blacks for black-owned units and reflects the weakness of white demand for such units.

The sale price pattern that emerges when considering the effects of buyer/ seller interaction reveals the structure of demand for biracial suburban housing. Blacks buying from other blacks in All-Black areas are relatively indifferent to neighborhood racial composition but are attracted by housing prices that are nearly 20 percent lower than prices in All-White neighborhoods.

Black households purchasing in Inter-Racial neighbohoods obtain a 12 to 13 percent discount (depending on whether they buy from blacks or whites) that, while less than the discount available in All-Black neighborhoods, is compensated for by access to an Inter-Racial rather than an All-Black neighborhood. White households overcome their distaste for buying a black-owned unit in an Inter-Racial area by paying nearly 20 percent less than would be required to buy a white-owned unit in an All-White neighborhood. At the same time, buying a white-owned rather than a black-owned unit represents enough of an improvement for whites in Inter-Racial neighborhoods that they reduce their discount by half, to 9 percent, relative to the markdown that would be available for buying a black-owned unit in the same neighborhood. The preference pattern in Black-Entry neighborhoods is straightforward: the substantial discount attached to black-owned units is indicative of the weakness of white demand. In sum, it is apparent that the large discounts available to blacks buying from other blacks depress the average black purchase price and account in large part for the negative black/white price differences observed at the neighborhood level.

EXHIBIT 8-6

SALE PRICE DIFFERENCES IN STANDARDIZED SUBURBAN HOMES <u>SOLD</u> BY BLACKS AND WHITES[a]

	Regression Coefficient	t-Value[b]	Percent Difference in Sale Price[c]
Relative to white sellers:			
Black sellers	−.1101**	−3.717	−10.4
Relative to white sellers in All-White neighborhoods:			
Black sellers in All-White blocks	−.0142	−0.158	−1.4
White sellers in Black-Entry blocks	−.0061	−0.305	−0.6
Black sellers in Black-Entry blocks	−.1161*	−1.531	−11.1
White sellers in Inter-Racial blocks	−.1092**	−4.911	−10.3
Black sellers in Inter-Racial blocks	−.1290**	−3.094	−12.1
White sellers in All-Black blocks	−.1307*	−1.445	−12.3
Black sellers in All-Black blocks	−.2057**	−3.511	−18.6
Relative to white-to-white sales in All-White neighborhoods:			
All-White neighborhoods			
Black-to-white sales	.0166	0.184	1.7
Black-Entry neighborhoods			
White-to-white sales	.0284	1.008	2.9
White-to-black sales	−.0317*	−1.285	−3.1
Black-to-white sales	−.0736	−0.639	−7.1
Black-to-black sales	−.1494*	−1.484	−13.9
Inter-Racial neighborhoods			
White-to-white sales	−.0976**	−3.796	−9.3
White-to-black sales	−.1365**	−3.575	−12.8
Black-to-white sales	−.2149*	−1.855	−19.3
Black-to-black sales	−.1219**	−2.752	−11.5
All-Black neighborhoods			
White-to-black sales	−.1343*	−1.485	−12.6
Black-to-black sales	−.2082**	−3.553	−18.8

Notes: a. Housing units standardized in regression of log sale price on five housing unit characteristics, four neighborhood characteristics, and six buyer characteristics, See Appendix Exhibit 8A-4.

b. Test that coefficient is significantly different from zero. The one-tailed .01 significance level (**) is 2.326 and the .10 significance level (*) is 1.282.

c. In the log-linear model, b (100) approximates the percent change in Y only when b is small. Otherwise, use $(e^b - 1)$ 100.

SALE PRICE CHANGES OVER TIME

A lower initial purchase price for blacks, coupled with a lower subsequent resale price, is problematic primarily if the intervening rate of price inflation is slower for black-owned units. The apparent savings in purchase price is illusory if the return on the initial investment lags behind that obtained by whites. We turn next, therefore, from a consideration of price levels to focus on relative rates of price change in suburban units owned by blacks and whites.

Measuring Price Change

The measure of price change used is the compounded monthly percent change in sale price for Recent Buyer Survey units for which the New Jersey State Treasury Department tax files recorded a prior sale during the period 1965 to 1977. The purchase price paid by survey respondents represents the latest (second) price measure. The annual tax files were searched in reverse chronological order back to 1965 (the earliest year with available date) to identify the most recent prior sale recorded for the sample units. This procedure yielded the month, year, and sale price for two consecutive transfers of all sample units for which a prior sale occurred since 1965.

The possible elapsed time between sales ranged from one month to twelve years; only units with a year or more between sales were retained for analysis in order to eliminate distortions introduced by speculative holding, distress sales, and the like. Then, to account for inflation over the twelve-year period, both current and prior sales prices were expressed in constant 1967 dollars, calculated separately for each case-study community and based on an annual price index of all units sold in each community over the 1965-77 period. The dependent variable is thus the monthly compounded percent change in adjusted sale price for individual units sold twice between 1965 and 1977, where the adjustment is for local inflation and prices are expressed in constant 1967 dollars. Thus, a price change exactly equal to the local rate of inflation would take a value of zero.[30] Of the 1,004 sample units, the state tax files recorded a prior sale (a year or more apart) for a total of 387 units, for which the adjusted price change measure could be computed. This measure has a mean value of .0181, ranging from a minimum of −1.383 to a maximum of 3.143.

The price change model used to control for unit and neighborhood characteristics is a variant of the price level model (see Appendix Exhibit 8A-5). Given the nature of change measures, the most significant determinant of rate of change is the initial sale price: lower-value units appreciate at a faster rate, after controlling for local inflation. The coefficient for previous selling price indicates that the monthly rate of change in sale price, in constant dollars, increases by .013 percentage points for every $1,000 decrease in the base sale price.

Inclusion of the initial sale price variable in the price change model, however, introduces serious problems of multicollinearity with the unit size measures shown to be closely related to sale price in the price level models. Unit size characteristics have therefore been deleted and only variables measuring housing unit improvements retained. Similarly, the land assessed-value measure has been deleted and the community type variable has been replaced by separate dummy variables corresponding to each of the case study communities. These separate housing market dummies indicate that, controlling for the initial sale price level, units in the two dormitory residential communities (Montclair and Teaneck) appreciate at a faster rate than units in mid-priced Franklin and Ewing Townships, and the depressed market in Pleasantville is reflected in the slowest real increase (after inflation) of housing values.

The explanatory power of the price change model is modest, but it is equivalent to that obtained by Berry for Chicago and only slightly less than that achieved by Palm for the San Francisco Bay Area.[31] Perhaps the greatest short-coming is our inability, shared with Berry, to control for improvements made to units over time.

The Effect of Race on Price Change

Analysis of the race effect in the price change model parallels our earlier examination of price levels. First, there appears to be no difference in the rate of price appreciation for units sold by blacks and whites not differentiated by neighborhood location (Exhibit 8-7). The coefficient of the dummy variable identifying black sellers is negative, suggesting that black units appreciate at a slower rate than white units, but the difference of .02 percentage points is not significant at the .10 level.

A significant difference does appear, however, when the model is reestimated with neighborhood-level dummies (Exhibit 8-7). Prices in Black-Entry neighborhoods increased at more than twice the rate of increase in all other neighborhood types: the compounded monthly percent change is .10, .11, and .08 in All-White, Inter-Racial and All-Black neighborhoods, respectively (no significant differences) but .23 in Black-Entry neighborhoods. This finding is consistent with interneighborhood prejudice models that suggest the upward pressure exerted on prices by demand for housing in black-expansion areas.

A faster rate of price appreciation in Black-Entry neighborhoods suggests that white sellers are benefiting from above-average increases generated by black buyer demand pressures. This hypothesis was tested with two further re-specifications of the price change model. First, the model was reestimated with dummy variables differentiating race of the seller within each neighborhood type. This revealed, as expected, that *white sellers* account for the entire ac-celeration of housing prices attributable to Black-Entry neighborhoods. The monthly rate of price increase in units sold by Black-Entry whites was .12 percentage points higher than in units sold by whites in All-White neighborhoods, a figure identical to that obtained with the neighborhood dummy for all Black-Entry units not differentiated by race of seller. The coefficient for units

EXHIBIT 8-7

DIFFERENCES IN SALES PRICE APPRECIATION RATES IN STANDARDIZED SUBURBAN HOMES SOLD BY BLACKS AND WHITES[a]

	Regression Coefficient	t-Value[b]	Compounded Monthly Percent Change in Sale Price After Inflation[c]
Relative to white sellers·			(.1488)
Black sellers	−.0239	−0.346	.12
Relative to All-White neighborhoods:			(.1043)
Black-Entry neighborhoods	.1237**	3.054	.23
Inter-Racial neighborhoods	.0080	0.167	.11
All-Black neighborhoods	−.0287	−0.210	.08
Relative to white sellers in All-White neighborhoods:			(.1155)
White sellers in Black-Entry neighborhoods	.1238**	3.008	.24
White-to-white sales	.0650	1.213	.19
White-to-black sales	.1792**	3.423	.30
Black sellers in Black-Entry neighborhoods	.1389	0.913	.25
White sellers in Inter-Racial neighborhoods	.0226	0.431	.14
Black sellers in Inter-Racial neighborhoods	−.0472	−0.507	.07
White sellers in All-Black neighborhoods	−.1423	−0.656	−.03
Black sellers in All-Black neighborhoods	.0418	0.241	.16

Notes: a. Housing units standardized in regression of compound monthly percent change in selling price (in constant 1967 dollars) on four housing unit characteristics and five neighborhood characteristics. See Appendix Exhibit 8A-5.

b. Test that coefficient is significantly different from zero. The one-tailed .01 significance level (**) is 2.326 and the .10 significance level (*) is 1.282.

c. Intercept from regression equation (price change rate when the dummy variable equals zero) plus or minus the dummy variable coefficient. Figures in parentheses show relevant intercepts (change rates) for white sellers, All-White neighborhoods, etc. See Appendix Exhibit 8A-5.

sold by Black-Entry neighborhood blacks is equivalent to that of whites, but is not significantly different from zero even at the 10 percent level. *While white sellers are therefore benefiting from rapid price increases, a final run of the price change model indicates that these increases are fully accounted for by units purchased by blacks* (Exhibit 8-7). When Black-Entry units sold by whites are disaggregated by race of buyer, the coefficient for white-to-black sales registers a substantial .18 percentage point supplement to the rate of price inflation. In contrast, white-to-white sales within Black-Entry neighborhoods appreciate at no better than the rate in All-White neighborhoods. Black-Entry units sold by whites to blacks experience a compounded monthly increase of .30 percent, or an annual increase of 3.5 percent above the local rate of inflation.

SUMMARY

Earlier studies of black/white housing price differences have lacked data on race of the seller, and as a result have inadequately assessed the price effects of white-to-black or black-to-white transfers within varying conditions of neighborhood racial composition. These studies have limited the hypothesized effect of white buyer prejudice to interneighborhood racial price differentials. They have assumed further that differences within neighborhoods are solely a function of discrimination in the transfer of units from white to black occupancy. As a result, they have generally failed to extend present race/price theories to consider possible intraneighborhood effects of white buyer prejudice, and they have been unable to directly relate purchase price differentials to the important issue of seller equity accumulation.

Our analysis of racial price differences in a sample of suburban single-family homes has identified substantial black purchase price discounts, both between and within neighborhoods, relative to prices paid by whites. Prices decrease for both blacks and whites as the neighborhood black population increases; the resulting interneighborhood price differences support prejudice models that ascribe lower prices in black neighborhoods to the weakness of white demand. The discount prevailing in each neighborhood type, however, is consistently greater for blacks than for whites. As a consequence, intraneighborhood black premiums posited by models of white seller discrimination are not revealed by the data; instead, black households in our suburban sample pay less than whites for equivalent housing within the same neighborhood.

Extension of the prejuduce model to consider within-neighborhood black discounts shows these apparent purchase-price savings to be illusory. The lowest prices prevailing within each neighborhood type are for units sold by black owners, which suggests that white avoidance of black or integrated neighborhoods extends to avoidance of black-owned units within neighborhoods as well. The largest observed markdowns are in units transferred between two black households, indicating the severe negative price effect resulting when units are removed entirely from the white market. An exception is for black units in Inter-Racial neighborhoods, where white buyers overcome their avoidance preferences by obtaining a 20 percent markdown in purchase price.

The negative consequences for black equity accumulation are substantial. The discount obtained by black buyers is exceeded by the markdown confronting black sellers in every neighborhood type. That is, although black households pay less than whites when purchasing a suburban house, they also obtain less when selling, and the latter markdown exceeds the former regardless of neighborhood racial composition. The price spread is most noticeable in Black-Entry neighborhoods, where the 3.6 percent discount obtained by black buyers is far exceeded by the 11 percent loss experienced by black sellers.[32] This is reflected in analysis of price changes, where white-occupied units appreciate at a faster rate than black units or units in integrated or black neighborhoods.

If racial price differences in suburban housing units are attributable to the weakness of white demand for integrated housing, then white preferences must be viewed in a broad institutionalized context. Overt white avoidance is certainly a major component of market weakness, as indicated by the data on expressed white preferences for integrated neighborhoods reported in Chapter 6. Also at issue, however, are the institutionalized market mechanisms that both arise from and reinforce white preferences. As indicated in Chapter 7, real estate brokers effectively mediate the level of demand for black-owned units by steering whites away from integrated areas. Even if a unit is included in a Multiple Listing Service, agents have complete autonomy in recommending listings to prospective buyers. Since MLS information is deemed confidential, dissemination of information about the availability of a listed unit rests entirely on the discretion of participating brokers. As a result of steering, the dissemination of information about black-owned units is substantially more restricted than that provided for units owned by whites.

In addition to real estate agents steering away prospective white buyers, the original listing broker can contribute directly to differential price levels for black units or units in integrated neighborhoods. Thus, in a form of self-fulfilling prophesy, the listing broker can perpetuate price differences by insisting that the unit be listed at a lower asking price because of its location. Respondents report:

> My parents recently sold their home and had a negative experience with brokers who said that they could ask the price that they wanted to ask if the home was in Tenafly [a predominantly white community] but not in Teaneck.

> In the two experiences we've had trying to sell our home since we've been here, the real estate people that have come into our home to sell it for us have told me that we could get a lot more money for our house if it wasn't in Franklin.

White demand may be further curtailed if black sellers list their house with a black real estate agent who has only limited access to a pool of prospective white buyers. Information on the role filled by black real estate agents in the housing market is completely lacking and remains largely conjectural. Several survey respondents, however, reported their dissatisfaction and disillusionment when black real estate agents contacted during the search for housing restricted their offerings to black-owned units in predominantly black neighborhoods. It is therefore conceivable that black sellers may experience a similar partitioning of the market by listing with a black broker. In sum, both overt white prejudice and institutionalized practices contribute to the weakening of white demand that, while forcing down prices, severely limits the potential for equity accumulation in suburban black homeownership.

APPENDIX EXHIBIT 8A-1

EFFECT OF RACE ON SELLING PRICE
WITH AND WITHOUT CONTROLLING
FOR NEIGHBORHOOD PROBLEMS AND SERVICES

| | WITHOUT CONTROLLING | | CONTROLLING FOR: | | | |
| | | | Services & Problems | | Houses, Traffic, Crime | |
	Regression Coefficient	t-Value	Regression Coefficient	t-Value	Regression Coefficient	t-Value
Race of buyer	−.0758	−4.086	−.0718	−3.601	−.0759	−3.856
Neighborhood:						
Black-Entry	−.0145	−0.759	−.0193	−0.952	−.0168	−0.855
Inter-Racial	−.1158	−5.745	−.1148	−5.441	−.1153	−5.512
All-Black	−.1811	−3.755	−.1796	−3.660	−.1908	−3.817
Race and Neighborhood:						
Whites in Black-Entry	.0159	0.587	.0122	0.428	.0157	0.568
Blacks in Black-Entry	−.0370	−1.574	−.0420	−1.700	−.0416	−1.714
Whites in Inter-Racial	−.1052	−4.251	−.1077	−4.157	−.1046	−4.036
Blacks in Inter-Racial	−.1331	−4.426	−.1268	−4.055	−.1326	−4.295
Blacks in All-Black	−.1839	−3.814	−.1820	−3.706	−.1935	−3.870

Notes: *Services* is a continuous variable measuring respondent's mean rating of the quality of seven municipal services.

               Problems is a continuous variable measuring respondent's mean rating of the seriousness of six neighborhood problems.

               Houses, Traffic and Crime are separate dummy variables coded "1" if respondent reported rundown houses, heavy street traffic, or street crime to be very serious or fairly serious problems, and "0" otherwise.

APPENDIX EXHIBIT 8A-2

EFFECT OF RACE OF BUYER ON PURCHASE PRICE

INDEPENDENT VARIABLES	DEPENDENT VARIABLE: *In SELLING PRICE*			
	I	*II*	*III*	*IV*
HOUSING UNIT CHARACTERISTICS				
Number of rooms	.0238**	.0251**	.0250**	.0255**
Number of bedrooms	.0275**	.0268**	.0271**	.0273**
Number of bathrooms	.0805**	.0786**	.0799**	.0780**
Age of house (years)	−.0049**	−.0052**	−.0050**	−.0051**
Garage (Yes=1)	.1353**	.1296**	.1276**	.1248**
NEIGHBORHOOD CHARACTERISTICS				
Land assessed value (*In*)	.0505**	.0496**	.0501**	.0501**
Community type (Montclair or Teaneck=1)	.1279**	.1404**	.1364**	.1390**
Journey-to-work (≤ 10 min=1)	−.0178	−.0232	−.0270*	−.0308*
Journey-to-work (≥ 1 hr.=1)	.0220	.0230	.0261	.0264
HOUSEHOLD CHARACTERISTICS				
Length of residence (months)	−.0035**	−.0036**	−.0034**	−.0035**
Blue-collar occupation (Yes=1)	−.1265**	−.1097**	−.1107**	−.1064**
Total family income ($1,000's)	.0046**	.0047**	.0044**	.0045**
Previous tenure (Own=1)	.0530**	.0462**	.0398*	.0384*
Age of head (years)	.0012	.0015*	.0017*	.0019*
Total family size	−.0072	−.0044	−.0029	−.0027
RACE OF BUYER *(Black=1)*		−.0758**		
NEIGHBORHOOD COMPOSITION				
Relative to All-White neighborhoods:				
Black-Entry neighborhoods			−.0145	
Inter-Racial neighborhoods			−.1158**	
All-Black neighborhoods			−.1811**	
RACE AND NEIGHBORHOOD				
Relative to whites in All-White neighborhoods:				
Whites in Black-Entry neighborhoods				.0159
Blacks in Black-Entry neighborhoods				−.0370*
Whites in Inter-Racial neighborhoods				−.1052**
Blacks in Inter-Racial neighborhoods				−.1331**
Blacks in All-Black neighborhoods				−.1839**
Constant	9.8087	9.8146	9.8106	9.8087
F	83.7835	81.2906	74.1412	66.9894
R^2	.634	.642	.658	.659
Number of cases	741	741	714	714

Note: Significance levels show (one-tailed test) that coefficient is significantly different from zero. Indicated absolute values for t: ** ≥2.326 (one percent); * ≥1.282 (ten percent).

APPENDIX EXHIBIT 8A-3

PURCHASE PRICE MODELS IN FOUR NEIGHBORHOOD TYPES
(Dependent variable = log Selling Price)

Independent Variables	All-White Neighborhoods White Buyers	Black-Entry Neighborhoods			Inter-Racial Neighborhoods			All-Black Neighborhoods Black Buyers
		Total	White	Black	Total	White	Black	
Length of residence (months)	-.0022 (.0008)	-.0029 (.0010)	-.0025 (.0015)	-.0037 (.0015)	-.0075 (.0014)	-.0081 (.0017)	-.0058 (.0024)	-.0024 (.0020)
Number of rooms	.0208 (.0083)	.0288 (.0085)	.0312 (.0158)	.0292 (.0106)	.0120 (.0127)	.0327 (.0189)	.0028 (.0180)	-.0466 (.0328)
Number of bedrooms	.0332 (.0143)	.0383 (.0188)	.0433 (.0255)	.0196 (.0282)	.0215 (.0245)	.0007 (.0306)	.0400 (.0465)	.0443 (.0523)
Number of bathrooms	.1509 (.0182)	.0945 (.0204)	.0666 (.0274)	.1115 (.0313)	.1189 (.0285)	.1031 (.0382)	.1112 (.0435)	.1206 (.0823)
Age of house (years)	-.0052 (.0006)	-.0059 (.0010)	-.0065 (.0014)	-.0054 (.0014)	-.0063 (.0009)	-.0076 (.0011)	-.0073 (.0021)	-.0105 (.0023)
Garage (Yes=1)	.1078 (.0291)	.1983 (.0466)	.1560 (.0983)	.1746 (.0581)	.2522 (.0434)	.2558 (.0579)	.1998 (.0692)	.0730 (.0838)
Land assessed value (ln)	.0695 (.0137)	.0196 (.0151)	-.0214 (.0308)	.0348 (.0187)	.0636 (.0202)	.0749 (.0324)	.0812 (.0288)	.0877 (.0376)
Community type (Montclair or Teaneck=1)	.1598 (.0342)	.2198 (.0442)	.3109 (.0798)	.2211 (.0586)	.2047 (.0522)	.1822 (.0875)	.2269 (.0724)	.3433 (.1049)
Constant	9.6842	10.0535	10.4517	9.9592	9.8303	9.8026	9.6518	9.8812
F	78.3774	30.8689	9.7120	20.4268	38.4631	27.4272	13.4738	6.7481
R^2	.542	.553	.476	.607	.659	.721	.624	.771
Number of cases	539	209	94	115	168	94	74	25

Note: Standard errors of regression coefficients are indicated in parentheses.

APPENDIX EXHIBIT 8A-4

EFFECT OF RACE OF SELLER ON SELLING PRICE

INDEPENDENT VARIABLES	DEPENDENT VARIABLE: ln SELLING PRICE		
	I	II	III
HOUSING UNIT CHARACTERISTICS			
Number of rooms	.0232**	.0239**	.0245**
Number of bedrooms	.0287**	.0283**	.0283**
Number of bathrooms	.0746**	.0766**	.0733**
Age of house (years)	-.0051**	-.0050**	-.0051**
Garage (Yes=1)	.1318**	.1287**	.1275**
NEIGHBORHOOD CHARACTERISTICS			
Land assessed value (ln)	.0510**	.0503**	.0509**
Community type (Montclair or Teaneck=1)	.1298**	.1346**	.1358**
Journey-to-work (< 10 min=1)	-.0172	-.0229	-.0266
Journey-to-work (≥ 1 hr.=1)	.0244	.0281*	.0298*
BUYER CHARACTERISTICS			
Length of residence (months)	-.0035**	-.0035**	-.0035**
Blue-collar occupation (Yes=1)	-.1148**	-.1072**	-.1040**
Total family income ($1,000's)	.0050**	.0047**	.0047**
Previous tenure (Own=1)	.0507**	.0413*	.0401*
Age of head (years)	.0011	.0016*	.0017*
Total family size	-.0071	-.0046	-.0041
RACE OF SELLER (Black=1)	-.1101**		
RACE OF SELLER BY NEIGHBORHOOD			
Relative to white sellers in All-White neighborhoods:			
Black seller in All-White neighborhoods		.0142	
White seller in Black-Entry neighborhoods		-.0061	
Black seller in Black-Entry neighborhoods		-.1161*	
White seller in Inter-Racial neighborhoods		-.1092**	
Black seller in Inter-Racial neighborhoods		-.1290**	
White seller in All-Black neighborhoods		-.1307*	
Black seller in All-Black neighborhoods		-.2057**	
RACE OF BUYER AND SELLER BY NEIGHBORHOOD			
Relative to white-to-white sales in All-White neighborhoods:			
Black-to-White Sales			.0166
Black-Entry neighborhoods			
White-to-white sales			.0284
White-to-black sales			-.0317*
Black-to-white sales			-.0736
Black-to-black sales			-.1494*
Inter-Racial neighborhoods			
White-to-white sales			-.0976**
White-to-black sales			-.1365**
Black-to-white sales			-.2149*
Black-to-black sales			-.1219**
All-Black neighborhoods			
White-to-black sales			-.1343*
Black-to-black sales			-.2082**
Constant	9.8189	9.8205	9.8117
F	77.9901	58.4913	49.7206
R²	.640	.658	.660
Number of cases	718	693	693

Note: Significance levels show (one-tailed test) that coefficient is significantly different from zero. Indicated absolute values for t: ** ≥ 2.326 (one percent); * ≥ 1.282 (ten percent).

APPENDIX EXHIBIT 8A-5

EFFECT OF RACE ON SELLING PRICE APPRECIATION RATE

Independent Variables	DEPENDENT VARIABLE: COMPOUNDED MONTHLY PERCENT CHANGE IN SELLING PRICE, IN CONSTANT 1967 DOLLARS			
	I	II	III	IV
HOUSING UNIT CHARACTERISTICS				
Previous selling price ($1,000's)	-.0132**	-.0132**	-.0126**	-.0126**
Number of bathrooms	.0564*	.0573*	.0501*	.0493*
Age of house (years)	.0003	.0002	.0003	.0002
Garage (Yes=1)	-.0547	-.0550	-.0712*	-.0800*
NEIGHBORHOOD CHARACTERISTICS				
Rating of municipal services	.0195	.0182	.0224	.0215
Montclair housing market (Yes=1)	.1394*	.1415*	.1479*	.1521*
Teaneck housing market (Yes=1)	.1098*	.1130*	.1118*	.1153*
Ewing housing market (Yes=1)	.0263	.0265	.0565	.0570
Pleasantville housing market (Yes=1)	-.1692*	-.1704*	-.1548	-.1645*
RACE AND NEIGHBORHOOD				
Race of seller (Black=1)		-.0239		
Black-Entry neighborhood			.1237**	
Inter-Racial neighborhood			.0080	
All-Black neighborhood			-.0287	
Black-Entry neighborhood				
White seller				.1238**
Black seller				.1389
Inter-Racial neighborhood				
White seller				.0226
Black seller				-.0472
All-Black neighborhood				
White seller				-.1423
Black seller				.0418
Constant	.1427	.1488	.1043	.1155
F	5.6994	5.1267	5.2295	4.2168
R^2	.144	.145	.173	.175
Number of cases	314	314	314	314

Note: Significance levels show (one-tailed test) that coefficient is significantly different from zero. Indicated absolute values for t: ** $\geq$ 2.326 (one percent); * $\geq$ 1.282 (ten percent).

NOTES

1. For reviews of recent literature see Peter Mieszkowski, *Studies of Prejudice and Discrimination in Urban Housing Markets* (Boston: Federal Reserve Bank of Boston, 1979); John Yinger, "Prejudice and Discrimination in the Urban Housing Market," in *Current Issues in Urban Economics,* ed. Peter Mieszkowski and Mahlon Straszheim (Baltimore, Md.: Johns Hopkins University Press, 1979), pp. 430-68.
2. Village of Oak Park, Ill., "Ordinance Providing for an Equity Assurance Plan for Single Family Residences in the Village of Oak Park," September 1977.
3. Gary Becker, *The Economics of Discrimination* (Chicago: University of Chicago Press, 1957); Chester Rapkin, "Price Discrimination Against Negroes in the Rental Housing Market," in *Essays in Urban Land Economics* (Los Angeles: Real Estate Research Program, University of California, 1966), pp. 333-45; Ronald Ridker and John Henning, "The Determinants of Residential Property Values with Special Reference to Air Pollution," *Review of Economics and Statistics* 44 (May 1967): 245-55; Richard Muth, *Cities and Housing* (Chicago: University of Chicago Press, 1969); John F. Kain and John M. Quigley, "Measuring the Value of Housing Qualities," *Journal of the American Statistical Association* 5 (June 1970): 532-48.
4. Ann B. Schnare, "Racial and Ethnic Price Differentials in an Urban Housing Market," *Urban Studies* 13 (June 1976): 107-20; Ann B. Schnare, *Externalties, Segregation, and Housing Prices* (Washington, D.C.: The Urban Institute, 1974); Brian J.L. Berry, "Ghetto Expansion and Single-Family Housing Prices: Chicago, 1968-1972," *"Journal of Urban Economics* 3 (October 1976): 397-423.
5. James R. Follain, Jr. and Stephen Malpezzi,, *Dissecting Housing Value and Rent: Estimates of Hedonic Indexes for Thirty-Nine Large SMSAs* (Washington, D.C.: The Urban Institute, 1980).
6. Ann B. Schnare and Raymond J. Struyk, "An Analysis of Ghetto Housing Prices Over Time," in *Residential Location and Urban Housing Markets,* ed. Gregory K. Ingram (New York: National Bureau of Economic Research, 1977), pp. 95-133.
7. Mieszkowski, *Studies of Prejudice and Discrimination.*
8. John Yinger, "The Black-White Price Differential in Housing: Some Further Evidence," *Land Economics* 54 (May 1978): 187-206; Yinger, "Prejudice and Discrimination in the Urban Housing Market."
9. Martin J. Bailey, "Effects of Race and Other Demographic Factors on the Value of Single-Family Homes," *Land Economics* 42 (May 1966): 215-20; Martin J. Bailey, "A Note on the Economics of Residential Zoning and Urban Renewal," *Land Economics* 35 (August 1959): 288-92.
10. It is immaterial to this formulation whether a black preference for resi-

dential location near whites is motivated by a desire for integration or by a perception that municipal services, environmental benefits, and similar residential amenities are often superior in white neighborhoods.

11. John Yinger, "Racial Prejudice and Racial Residential Segregation in an Urban Model," *Journal of Urban Economics* 3 (October 1976): 383-96.

12. Robert Schafer, "Racial Discrimination in the Boston Housing Market," *Journal of Urban Economics* 6 (April 1979): 176-96.

13. Mieszkowski, *Studies of Prejudice and Discrimination,* pp. 19-21; Thomas A. King and Peter Mieszkowski, "Racial Discrimination, Segregation, and the Price of Housing," *Journal of Political Economy* 81 (May/June 1973): 590-606.

14. George Sternlieb and Robert W. Lake, "Aging Suburbs and Black Homeownership," *Annals of the American Academy of Political and Social Science* 422 (November 1975): 105-17.

15. Risa Palm, "Financial and Real Estate Institutions in the Housing Market: A Study of Recent House Price Changes in the San Francisco Bay Area," in *Geography and the Urban Environment: Progress in Research and Applications, Volume II,* ed. D.T. Herbert and R.J. Johnston (New York: John Wiley and Sons, 1979), pp. 83-123.

16. Berry, "Ghetto Expansion and Single-Family Housing Prices."

17. Follain and Malpezzi, *Dissecting Housing Value and Rent;* Larry Ozanne, Marcellus Andrews, and Stephen Malpezzi, *An Assessment of Annual Housing Survey Hedonic Indexes Using Demand Experiment Data* (Washington, D.C.: The Urban Institute, 1979); C. Lance Barnett, *Using Hedonic Indexes to Measure Housing Quantity* (Santa Monica, Calif.: Rand Corporation, 1979).

18. John F. Kain and John M. Quigley, *Housing Markets and Racial Discrimination* (New York: National Bureau of Economic Research, 1975); Yinger, "The Black-White Price Differential in Housing."

19. Mieszkowski, *Studies of Prejudice and Discrimination,* p. 63.

20. William Alonso, "A Theory of the Urban Land Market," *Papers and Proceedings of the Regional Science Association* 6 (1960): 149-57.

21. This is consistent with Follain and Malpezzi's findings in 39 SMSAs: see Follain and Malpezzi, "Dissecting Housing Value and Rent," pp. 45-46; and with Berry's findings on the significance of air pollution as a neighborhood quality measure in Chicago: Berry, "Ghetto Expansion and Single-Family Housing Prices."

22. Since the neighborhood quality ratings measure respondents' perceptions rather than "objective" measures (such as crime reports or educational testing levels, for instance) the possibility of respondent bias cannot be ignored. Such bias would be most damaging if highly correlated with race. Some evidence is available, however, that racial differences are uncorrelated with perceptions of neighborhood quality, i.e., that reported differences in neighborhood quality reflect objective environmental differences and not racial

differences in perceptions. See Stephen C. Casey, "The Effect of Race on Opinions of Housing and Neighborhood Quality," in *America's Housing: Prospects and Problems,* ed. George Sternlieb and James W. Hughes (New Brunswick, N.J.: Center for Urban Policy Research, 1980), pp. 485-542.

23. For instance, inclusion of the three specific problem dummies (crime, street traffic, and rundown houses) contributes only .0018 to a total R^2 value of .6359, or approximately 0.3 percent of the total variation in selling price explained by the basic housing unit, neighborhood, and buyer characteristics.

24. Yinger, "The Black-White Price Differential in Housing."

25. Schafer, "Racial Discrimination in the Boston Housing Market."

26. The curtailed variable set also has the advantage of accommodating the smaller sample sizes in the neighborhood submarkets.

27. Schafer, "Racial Discrimination in the Boston Housing Market," pp. 184-88.

28. In his prototype analysis of the Boston Urbanized Area, Schafer compared prices paid by whites in each neighborhood type with white prices in the suburbs, and prices paid by blacks in each neighborhood with black prices in the suburbs. The rationale for the latter comparison is unclear, since it incorporates into the analysis the possible confounding effects of suburban black/white price differences. Indeed, the suburban black discounts uncovered in the New Jersey case would account for Schafer's finding of a markup for central-city blacks relative to whites, since the black benchmark was lower. For instance, equivalent black/white central-city prices would show a black premium if the price difference between central city and suburb was greater for blacks than for whites due to a lower suburban black price level. See Schafer, "Racial Discrimination in the Boston Housing Market," pp. 188-91.

29. Information on the race of the previous owner was furnished by 96 percent of survey respondents, of whom only 1 percent reported purchasing their unit from other than a private party.

30. A similar adjustment using the U.S. Consumer Price Index for homeownership proved to be unsatisfactory, yielding results closer to those obtained with unadjusted values than with the local adjustment. U.S. Bureau of the Census, *Statistical Abstract of the United States: 1978,* Table 792 "Consumer Price Indexes, by Major Groups: 1950 to 1978."

31. Berry, "Ghetto Expansion and Single-Family Housing Prices," pp. 457-64; Palm, "Financial and Real Estate Institutions in the Housing Market," pp. 102-7.

32. This comparison, of course, applies to buyers and sellers a generation apart in terms of their occupance of the unit. We are not comparing here the price spread obtained when the same unit is bought and then subsequently sold, but rather average prices paid and recorded in a single turnover of the unit between two generations of occupants.

9

THE REAL ESTATE
AGENT'S PERSPECTIVE

INTRODUCTION

Preceding chapters have documented racial differences in suburban housing
search and housing market operations that cannot be attributed to socioeconomic or mobility characteristics. This chapter turns to institutionalized patterns within the real estate industry that perpetuate black/white differences in
the terms and conditions of home purchase. Neither overt discriminatory acts
nor an intent to discriminate are necessary for the structure of the real estate
industry to impact negatively on black home purchase. Racially differentiated
treatment by brokers is less a function of discriminatory intent than of rational
competitive behavior based on the structure of the industry and on the broker's
perception of white prejudice.[1] From the real estate agent's perspective, race is
a dominant concern of both clients (sellers) and prospects (buyers). The racial
identity of buyer, seller, and neighborhood is thus a salient consideration of
most real estate agents, and this salience is internalized in day-to-day operations.

This chapter examines the incentives to discriminate inherent in everyday real estate operations. Data for this discussion were obtained from twenty intensive open-ended interviews conducted with major real estate brokers in the five case study communities. This survey was not directed explicitly at racial practices per se but rather was aimed at providing an overview of day-to-day agency operations. The hypothesis was that insight into the normal *modus operandi* of the real estate agent would reveal the underlying pressures and incentives that make discriminatory behavior a rational response on the part of the individual agent.

The discussion begins with a brief overview of racial patterns and practices of real estate brokers and the following section summarizes the methodology used in implementing the real estate broker survey. Survey results are then discussed in terms of several broad categories of issues. These include the importance of obtaining listings as the basis of the real estate business; the broker's perception of racial submarkets; the importance of community reputation and of maintaining close social and personal ties within the community; the broker's attitude regarding showing houses to black prospects in light of a perceived responsibility to cater to community preferences; and the broker's method of selecting houses to show prospects.

ATTITUDES AND PRACTICES OF
REAL ESTATE BROKERS

The literature on real estate broker attitudes and practices provides information on both the organizational structure of the industry as well as the racial policies and ideology of individual brokers. These two facets—the structural and the attitudinal—have, however, rarely been considered together in the same study.

General Brokerage Operations

Several studies have focused on the general functioning and operation of the real estate industry with the goal of explaining the role of the broker in the housing market. Hempel's survey of a 100 housebuyers in southeastern Connecticut documented the importance of the real estate agent in helping buyers define their housing needs and appropriate price range and in providing information on housing prices and vacancies.[2] Barresi focused on the equally important role of the broker in recommending particular neighborhoods to prospective buyers and thereby influencing neighborhood destinations.[3] Other studies have examined the interpersonal dynamics that evolve between broker, buyer, and seller, given the often conflicting goals of each of these parties in a real estate transaction.[4]

The spatial pattern of broker activity has been examined in a perceptive series of studies by Risa Palm.[5] Large samples of brokers in two metropolitan areas (450 in San Francisco and 250 in Minneapolis) were asked to recommend appropriate neighborhoods for each of eight hypothetical families differing in occupational and social status along a continuum from a dentist to a delivery-man. The surveyed brokers belonged to the largest real estate firms in their respective areas, had access to multiple listing information, and served a metro-politan-wide clientele. Nevertheless, Palm found a highly localized pattern of recommendations:

> Real estate agents have a strong tendency to bias their recom-mendations in favor of territories with which they are most familiar, giving a strong local effect to the pattern of neighborhood recom-mendations.[6]

This highly localized pattern of activity is indicative of strong local-area ties developed by most brokers and has important consequences for broker practices and day-to-day operations.

Racial Practices

Evidence on the explicit racial attitudes and practices of brokers is extensive but is growing increasingly dated. The most extensive and widely quoted study of this type is that by Helper, based on highly detailed interviews with ninety Chicago real estate brokers in 1955-56.[7] Helper defined three types of racial ideology held by brokers and termed them exclusionist, intermediate, and integrationist. Brokers were assigned to these categories on the basis of their stated beliefs and perceptions regarding white attitudes toward blacks, the effect of black residence on neighborhoods and property values, the possibility of successful residential integration, and similar issues. Most brokers were classified as exclusionist, which reflects the strict residential segregation in effect at the time, the brokers' perception of white expectations, and their belief that pro-tecting white neighborhoods from black entry was an ethical duty. More recent surveys of racial practices in the San Francisco and New York metropolitan areas in the late sixties and early seventies showed that exclusionary practices became more subtle but not less effective.[8]

Stronger enforcement of civil rights laws and changing rhetoric on the acceptability of discrimination made it increasingly difficult to obtain data on racial practices through direct survey techniques. Some studies turned instead to assessing broker attitudes on local and federal open housing laws. A survey of 164 Pittsburgh realtors in 1965 showed that those who had dealt with non-white buyers were more likely to have positive attitudes toward a local open housing ordinance but that 73 percent of brokers interviewed had never sold a house in a white neighborhood to a black buyer. Overall, 58 percent were opposed to the fair housing ordinance and 33 percent were opposed to the "concept of a non-discriminatory housing market."[9] In a more recent study conducted after passage of the federal Fair Housing Act, Schechter found that brokers in two predominantly white Boston suburbs had little knowledge of open housing laws and consequently were unable to evaluate them.[10]

The National Association of Realtors

Numerous authors have argued that the attitudes and ideology of individual brokers are simply a reflection of the official position of the National Association of Realtors (NAR), the primary national professional organization of realtors (formerly the National Association of Real Estate Boards, or NAREB). Several authors, beginning with Charles Abrams in 1955, have traced official NAREB opposition to introducing black residents into white neighborhoods; the NAREB code of ethics prohibited such action explicitly until 1950 and implicitly until the early 1960s.[11] A discussion by William Brown serves as a reminder that official industry opposition to integration has persisted into the 1970s.[12] For example, Brown reports that black brokers were barred from membership in the Oakland (Calif.) Real Estate Board until 1962 and cites testimony before the U.S. Commission on Civil Rights by recently admitted black brokers who were "amazed to discover that the OREB (Oakland Real Estate Board) used 'Caucasians Only' on their multiple listings."[13] Helper documents the active real estate board opposition to state and local enactment of fair housing laws in Illinois, California, Ohio, and Michigan, and Brown describes the California Real Estate Board's campaign to overturn through referendum the 1963 Rumford Fair Housing Act in that state. NAREB lobbied actively against inclusion of the Fair Housing Title in the federal Civil Rights Act of 1968 on the grounds that "forced housing" violated the rights of property owners to dispose of their property in any way they saw fit. The NAREB president called the law "a loosely drawn and unsound legislative attack on the human rights of private property owners."[14] Two months after passage of the Civil Rights Act of 1968, the Supreme Court ruled in *Jones v. Mayer* that the Civil Rights Act of 1866 prohibits any discrimination in the sale of housing. This decision prompted the executive secretary of NAREB to acknowledge, albeit belatedly, that "the Negro in America is henceforth a free man, or, if there be any further impediment to that freedom in the future, the court noted the means by which it would be struck down."[15]

Official NAR rhetoric regarding fair housing was reversed in 1972 with the recommendation of a five-point Code for Equal Opportunity for adoption by local boards.[16] Local board adoption of the code requires board members to "offer equal service to all clients and prospects without regard to race" and to refrain from panic peddling, from using racially biased advertising, and from volunteering information on neighborhood racial composition. These prohibitions reflect the list of discriminatory practices explicitly proscribed under Title VIII of the Civil Rights Act of 1968, so that adoption of the code is little more than a stated agreement to abide by the law. By late 1978, however, 36 percent of NAR member boards had not yet adopted the code.[17]

In addition to the Code for Equal Opportunity, the NAR drafted an Affirmative Marketing Agreement in 1975 for voluntary adoption by its member boards. The agreement calls for participating brokers to use the HUD-approved equal opportunity logo in advertising, to develop educational materials to inform salespersons and employees of their obligations under Fair Housing Laws, to implement office procedures to facilitate dissemination of information to minority prospects and clients, and to recruit minority brokers and salespeople.

The Affirmative Marketing Agreement was drafted jointly by the NAR and HUD to encourage voluntary adoption by realtors of the principle of equal housing opportunity. Development of a voluntary mechanism was effective in forestalling pressure from HUD and private fair housing groups for mandated affirmative action by brokers. In the NAR's view:

> ...the success of the Agreement depends on a "voluntary" as opposed to a "coerced" commitment to the spirit and intent of the concept of affirmative marketing in support of equal opportunity in housing. It is no answer to the National Association's condemnation of governmental coercion to substitute its own form of private coercion.[18]

As a consequence of this position, implementation of the Affirmative Marketing Agreement is extremely diffused since it first requires each local board to adopt the agreement and subsequently requires each individual realtor member to subscribe to the local board's adoption.[19] The fact that the NAR is composed of 1,735 local boards comprising over 700,000 realtor members raises obvious questions as to the efficacy of such a procedure. The NAR position is that this procedure is required by the independent corporate nature of the individual brokerage firms comprising its membership, and that requiring adoption of the agreement as a condition for membership would constitute unwarranted interference in the internal operations of member firms.[20]

The principal argument put forth by the NAR to induce its local boards and members to subscribe to the Affirmative Marketing Agreement is that adoption represents valuable insurance against any litigation charging discriminatory treatment. Adoption is described as "a wise business decision ... just like insurance,"[21] and substantial savings in defense costs are seen to accrue from adoption:

> The mere filing of a fair housing complaint against a realtor commits him to often prohibitive defense costs regardless of the merits of the case. To the extent adoption of affirmative marketing reduces the realtor's exposure to such suits or enhances his ability to defend them, it is valuable insurance.[22]

Not only will adoption result in cost savings in the event of litigation, but it will also make it more difficult for a complainant to substantiate a case:

> It will force the plaintiff to prove specific violation of the law rather than merely a set of ambiguous practices or procedures which, in the context of *de facto* community segregation, permits an inference of misconduct sufficient to survive summary judgement ... the Affirmative Marketing Agreement will shift the burden of proof back to the plaintiff where it rightly belongs.[23]

In addition to aiding in defense against charges of discriminatory treatment brought by individuals, adoption of the Affirmative Marketing Agreement will also defend the realtor against suits brought by the Justice Department that charge a broad "pattern or practice" of discrimination. According to the NAR's advice to its members, signing the agreement

> ... enables the Realtor to establish a *prima facie* case that any violation of law by a salesperson was *not* part of a pattern or practice for which he should be held responsible ... perhaps the most vital protection it offers is the opportunity to distinguish the "isolated, unauthorized aberrant," civil rights violation from the "pattern or practice".... In the face of such Agreement, it is not enough for the government to infer a pattern from isolated violations; it is necessary to prove that the commitment represented by the Agreement was illusory and the program to implement it was a sham.[24]

In other words, adoption of an Affirmative Marketing Agreement shifts the focus of litigation away from the broker's practices and onto the terms and implementation of the agreement.

Despite these arguments, however, and perhaps as a consequence of the extremely diffused nature of the industry, adoption of the agreement has not been widespread. As of October 1978 only 430 of 1,735 member boards or 24.8 percent had signed.[25]

Recent Evidence

Recent studies have shown that de facto discriminatory practices remain prevalent within the real estate industry. The 1977 HUD Housing Market Practices Survey utilized matched pairs of black and white "testers" to simulate housing search in forty metropolitan areas.[26] As indicated in preceding chapters above, the HUD survey compared the treatment of black and white testers by rental and sales agents in terms of housing availability, courtesy, and the quality and quantity of service provided. Focusing primarily on the issue of housing availability, HUD found that blacks encountered discrimination from 27 percent of rental agents and 15 percent of sales agents, and that the probability of discriminatory treatment was cumulative given the likelihood of visiting several agents in the course of housing search. In terms of courtesy and the quality of service provided, the study found that agents were more likely to attempt to establish a continuing relationship with the white than with the black auditor. In a similar study, Diana Pearce sent paired testers to 97 randomly selected brokers in the Detroit metropolitan area and found similar results.[27] Despite Palm's finding of the highly localized nature of realtor recommendations, Pearce found that "blacks more often than whites were shown houses *not* located in the city where the sales agent's office was located; that is, they were steered 'out of town' .... when blacks were 'steered out,' two-thirds of the houses shown were in the racially mixed cities of Inkster and Detroit."[28] In short, in addition to the evidence of steering and market segmentation, both audit studies showed that brokers are unlikely to see black prospects as potential future clients, a finding that will take on additional meaning in the discussion of day-to-day agency operations below.

In light of the existence of federal and local legislation prohibiting housing discrimination, it is necessary to ask why the evidence continues to point to widespread discrimination on the part of brokers. The National Association of Realtors has offered two responses. The first has been to discredit the evidence collected by testers. Although charges of entrapment have been laid to rest by the courts, the NAR warns its members of the activities of testers who "use a variety of techniques designed to induce the salesman into making illegal racial representations or otherwise engaging in discriminatory conduct."[29] The NAR similarly denigrates the attempts to expose discrimination undertaken by the "innumerable public and private 'human rights' agencies with staffs of lawyers whose job security depends on the initiation of civil rights complaints."[30] The imputation is that the evidence assembled by testers and the cases brought by fair housing groups overplay the actual amount of broker discrimination.

A second and somewhat more credible position adopted by the NAR is that discrimination undoubtedly persists, but that this is simply a reflection and consequence of deepseated societal prejudice that until recently was supported by government action. The NAR cites the period of "102 years of legalized housing discrimination" during which "the decisions of the Supreme Court and the policies of federal, state, and local government affirmatively created, or at least countenanced, a segregated and discriminatory housing market."[31] According to this argument, real estate agents should not be faulted for simply reflecting societal values and government policy.

A third and more fundamental explanation is that incentives to discriminate are inherent in the organization of the real estate industry and the nature of the real estate business. From the broker's perspective, the pervasiveness of white prejudice expressed in an overwhelming white preference for residential segregation makes the failure to discriminate an economically irrational act.[32] Once this belief becomes internalized as a basic business precept, then discriminatory treatment arises not from an overt intent to discriminate but simply as an expression of the broker's instinctual knowledge of successful business operations.

Incentives to discriminate are contained throughout the most basic elements of brokerage. These include the fundamental importance of and methods for obtaining listings; the significance of the broker's social and personal reputation in the community as a primary business asset; the highly localized nature of brokerage activities; the perception of racial submarkets among brokers; the broker's belief in a responsibility for ensuring neighborhood compatability; methods for selecting neighborhoods and houses to show prospects; and beliefs regarding the problem of showing houses in white neighborhoods to black prospects.

In order to assess the incentives to discriminate inherent in each of these issues of day-to-day brokerage operations, we conducted intensive open-ended interviews with twenty major realty firms in the five case study communities. The methodology used in the real estate broker survey is described below and the findings are presented in the following section.

THE REAL ESTATE BROKER SURVEY

Respondents to the Recent Buyers Survey conducted in five New Jersey suburban communities were asked for the name and location of the real estate broker that they finally used in purchasing a house. After excluding respondents who did not use a broker at all or could not recall or would not identify the broker, a total of 691 respondents provided the requisite information. These 691 homebuyers in five communities named 221 different brokerages as the firm that handled their home purchase. This is an average of only 3.1 sales per realty firm among the sampled sales, indicating the large number of firms active within particular communities and the difficulty facing attempts to monitor or control such a dispersed and individualized industry. Fully 74 percent of the brokers identified handled only one or two sales within the sample, while 6 percent of firms handled ten sales or more.

In order to identify the principal brokers operating within the case study communities, the survey focused on the thirty-three firms responsible for five or more sales within the sample. These included ten in Montclair, eleven in Teaneck, five in Franklin, six in Ewing, and one in Pleasantville. The survey goal was to complete five interviews within each community, with the exception of Pleasantville. An initial introductory letter was mailed to the principal in each firm with five or more sales that explained the purpose of the survey and indicated that an interviewer would call to arrange an appointment for an interview. Subsequent letters were sent and appointments arranged with brokers with less than five sales, since several of the initial contacts declined to be interviewed. The final tally of twenty completed interviews included fifteen brokers with five or more sales within the sample, one with four sales, three with three sales, and one broker with two sales. The survey thus included fifteen of the thirty-three brokers initially selected because of their volume of sales within the buyer sample, and five additional interviews were conducted with brokers with fewer than five sales in the sample. The twenty brokers interviewed represent 9.1 percent of brokers identified by survey respondents but account for 31 percent of purchases by the 691 respondents who identified their broker.

Interviews ranging from an hour-and-a-half to four hours in length were conducted with principals of each firm in the respective broker's office during August and September 1979. Several of the longer interviews were held in several sessions over a period of days. The survey schedule was semi-structured and open-ended, and used a list of topics and questions for discussion rather than a structured questionnaire. The schedule included questions on seven basic areas of brokerage operations: knowledge of local housing market conditions; average homebuyer characteristics and minimum affordability criteria; methods of attracting prospects (buyers); procedures in selecting and showing homes to prospects; assisting buyers to obtain financing, and relationships with lenders; methods of obtaining listings and relationships with clients (sellers); and relationships with other brokers (see Appendix B). The interviewers took detailed notes and immediately following each interview prepared a transcript of the interview in as close to verbatim form as possible. These transcripts, numbering over two hundred pages, provide the data for the discussion below.

REALTY OPERATIONS AND INCENTIVES TO DISCRIMINATE

Obtaining Listings

The primary activity of the residential real estate broker is obtaining listings of houses for sale. As stated in a recent real estate textbook, "listings make the brokerage business."[33] Listings represent the broker's inventory of stock in trade. Of course, the Multiple Listing Service (MLS) widens the broker's access to listings, but not all brokers are members of the local real estate board providing access to the MLS.[34] In addition, a broker selling his/her own listing receives the full commission while the commission on a unit listed by another broker must be split with the listing broker. Most MLSs allow the broker to maintain an "exclusive" on a listing (i.e., the exclusive right to sell the house and collect the commission) for a specified period agreed to by the seller. The incentive to find a buyer for the house during this period is great, of course, given that the entire commission accrues to the listing broker. As a result, the most attractive houses ("cream puffs") that the broker will easily sell are least likely to find their way into the MLS.

Brokers use two principal means of obtaining listings: referrals or repeats from previous clients and canvassing or "farming."[35] The real estate agents interviewed were nearly unanimous in their agreement that referrals and repeat sales were their most important source of listings:

> "Referrals are the most efficient way of getting saleable properties." (Broker No. 89)

> "We get listings from people we have previously sold houses to. And we have contacts—that is our main way of getting listings. By contacts I mean business, personal, and social contacts." (Broker No. 34)

> "I get listings through recommendations and referrals. Also through personal contacts. Most people call us—we don't have to go looking for listings." (Broker No. 30)

As a result of the importance of contacts and referrals for obtaining listings, the brokers interviewed were also unanimous on the overwhelming significance of their reputation in the community and of the importance of spending considerable effort on maintaining and developing that reputation. Indeed, a major lesson in real estate texts is that marketing oneself is the key to marketing real estate: "The broker's objective in marketing real estate is primarily to market himself or herself as a proper intermediary in the real estate transaction."[36] The lesson has clearly been learned by the surveyed brokers:

> "Our image in the market is vital to us—it has a tremendous influence on our business.... My community reputation is important, substantially important. I encourage everyone in my office to participate in civic, charitable and social organizations. A huge percentage of my business comes from my community reputation and activities." (Broker No. 2)

> "A broker's reputation is the most important thing to him. Real estate is localized, and a local reputation is important." (Broker No. 30)

> "We want people to think we are interested in the community—that we are not outsiders." (Broker No. 151)

Numerous brokers seem to go to extraordinary lengths to involve themselves in community activities and to achieve exposure, and many expect their salespeople to do the same. Often the broker's involvement is so extensive that the boundary between business and personal life becomes indistinguishable:

> "Community reputation is of the utmost importance. Absolutely. A broker must build a feeling of trust in all business relationships.... It is to every advantage to be active and outgoing.... It is good advice to keep up community contacts. I have been PTA president, taken courses at the Y, been a teacher in the area, choir director, taught piano. The contacts my children have in sports are important. I'm an active member of my church. I keep in touch with everyone." (Broker No. 153)

Nor is this an exceptional case, as other brokers reported a similar degree of personal and social involvement in the community:

> "I sit on the board at the Y, community hospital, community chest, Red Cross, Welfare Board, Boy Scouts, the Church. It is definitely important. There are few people in _____ who don't know me." (Broker No. 12)

One result of such intense community activity is a blurring of the distinction between personal and business concerns for many brokers, for whom a great deal of personal and social life is invested in creating the positive community reputation necessary for a successful business.

Canvassing or soliciting is the second most important method of obtaining listings for most brokers. In Teaneck, an antisolicitation ordinance enacted in

1966 to control block-busting effectively limits the use of this technique, but it is an important tool elsewhere. Canvassing takes several forms, from mail brochures extolling the services provided by the firm to active door-to-door solicitation. The latter is also known as "farming," as explained by several brokers:

> "We also do farming: to canvass in a specific area and become familiar with every household so that for the people that live there, real estate becomes synonymous with (agency name)." (Broker No. 89)

> "We do something called farming. Every area in town is divided into 500-house sections. Each realtor is given those 500 houses to canvass. We keep in touch with the residents, go around ringing doorbells, ask them to call on me if I can be of help to them. Recently ... an ordinance was passed that said every house that is sold from now on must have smoke detectors. So I am making copies of the ordinance and distributing them to my farm." (Broker No. 4)

> "(In addition to referrals) the other fifty percent come through the agent's activity or canvassing .... In some cases the agent will work a 'farm' area. In one area, say with a hundred homes, during the course of a year the agent will visit every home." (Broker No. 88)

This type of activity clearly represents a substantial investment of effort and personnel in a narrowly defined territory. It contributes further to the broker's control of and identification with particular territories within the community or region. Such territorial control breaks down only in unusual circumstances. One broker continued his discussion of farming by describing one such circumstance:

> "But I have many relatives in town. They know and the brokers know that if one of my relative's houses is listed, it will be my territory and no one else's." (Broker No. 4)

Both methods of obtaining listings—referrals based on reputation and canvassing—generate strong local ties to a well-defined but relatively circumscribed area. Both represent a substantial investment in the stability and continuity of the area. In many cases, the investment is a highly personal one in which personal and professional ties cannot be separated. These conclusions go a long way in explaining Risa Palm's finding of the localized nature of realtors' recommendations.

At the same time, these conclusions explain in part the resistance of many brokers to integration of all-white neighborhoods in their territory. If the broker's business relies greatly on close community ties, and if whites and blacks tend to be relatively isolated (see Chapter 5), then the white broker will have few ties within the black community and will consequently obtain few if any listings from black clients. The evidence from testing described above indicating that white realtors do not see black homebuyers as potential future clients suggests that they will be unlikely to encourage black entry into their territory.

A potential recourse for the broker facing a breaking off of social ties and loss of listings from his/her territory is to move operations to a new locale. A recent HUD study documented the shift that occurs in real estate broker activity in neighborhoods undergoing racial change.[37] Analyzing neighborhood racial change in three cities, the study found a "perceptible if not pervasive shift among real estate firms handling study neighborhood properties," such that established firms were replaced by others specializing in low-priced housing attractive to first-time homebuyers.[38]

If brokers do indeed shift their operations to new locations because of racial change, it is only at considerable expense given their prior investment in their original territory. The personal ties and social contacts already established are extremely difficult to duplicate elsewhere. To the extent that personal and professional ties have merged, reestablishing a new professional identity in a new locale may involve substantial personal uprooting as well.

An added disincentive to moving into a new territory derives from the highly competitive nature of the industry and the difficulty of competing with an already entrenched broker. The realtors surveyed were unanimous in citing the extreme competition among brokers to obtain listings. The services that would be provided the client in marketing the house were an important consideration, but most brokers agreed that style and personality were ultimately the crucial factors in getting the listing:

> "Most people will call more than one broker to hear them present their case. I'll tell a seller I'll use the *New York Times,* but it boils down to personalities, whether they like you or not." (Broker No. 29)

An established broker with a local reputation clearly has an advantage over a newcomer in such a situation.

Racial Submarkets

Given the extreme difficulty of reestablishing operations in a new locale, broker opposition to integration of their present territory may be largely motivated by the expectation that they will be unable to establish ties with—and get listings from—black clients. This is in fact their present experience with the predominantly black areas of the study communities:

> "I don't get listings in the black areas. They are very stable .... Whether or not the property doesn't change hands or just without brokers, I don't know." (Broker No. 153)

Several brokers considered the development of racial submarkets as a natural occurrence, based on demographic verities and personal preferences:

> "It's just natural that there would be submarket areas within the township. There are more whites in the the world than blacks. The

whites don't want to move into black neighborhoods. So the black areas have a small supply, low prices, and low demand." (Broker No. 91)

The result of racially defined submarkets is that white brokers consider predominantly black neighborhoods as outside their territory:

"Yes, there are submarket areas by racial composition. These are areas where I am not active in the residential market, because they are serviced by brokers of their own race." (Broker No. 2)

"One major area in _____ is non-integrated, all-black. There are very few MLS listings from that area. White brokers don't see property (there) but that's okay because few black prospects come to my office. They don't respond to the ads." (Broker No. 5)

These brokers went on to explain that sales in predominantly black neighborhoods were handled by black realtors:

"Two brokers from there are members of the board and subscribe to MLS .... I'm sure those two brokers keep listings in their desk drawers. But I have no demand for that property so it's all right." (Broker No. 5)

"It's really a matter of different marketing. Don't get me wrong—this is nothing like segregation. The distinctions are of broker sales—it's the broker control. I don't care that we don't list houses in the black area and the black brokers don't care either. It's a market peculiarity. The (black neighborhood) is for black brokers. It's a corner we know little about." (Broker No. 2)

The experience of white brokers is that predominantly black areas are lost to them as a source of listings and that there is no demand from white prospects for homes in black neighborhoods.

From the white broker's perspective, then, assisting black entry into a white neighborhood within his/her territory is to initiate a process that will ultimately result in the loss of that territory. White demand will decline and it will be more difficult to find buyers for his listings. Black households who do purchase homes in the area will be tied into a different set of community institutions and the broker's carefully developed social networks will begin to unravel. The process of shifting to a new territory is frought with difficulty, compounded by competition from other brokers and the necessity of recreating a broad spectrum of personal, social, and professional relationships in the new locale. For all of these reasons, brokers tend to protect the stability and constancy within their territory, and for most white brokers this translates into the discouragement of black entry.

Responding to White Preferences

An added incentive to discourage blacks from buying in white neighborhoods is a need felt by many brokers to respond to the preferences of the white community. In general terms, this is seen as one component of building a good reputation:

> "We have a good reputation and it's very important to maintain good will with the community .... A lot of our agents are involved locally politically, in the Chamber of Commerce, on zoning commissions. It enhances our reputation to have our agents doing things like that. We have to somewhat cater to community preferences. Otherwise we'll go out of business." (Broker No. 85)

In practice, maintaining neighborhood homogeneity is an important component of catering to community preferences. The NAR's Code of Ethics no longer considers introducing incompatible racial groups into a neighborhood as an unethical practice but this is still clearly viewed by many brokers as an important part of their function and is necessary for maintaining ties to the neighborhood:[39]

> "It's a given fact that it's important to cater to neighborhood preferences. A community is a political subdivision but a neighborhood is different. Compatability with neighbors is vital—that's how people live." (Broker No. 89)

Because of the broker's dependence on community good will to ensure a future supply of listings, the broker is wary of antagonizing potential clients by introducing an "incompatible" black family into the neighborhood.

At this point, the realtor's role has extended substantially beyond that of intermediary in a financial transaction and has taken on the aspect of neighborhood gatekeeper. The gatekeeper role relies on a great amount of subjective, intuitive understanding of both buyers and neighborhoods: many brokers view their capacity to achieve such understanding as one of their primary professional skills.

> "Aside from racism, I feel I've got to put a person in a neighborhood where he fits. *I can just tell by looking at a person whether he belongs in a certain neighborhood.* We do a lot of integrated business but frankly a lot of colored don't want to bother moving into all-white neighborhoods." (Broker No. 212)

The broker's gatekeeper role is operationalized in the process of selecting homes to recommend to the prospect. This essential component of salesmanship—perceiving the prospect's needs better than the prospect himself can and selecting the appropriate house/neighborhood from among the alternatives available—is a major component of the broker's self-image of his abilities as a professional.

Recommending Houses to Buyers

The issue of selecting houses to show the prospect reduces to how completely the broker will convey the range of available alternatives. The most frequently used procedure is the most constrained in total information provided. The broker simply selects two to three houses to show the prospect and then goes on to two to three more if the first are unacceptable. The other end of the information continuum is to go through the MLS book together with the prospect, pointing out the pros and cons of the houses listed and clearly establishing the full range of alternatives.[40]

In line with the broker's certainty in knowing the prospect's needs, most brokers surveyed prefer not to show the listing book at all but rather to select a small number of units to show the prospect:

> "If I can avoid it, I never show the listing book to prospects. I don't want the prospect to have the privilege of selecting houses they think they'd be interested in. I know what they should buy." (Broker No. 2)

In the brokers' experience most buyers have only a poorly formed idea of what they are looking for and are unable to specify preferences if confronted with too large a range of options. That the "broker knows best" is an often repeated theme:

> "I could go through the listing book with a buyer but I usually don't. A buyer doesn't really know what he really wants and showing him the listing book confuses him. I try to show three houses at most at a time to a buyer. I know what they're going to buy before I show it to them." (Broker No. 212)

Some brokers argue against showing the book to prospects on grounds of confidentiality or protecting clients. In some cases this is stated as a blanket prohibition: most Multiple Listing Services characterize their listings as confidential information not to be revealed to unauthorized parties under penalty of a fine or expulsion from the service. One broker argued that

> "It's illegal to go through the listing book with the buyer, that is, it violates the contractual relation of the Multiple Listing Service." (Broker No. 89)

In other cases brokers argued that the listing book contained information that might be damaging to clients if made public:

> "The listing book never leaves the office. The information is private in the book. There are mortgage amounts, balances of mortgages, and that's nobody's business." (Broker No. 152)

> "Some people will grab it or will ask to see it. I'm reluctant to do this. I am exposing them to telephone numbers and information about who is on vacation or moving. These buyers could be potential thieves." (Broker No. 38)

> "I don't like to give the listing book to a buyer because of the

private information that is included like phone numbers or listing
expiration dates. People will see a date, go see the house, and wait
until the contract expires, then buy the house." (Broker No. 34)

Notwithstanding the legitimacy of some of these concerns, however, the over-
riding reason for not releasing the listing book to prospects centers on the
broker's standing as a professional. The listing book is a professional tool requiring special expertise, and it is precisely to avail himself of this expertise and
the information that it provides that has motivated the buyer to seek out the
broker in the first place:

> "No, I never show the listing book to a buyer. I feel that I'm the
> professional, that's why they come to me. I know how to use the
> book . . . . I pay for the listing book. It is part of my tools. You
> don't go to a garage and take the mechanic's tools to fix your car."
> (Broker No. 38)

The analogy between the listing book and the hallmarks of other professionals
was repeated by several brokers:

> "If you let them look, you are no longer the pro. The doctor doesn't
> give the stethoscope to the patient." (Broker No 30)

> "When you go to a doctor's office, the doctor doesn't give you a
> book and say, 'see if any of these looks like your disease.' You ask
> the doctor for a cure . . . . You can't tell by pictures in a book."
> (Broker No. 91)

As a consequence of these beliefs, most brokers maintain complete control of
information on housing vacancies: buyers learn only of those houses in those
neighborhoods that the broker selects as appropriate. Both the control over
information and the ability to recommend units to buyers are central to the
broker's conception of him/herself as a professional and are thus deeply in-
grained in day-to-day operations.

Introducing Blacks into White Neighborhoods

The broker's information monopoly and the necessity of maintaining a community reputation coalesce in the issue of introducing a black household into a
white neighborhood. The governing consideration is the broker's perception of
the intransigence of white prejudice:

> "I am shocked at the deep racial hatred in the mind of John Q.
> Public. You wouldn't know that it is your neighbor, that nice, fair-
> minded, democratic guy next door. It's so deepseated." (Broker No.
> 153)

This same broker described his reaction when encountering prejudice among
white sellers:

> "Sometimes there is a severe backlash here. Sometimes when we go

to list a house the owners tell us they only want 'nice people' here. It's easy to pick up their drift. So we either don't take the listing or we explain that we are not in the position to discriminate. If they cannot open their house to the general market, we can't list it." (Broker No. 153)

Such experiences reinforce the broker's perception of white attitudes and expectations. To the extent that this is perceived as the dominant white attitude, brokers conscious of "neighborhood compatibility" will "just know" that black families would be unwelcome and thus will be unlikely to recommend available homes in such neighborhoods to black prospects. In addition, if a large proportion of white sellers expresses a desire for the broker to screen out all but "nice people," the broker will not long be in a position to refuse listings and alienate potential clients. Thus, given the structure of the realtor-client relationship, there is some truth to the real estate industry's claim that discrimination is forced upon brokers by the prejudice of white society.

In order to connect these various threads of information directly to the issue of discriminatory treatment, we added an explicit question at the end of the survey as to whether there would be a problem showing a black family a home in a white neighborhood. An extremely small minority of brokers vigorously and forcefully displayed an evident strong commitment to equal access:

"This is not an issue. I will show the house. If they want it I'll tell them to make an offer. There may be a hard time with the homeowner to take the offer. We see this, and we're up against it. I've seen a black couple looking in a white area with the owner shaking. The people didn't want to pursue the matter. I told them to take it to (the) Fair Housing (Council). A family has every right and I will get any house for him. I never have to tell a black family about this type of situation, they will tell me. Most black people feel they can handle this situation. If they want to go ahead, I don't care." (Broker No. 29)

Brokers in this category clearly must be willing to ignore considerable community pressure and white backlash:

"If there is a conflict in the community, there certainly is not one in my mind. If they qualify financially, they are entitled to the house. There very well may be repercussions. The town might make me feel bad but I won't change my mind. When I take anyone to a house I tell them to ride around the neighborhood. I would say it to this family also, so they could notice without being told. Afterwards I could predict whether this would bother them. A lot of people don't want to be pioneers. But this area is integrated. They'll know if they like the neighborhood. It's not my decision to make. Any repercussions would not change anything for me." (Broker No. 34)

A strong unequivocal commitment to a color-blind market is quite definitely a minority viewpoint among brokers surveyed, however. One broker professed a pro-integration sentiment but found it necessary to impose qualifications:

> ".... if any man picked himself up by the bootstraps and made enough money, I wouldn't care if he lived next door to me, as long as he was a gentleman and behaved himself, that fast I'd sell it to him." (Broker No. 151)

To this same broker, however, it appeared that these may be difficult criteria to meet satisfactorily:

> "One old lady said she wouldn't sell to blacks. But we sold it to a black woman anyway, and the neighbors love her. She's a lawyer at_____. It might sound like I love blacks. I don't. But this lady has been to my house for dinner and I think she is a tremendous person. But the blacks from the city—I wouldn't live next to them if they were pink." (Broker No. 151)

Other brokers who professed a commitment to integration nonetheless indicated in their response that the service provided a black prospect would be minimal:

> "Steering is a controversial issue. Some will not introduce a black family to a white neighborhood. The blacks are as concerned as the whites .... This office doesn't discriminate about color at all. We will answer all questions. We will show and we will sell. The buyer probably already knows what to ask and look for." (Broker No. 153)

That this broker will "answer all questions" represents a substantially different standard of service than the counselling, recommendations, and information volunteered to white prospects. The statement supports black homebuyers' reports of obtaining information from brokers concerning only those units they specifically asked about and also supports the finding that black homeseekers often first obtain information that a unit is available and only then contact a broker regarding price and access to the unit. The statement is also reminiscent of the argument advanced by the NAR following passage of the 1968 Fair Housing Act that no discrimination can occur regarding a house that the prospect does not know exists.[41] In addition, the broker's contention that "the buyer probably already knows what to ask and look for" is here in striking contrast to the earlier consensus that buyers do not know what they want and it is the broker's professional expertise that helps the buyer define his/her needs. Black homebuyers are evidently far less likely to benefit from such expertise.

The response of most brokers surveyed to the question of introducing a black family into a white neighborhood focused on the issue of warning the black prospect of a potentially inhospitable white reception. Volunteering such information, whether real or imagined, is a subtle form of steering of blacks away from white neighborhoods. The imputation is that the broker serves as spokesperson for the white neighborhood's anti-black prejudice, turning the black prospect away from the neighborhood before the imputed prejudice can be manifested.

The few brokers expressing a commitment to open housing abjured the gatekeeper responsibility and stated that they would inform the family of potential problems only if asked:

> "I would write it up as a regular transaction. I wouldn't mention anything unless they ask me. I don't know of any cross burnings around here. There is none of that. I'd let them deal with the problems themselves. It's my job to sell houses." (Broker No. 38)

> "Let it be a melting pot. I don't steer customers—you can lose your license for that. Steering is practiced subtly but I don't do it. If a buyer asks me about the racial or ethnic composition of a neighborhood, then I'll tell him the specifics. Otherwise I won't." (Broker No. 85)

> "I could care less that the white residents would not be happy to see a black family move in. If the black couple didn't ask if the neighborhood was prejudiced against blacks, I wouldn't tell them. Only if they asked would I tell them. My job is to find people houses that suit their needs." (Broker No. 86)

This view again is definitely in the minority. For most brokers, the gatekeeper role extends far beyond the more limited (but less subjective) role of middleman in the housing transaction. The concern for neighborhood compatability represents an "obligation" on the part of the broker to warn black buyers about potential white hostility:

> "I would tell them about the prejudice they will encounter because of my obligation to them. If they still wanted to buy I wouldn't stop them. That's not considered steering. We have worked with a few minorities, and those we do work with we have good relations with." (Broker No. 88)

Some brokers differentiate between "pioneers" and those they feel may be unaware of possible harassment:

> "Some minority groups are pioneers—they are doing it on purpose. If this is the case, I'll help them. But if the buyer is innocent of the possible reception, I feel it would be my place to say to them what may happen. If wouldn't be fair to keep that information a secret." (Broker No. 4)

Most commonly, however, brokers feel it is their responsibility to transmit their perceptions of white neighborhood sentiment to their black customers:

> "It's not fair to the buyer not to tell them what they are getting

into. I would definitely tell them about it and let them make up
their own minds." (Broker No. 91)

"I would take the family and show the house. I must abide by the
law even if the seller gives us a hard time. But I would forewarn the
(buyer) so they would be prepared." (Broker No. 152)

It's up to them to decide if they want to move into that neighborhood. But I want them to know what's going on there." (Broker
No. 212)

In each of these cases, the brokers distinguish between overt steering—barring
blacks from white neighborhoods—and warning blacks of potential white hostility. This is a moot distinction. First, the effect is likely to be the same, since few
homebuyers are of the pioneer persuasion. More significantly, volunteered inter-
vention no less than overt steering involves the broker in the role of social arbiter
in a race-conscious fashion. As soon as the broker moves from the role of
intermediary in a business transaction to that of neighborhood gatekeeper, racial
discrimination is inevitable.

SUMMARY

Racial discrimination is inherent in the structure of the real estate industry,
the nature of day-to-day realty operations, and the broker's perception of his/
her professional role as guardian of neighborhood compatability. To not discriminate puts a broker at a competitive disadvantage in a highly competitive
and localized industry.

The overwhelming importance of close local ties and the broker's heavy investment in localized marketing constitute irrefutable incentives to protect local
stability and the continuity of the status quo. From the white broker's perspective, black prospects (buyers) are not seen as potential future clients. To intro-
duce blacks into one's territory is to risk alienation of potential white clients and
to replace whites with blacks in whose social networks one does not participate.
The consequence for the broker is to undermine the carefully developed local
contacts necessary to continue to obtain listings.

In addition, most brokers view their professional role as encompassing far
more than that of a technical intermediary in a financial transaction. A major
element of salesmanship involves recommending houses in the "right" neighborhood; the broker's professional self-concept rests largely on being able to
intuitively select appropriate neighborhoods for particular prospects. Given the
broker's perception of strong racial preferences held by both prospects and
neighborhood residents, selection of appropriate neighborhoods inevitably involves racial considerations.

The potential for eliminating racial discrimination without altering these
deeply rooted incentives to discriminate is minimal. As long as brokers are

subject to economic reprisals by prejudiced sellers, brokers will discriminate. As long as brokers are cast in the role of arbiter of neighborhood social compatability, brokers will discriminate. The necessity for development of alternative institutional mechanisms to free the real estate industry from these pressures is addressed in the following chapter.

NOTES

1. The terms *agent, realtor, broker,* and *salesperson* are used interchangeably throughout this book. The term *realtor* in capitalized form is a registered mark of the National Association of Realtors.

2. Donald J. Hempel, *The Role of the Real Estate Broker in the Home Buying Process* (Storrs, Conn.: Center for Real Estate and Urban Economic Studies, University of Connecticut, 1969).

3. Charles M. Barresi, "The Role of the Real Estate Agent in Residential Location," *Sociological Focus* 1 (Summer 1968): 59-71.

4. J. Douglas House, *Contemporary Entrepreneurs: The Sociology of Residential Real Estate Agents* (Westport, Conn.: Greenwood Press, 1977); J. Douglas House, "Middlemen in Housing Exchanges: The Social Role of the Real Estate Agent," *Western Canadian Journal of Anthropology* 4 (1975): 37-52.

5. Risa Palm, "Real Estate Agents and Geographical Information," *Geographical Review* 66 (July 1976): 266-80; Risa Palm, *Urban Social Geography from the Perspective of the Real Estate Salesman* (Berkeley, Calif.: Center for Real Estate and Urban Economics, University of California, 1976).

6. Palm, "Real Estate Agents and Geographical Information," p. 278.

7. Rose Helper, *Racial Policies and Practices of Real Estate Brokers* (Minneapolis, Minn.: University of Minnesota Press, 1969).

8. John H. Denton, *Apartheid American Style,* (Berkeley, Calif.: Diablo Press, 1967); Joel Mandelbaum, "Race Discrimination in Home Buying Resists Tough Laws," *New York Times,* December 3, 1972. These surveys are summarized in Donald L. Foley, "Institutional and Contextual Factors Affecting the Housing Choices of Minority Residents," in *Segregation in Residential Areas,* ed. Amos H. Hawley and Vincent P. Rock (Washington, D.C.: National Academy of Sciences, 1973), pp. 85-147. See also John Yinger, *An Analysis of Discrimination by Real Estate Brokers,* Discussion Paper 252-75 (Madison, Wisc.: Institute for Research on Poverty, University of Wisconsin, 1975).

9. Margery R. Boichel, et al., "Exposure, Experience, and Attitudes: Realtors and Open Occupancy," *Phylon* 30 (Winter 1969): 325-37.

10. Alan H. Schechter, "Impact of Open Housing Laws on Suburban Realtors," *Urban Affairs Quarterly* 8 (June 1973): 439-63.

11. Charles Abrams, *Forbidden Neighbors—A Study of Prejudice in Housing* (New York: Harper, 1955); see also Helper, *Racial Policies and Practices of*

Real Estate Brokers; Yinger, *An Analysis of Discrimination by Real Estate Brokers.*

12. William H. Brown, "Access to Housing: The Role of the Real Estate Agent in Residential Location," *Economic Geography* 48 (January 1972): 66-78.

13. Brown, "Access to Housing," p. 70.

14. Quoted in George W. Grayson and Cindy Long Wedel, "Open Housing: How to Get Around the Law," *The New Republic,* June 22, 1968, p. 15.

15. "Realtor's Headlines," National Association of Real Estate Boards, 35 (July 1, 1968), cited in Brown, "Access to Housing," p. 74.

16. *Realtors Guide to Practice Equal Opportunity in Housing* (Chicago: National Association of Realtors, 1976).

17. Letter from Edward E. Simmons, Jr., Director of Member Activities, National Association of Realtors, Chicago, Illinois, October 30, 1978.

18. *Realtors Guide,* p. 27.

19. "Each Member Board or State Association of Realtors must make an individual decision to adopt the Agreement and, in those Member Boards which adopt it, each Realtor must make a voluntary decision to subscribe to the Agreement and accept the responsibilities defined therein. Member Board adoption does not, in and of itself, obligate the Realtor member to adopt the Agreement." *Affirmative Marketing Handbook* (Chicago: National Association of Realtors, 1975) p. 5.

20. *Realtors Guide,* p. 19.

21. *Affirmative Marketing Handbook,* p. 21.

22. *Realtors Guide,* p. 20.

23. *Affirmative Marketing Handbook,* p. 37. Note that Title VIII of the Civil Rights Act of 1968, the Fair Housing Act, specifically states that the burden of proof in discrimination cases is on the complainant. See Chapter 10.

24. *Affirmative Marketing Handbook,* pp. 32-34.

25. Letter from Edward E. Simmons, Jr.

26. Ronald E. Wienk, et al., *Measuring Racial Discrimination in American Housing Markets: The Housing Market Practices Survey* (Washington, D.C.: U.S. Department of Housing and Urban Development, 1979.

27. Diana M. Pearce, "Black, White, and Many Shades of Gray: Real Estate Brokers and their Racial Practices" (Ph.D. diss.) University of Michigan, 1976; Diana M. Pearce, "Gatekeepers and Homeseekers: Institutional Patterns in Racial Steering," *Social Problems* 26 (February 1979): 325-42.

28. Pearce, "Gatekeepers and Homeseekers," p. 335.

29. *Realtors Guide,* p. 51. For a review of judicial decisions supporting the legitimacy of evidence collected by testers, see National Committee Against Discrimination in Housing, *Guide to Fair Housing Law Enforcement,* Appendix E (Washington, D.C.: U.S. Department of Housing and Urban Development, 1979).

30. *Affirmative Marketing Handbook,* p. 36.

31. *Realtors Guide,* p. 21.

32. For a discussion of this perspective, see Yinger, *An Analysis of Discrimination by Real Estate Brokers.* A recent discussion of provisions in the Federal Fair Housing Act explicitly prohibiting racial steering concludes with a pessimistic note as to the efficacy of the law in the face of economic incentives to discriminate: "Since residents of white areas may prefer to list their homes with brokers who will steer black buyers away from their neighborhoods, brokers who comply with the law are likely to be at a competitive disadvantage relative to brokers who do not comply." T. Alexander Aleinikoff, "Racial Steering: The Real Estate Broker and Title VIII," *Yale Law Journal* 85 (1976): 824.

33. Frank J. Parker and Norman P. Schoenfeld, *Modern Real Estate: Principles and Practices* (Lexington, Mass.: D.C. Heath, 1979), p. 240.

34. The criterion of local board membership as a requirement for access to the MLS has recently been successfully challenged in a New Jersey court, although appeals are likely. "Ruling Eases Access to Multiple Listings," *New York Times,* July 6, 1980.

35. Other methods used include display advertising, monitoring "For Sale by Owner" ads in local newspapers, and cultivating relationships with local builders, but these are decidedly secondary to the two techniques identified.

36. Parker and Schoenfeld, *Modern Real Estate,* p. 236.

37. U.S. Department of Housing and Urban Development, *The Role of the Real Estate Sector in Neighborhood Change* (Washington, D.C.: HUD Office of Policy Development and Research, 1979).

38. Ibid., pp. 153-54.

39. Until 1950, the NAR Code of Ethics stated that "A Realtor should never be instrumental in introducing into a neighborhood a character of property or occupancy, members of any race or nationality, or any individuals whose presence will clearly be detrimental to property values in that neighborhood." Cited in Helper, *Racial Policies and Practices of Real Estate Brokers,* p. 201.

40. The option of handing the MLS book to the prospect to look through on his/her own has the appearance of providing full information but is in fact confusing and relatively uninformative. With four selections to the page, an MLS book may run to several hundred pages, depending on turnover and the size of the MLS area. Abbreviations and notations used are confusing to the uninitiated. Showing the MLS book to a prospect is only informative if accompanied by a full explication of its contents.

41. A week after passage of the Fair Housing Act, a NAREB memorandum entitled "Some questions (and their answers) suggested by a reading of Title VIII of Public Law No. 90-284, related to forced housing," was distributed to local boards, The memorandum described a "would-be Negro purchaser" interested in a $20,000 home in a particular neighborhood. The broker is "well aware" of such properties, yet he "informs the prospect that the office has no listings in that category." According to the NAREB memorandum, no

law has been violated. "The law does not give any person the right to purchase or right to inspect dwellings whose identity is vague and uncertain. The essence of the offense is the discriminatory refusal to sell a dwelling which the purchaser wants to buy." Quoted in Grayson and Wedel, "Open Housing: How to Get Around the Law."

PART

III

CONCLUSIONS

10

SUMMARY AND
POLICY IMPLICATIONS

INTRODUCTION

The suburbanization of blacks is being accompanied by the increasing territorial differentiation of suburbia along racial lines—and not by integration. Comparison of the experiences of black and white suburban homebuyers at the end of the 1970s provides strong evidence of a suburban housing market explicitly and implicitly organized along racial lines. The significance of race is evident in the selection of destination communities by black suburban in-migrants, in the transition of suburban housing units from white to black occupancy, in the social isolation of blacks and whites within biracial communities, in the resegregation of interracial neighborhoods, in the housing search experiences of black homebuyers, in black-white differences in resale value and equity accumulation, and in the behavior of real estate agents as mediators of residential mobility. The mechanisms in place to enforce and reproduce a structural pattern based on race mean that at the individual level, suburbanization for blacks connotes constrained residential choice, a restricted and less efficient housing search process, and limited opportunities for housing equity and wealth accumulation. This chapter presents a brief summary of findings on these issues, examines the shortcomings of present federal legislation designed to counter discrimination in housing, and considers new policy directions suggested by the research findings.

STRUCTURAL AND INDIVIDUAL IMPLICATIONS
OF BLACK SUBURBANIZATION

The acceleration of suburban black population growth during the 1970s represents a reversal of longstanding trends of black concentration, and the characteristics of black in-migrants are contributing to dramatic improvements in suburban black socioeconomic levels. Nonetheless, a somber picture of black suburbanization emerges from the data. As a group, suburbanizing blacks are not replicating the patterns and experiences of suburban whites. Suburbanization is not the avenue to capital accumulation for blacks that it has provided for generations of whites for whom equity in a home represented the best guarantee of membership in the middle class. For the successful black homebuyer, entry costs in time and effort required for housing search are high, while the payoff in equity accumulation is disproportionately low. In structural terms, the pattern of black suburbanization is indicative of a continuing social differentiation and specialization of suburban territory, rather than of a decrease in social cleavages based on race. This parceling of suburban space along racial lines can be observed as it proceeds from the individual housing unit to the neighborhood to the community level.

At the broadest scale, the suburban black population increase of the 1970s is clearly not uniformly distributed throughout suburbia: blacks are moving to those suburban communities where blacks already live and from which whites are moving away. This is more than a simple effect of distance decay in which central city blacks move first to the closest-in adjacent suburbs. White out-migration from the older, denser inner suburbs appears to be a trigger mechanism, with lack of white demand a prerequisite for the weakening of barriers to black entry. White and black suburban growth trends are moving in diametrically opposite directions. Black gains and white losses in the older suburbs adjacent to central cities, coupled with white gains and black losses in the new growth areas in outlying rural suburbs, indicate that black suburbanization is contributing little to convergence in the residential distributions of blacks and whites.

The absence of racial convergence at the regional level is replicated within individual communities as well. Racially integrated suburban municipalities represent regional racial distributions in microcosm: each has a predominantly black area, extensive all-white areas, and a biracial transitional area in between. Social, religious, civic, and recreational institutions within these communities are bifurcated by race, and black and white social networks rarely overlap.

The pattern of housing unit transition within suburban communities indicates a strong trend toward resegregation and the perpetuation of a dual housing market for blacks and whites. Among a sample of recent homebuyers, blacks disproportionately purchased black-owned units in black or integrated neighborhoods while whites were concentrated almost exclusively in all-white neighborhoods. Even in black-entry neighborhoods with less than 5 percent black population, black homebuyers were twice as likely as whites to purchase a black-owned unit. Blacks *selling* a suburban house are far more likely than whites to sell to a black buyer. In brief, race is a potent variable in the differentiation of suburban space, be it at the level of the community, the neighborhood, or the individual housing unit.

These structural patterns both result from and reinforce a process in which socioeconomic convergence is overshadowed by divergent preferences for residential integration. Socioeconomic status characteristics of suburban homebuyers show greater differentiation by location of previous residence than between racial groups. Black families moving into predominantly white neighborhoods have higher median incomes than their white counterparts and reflect the highest socioeconomic status levels among suburban black homebuyers. Nonetheless, white preference for integrated neighborhoods lags black preference levels by twenty-five percentage points, even among homebuyers in biracial communities. Rather than an identifiable tipping point, the primary criterion for white stability is the perception that whites continue to move in and that the neighborhood continues to be defined as part of white residential space. Black preferences for integration are constrained by a concern to avoid situations of potential white hostility. Few black families choose to be the only black household in an all-white community. Accordingly, a move from renter to owner-occupancy within the same neighborhood is an important avenue to homeownership for suburban black households. A move of this type is based on personal knowledge that the unit is available—thus obviating dependence on potentially discriminatory formal sources of vacancy information—and is free from the uncertainties involved in moving to an unknown and potentially hostile suburban environment.

For the individual black household, these disparate white and black demand functions generate a less efficient and therefore more costly housing search and a substantial relative loss of equity in homeownership. The analysis indicates that greater search costs for blacks are not attributable to socioeconomic characteristics, previous tenure, experience in the housing market, or reasons for moving, but rather that they derive from discriminatory treatment by the guardians of housing information and/or the necessity of using these information sources differently, given the expectation of discrimination. The advantages of previous ownership in facilitating housing search for whites are not enjoyed by black homebuyers; use of a real estate agent broadens access to housing information for whites but yields no such benefits for blacks. Racial steering by real estate brokers occurs at the level of the community, the neighborhood, and the individual housing unit. Blacks report being steered to black-owned units in black neighborhoods within biracial communities and away from white neighborhoods and white communities. White buyers are steered away from biracial communities, integrated neighborhoods, and units sold by blacks.

Relative levels of housing demand resulting from preference patterns and institutional discrimination are best reflected in housing price levels and changes.

Controlling for housing unit, neighborhood, and buyer characteristics, housing prices decrease as the neighborhood percent black increases, reflecting the progressive weakening of white demand. Blacks pay less than whites for equivalent housing within neighborhoods as well, but this is attributable to the greater frequency with which blacks purchase black-owned units and the lower average price—again due to low white demand—obtained by blacks when selling a suburban house. The largest observed markdowns are among units transferred between two black households, indicating the severe negative price effect resulting when units are removed entirely from the white housing market. The negative consequences for black equity accumulation are substantial. Discounts obtained by blacks when buying are exceeded by the markdowns sustained when selling, and this relationship holds regardless of neighborhood racial composition.

The weakness of white demand is a function of overt white preferences for residential segregation coupled with institutionalized discrimination practiced by real estate brokers as market intermediaries. The notion of white preferences is multidimensional and encompasses racial prejudice per se, fear of negative economic consequences, fear of loss of status, and fear of becoming a new minority in a resegregated black neighborhood. This preference structure is augmented by the steering of white demand away from integrated housing regardless of white attitudes. Incentives for broker discrimination derive from the extremely localized and competitive nature of the industry, from the merger of the broker's personal and professional ties to the white community, from the monopoly on housing market information, and from the broker's self-conception of his/her role as arbiter of neighborhood compatability. Broker behavior and white attitudes are therefore complementary, with white preferences providing an incentive for realtor discrimination and such discrimination reinforcing and confirming white preferences.

The crucial role of the realtor as implementer of residential mobility indeed clarifies the significance of white attitudes as the fulcrum linking the structural and individual endproducts of black suburbanization. Majority white preference for racial residential segregation accounts for the racial differentiation of suburban territory accompanying the increase in the suburban black population. The strong local ties inherent in the nature of the real estate industry compel the broker to confirm in day-to-day operations the integrity of a territorial structure created to accommodate white racial preferences. For the broker to fail to discriminate not only is to alienate his/her potential white clientele but also to ignore the localized nature of the industry and the broader societal forces contributing to the territorial structuring of suburban space.

PRESENT FEDERAL FAIR HOUSING POLICY

The racial differentiation of suburban space and the pervasiveness of discriminatory mechanisms employed to perpetuate that differentiation raise unavoidable questions regarding the potential effectiveness of federal legislation designed to eradicate racial discrimination in housing.

Title VIII of the Civil Rights Act of 1968 states that it is unlawful to "make unavailable or deny a dwelling to any person . . ." or ". . . to discriminate against any person in the . . . sale or rental of a dwelling . . . because of race, color, religion, sex or national origin."[1] Considered landmark legislation at its enactment, Title VIII is unequivocally important as a remedy for individuals confronting overt discrimination in their search for housing. Congress considered but failed to adopt amendments in 1979 and 1980 designed to further strengthen the law by providing enforcement mechanisms lacking in the original legislation. Nonetheless, the findings reported here and in other recent studies suggest that Title VIII alone is insufficient in scope of coverage and in its programmatic approach to counter systemic patterns of housing market discrimination. The persistence of suburban racial differentiation and of racial differences in the suburban home purchase experience is evidence of the tenacity of housing market discrimination as a determinant of the residential location of whites and blacks. That such segregated patterns are developing in the suburbs more than a decade after enactment of Title VIII suggests the need for a new policy initiative based on a clear understanding of current conditions. In this section, we examine the scope, assumptions, and remedial approach implicit in Title VIII and show that further policy initiatives are required for a comprehensive attack on housing discrimination. The final section proposes some policy initiatives that may further the goal of eliminating racial discrimination in the housing market.

Title VIII of the Civil Rights Act of 1968

Declaring that "it is the policy of the United States to provide . . . for fair housing" (Pub. L. 90-284, Sec. 801), Title VIII explicity prohibits several discriminatory practices: racially motivated refusal to sell or rent, denial that a unit is available when in fact it is, racial steering by brokers, and statements of racial preference or exclusion in advertisements.[2] Individuals subjected to any of these practices may obtain injunctive relief and recover damages by filing suit in Federal court.

Title VIII is clearly important in providing redress for the individual home-seeker confronting unequal access to information about housing vacancies. Why, then, have its effects not been more evident? Shortcomings are threefold: in scope of coverage, in underlying assumptions about the nature of a discriminatory housing market, and in the implicit programmatic approach to reducing discrimination. These shortcomings are inextricably linked.

The statute underestimates the pervasiveness of discrimination in the housing market. To cite one example, it solely addresses discrimination against the *home-seeker* (buyer or renter) encountering unequal access to information about housing vacancies. It is mute on the issue of the black home *seller* confronting bias in the information dissemination channels used to market a unit and recover accumulated equity. Our analysis indicates that the black/white discrepancy in equity recapture is attributable at least in part to an inability by blacks to reach as wide and representative a market as is available to whites selling equivalent homes. Legislation currently in place is too narrow in scope of coverage to respond to this latter form of market inequality.

An overly restrictive scope of coverage may be linked to a faulty set of underlying assumptions about the nature of housing market bias. By identifying specific discriminatory practices and establishing penalties for their occurrence, the statute implies that these practices constitute a set of perverse actions within an otherwise impartial and color-blind market. If these particular practices were to be eliminated, it is assumed, the market would function in a nondiscriminatory manner.

Rather than being distorted by a discrete set of discriminatory practices susceptible to elimination, the information channels through which the market functions are structured and operate in a systematically biased fashion. As we have indicated, real estate brokers and other market mediators perceive strong incentives to discriminate when their livelihood is dependent on personal contacts and strong community ties and when they believe that majority white sentiment favors black exclusion. There is no inherent incentive within the structure of the market not to discriminate. The race of the buyer and the seller, and the racial composition of the neighborhood, are overtly or tacitly acknowledged in the overwhelming majority of residential real estate transactions. Despite the pervasive and inescapable influence of race, however, the law as written assumes a bias-free market structure from which aberrant discriminatory practices can be eliminated through punitive measures.

Following from the basic assumptions outlined above, the legislation moves to reduce discrimination through application of negative sanctions in individual cases. This case-by-case approach is noncumulative in that favorable resolution of one case has no direct impact on other instances of discrimination.

As a means of relief from overt discriminatory treatment, the present enforcement procedure is time-consuming and costly. An individual who experiences discrimination can file a complaint with HUD's Office of Fair Housing and Equal Opportunity. HUD's ability to resolve the problem is presently limited to "informal methods of conference, conciliation, and persuasion" [Sec. 810 (a)].[3] In states with "substantially equivalent" fair housing legislation, HUD is required to refer the complaint to the appropriate state agency for review and investigation.[4] If conciliation fails within thirty days, the complainant can file a civil action in Federal court. In line with the law's basic assumptions, section 810 (e) states in its entirety: "In any proceeding brought pursuant to this section, the burden of proof shall be on the complainant." As reported in Chapter 9, the method increasingly being adopted to establish such proof is the use of white "testers," often provided by a local fair housing group: the white tester's experience is contrasted to that of the black homeseeker to substantiate discriminatory treatment.[5] In the case of a discriminatory real estate broker, for instance, a local fair housing group can use a tester to document a particular instance of discriminatory behavior, litigate in Federal court, and obtain a judgment for damages for a particular plaintiff. If the proof is accepted, the court can issue a restraining order and award actual damages plus punitive damages to a limit of $1,000. Even when the plaintiff prevails, however, he/she must pay court costs and attorney's fees, unless "said plaintiff in the opinion of the court is not financially able to assume said attorney's fees" [sec. 812(c)], i.e., unless the complainant is indigent. Little in this procedure is likely to deter the same or another broker from repeating the same pattern of behavior in other cases, since the onus is again on the individual and the advocacy group to repeat the testing and litigating routine *de novo* in each case. Full costs of enforcement are borne by the victim of discrimination who must initiate the complaint.

Under the existing law, the attorney general can initiate civil actions independently of individual complaints. Such actions, however, are restricted by the statute to cases involving a broad "pattern or practice of resistance" to the rights provided by the Act and where violation "raises an issue of general public importance" (sec. 813). Preparation and documentation of "pattern and practice" cases taxes available resources. The Department of Justice has assigned thirteen attorneys to bring cases nationwide.[6] A Regional Plan Association report on fair housing practices in the New York region is skeptical about the effectiveness of these broad-based actions.[7] According to the report, most such cases are settled in pretrial consent agreements in which the defendant does not admit guilt but accepts certain court-ordered conditions designed to monitor future compliance. Enforcement of these conditions, however, is difficult for the same reasons that apply to the Title itself.

The Fair Housing Amendments Act of 1980

The shortcomings in the enforcement provisions of Title VIII have been subjected to extensive criticism from a wide number of sources. A report prepared by the U.S. Commission on Civil Rights criticized HUD's enforcement of Title VIII but concluded that the lack of credible sanctions in the conciliation process was the major obstacle.[8] The same criticism was echoed in a GAO report that concluded that "HUD lacks the authority it needs to enforce compliance."[9] In recognition of these criticisms, several attempts have been made in Congress beginning in 1978 to amend Title VIII to correct obvious enforcement deficiencies. After repeated setbacks, the Fair Housing Amendments Act of 1980 was adopted by the House but rejected in the Senate, and its future remains uncertain.[10]

The Fair Housing Amendments Act of 1980 aimed to eliminate the most egregious shortcomings in Title VIII enforcement provisions. The amendment proposed to increase the maximum limit on punitive damages to $10,000 and to award attorney's fees to a prevailing plaintiff. Most important, the amendment would substantially expand the Federal enforcement role by empowering HUD to initiate and adjudicate complaints in an administrative process, a considerable improvement over the earlier conciliation process.

Extensive Congressional debate developed over the appropriate form of administrative enforcement. The initial amendment introduced in the House empowered HUD to appoint administrative law judges with authority to investigate charges of discrimination, adjudicate cases, and award penalties and payment of damages. Opponents of the measure charged that this would in effect make HUD prosecutor, judge, and jury in antidiscrimination cases. An amendment to delete administrative enforcement entirely and require fair housing cases to be heard in Federal court was rejected by the House by a one-vote margin. This of course would represent no improvement over the existing statute. A compromise House measure was ultimatily adopted that allows HUD to initiate and prosecute cases but places the administrative law judges under the jurisdiction of the Justice Department. A Senate version approved by the Judiciary Committee also empowers HUD to initiate cases but envisions a staff of administrative law judges appointed by a three-member Fair Housing Review Commission created expressly for that purpose. Republican opposition to an administrative remedy led to ultimate defeat of the Bill in the Senate, although some form of administrative enforcement is clearly necessary to shift the burden of effort from the aggrieved individual to the government and to lend credibility to the sanctions against overt discrimination contained in the law.

Nonetheless, regardless of the form of enforcement adopted, the basic programmatic approach of the law would remain unchanged. *The case-by-case approach that underlies Title VIII and its proposed amendments is insufficient as an antidote to systemic bias that bars blacks as a group from participating in the housing market on equal terms with whites.* Transcending issues of implementation is the question of the appropriateness of the program to meet its objectives. The strengthened enforcement powers proposed in the Fair Housing Amendments Act are necessary if Title VIII is to provide relief for aggrieved individuals. Nonetheless, a case-by-case approach that seeks to eliminate discrimination by punishing its occurrence will not reduce systemic bias as long as the institutional incentives to discriminate prevail. The National Academy of Sciences has called for "measures to insure equal access to real estate board listings throughout the metropolitan area" and notes significantly that "this may involve the creation of new marketing institutions."[11] We consider the nature of such institutions in the final section.

DIRECTIONS FOR POLICY

Clarification of policy objectives is the first step in developing an appropriate strategy for countering racial discrimination in housing. The statement in Title VIII that the goal of federal fair housing policy is "to provide, within constitutional limits, for fair housing," is hopelessly ambiguous as a policy directive.

Two basic policy objectives nonetheless can be identified. These are: (1) to provide redress for victims of discrimination, and (2) to eliminate the incidence of discrimination by reducing the incentives to discriminate. Clearly, a policy designed to meet the first objective without addressing the second is doomed to the endless allocation of funds for alleviating the symptoms without treating the causes of discrimination. As currently being implemented, the machinery established by Title VIII is directed towards the first goal. Additional affirmative steps are required to establish institutional mechanisms that contribute directly to facilitating equal access to the housing market.

A major component of the housing discrimination examined in the preceding chapters reduces to the general issue of unequal access to and utilization of housing market information channels. Racial steering, seller discrimination, and nondisclosure by brokers limit black homebuyers to information on a biased subset of available units. When selling a house, blacks are limited by the same practices to a biased subset of potential buyers. The numerous forms of discrimination in the dissemination of vacancy information burden blacks with both excessive costs of housing search and with loss of equity when selling. In sum, restricted access to information channels for both buyers and sellers raises entry costs for blacks while simultaneously reducing the eventual payoff from homeownership.

An affirmative approach is required that encourages the development of conditions conducive to equal access to housing market information. As currently mediated through real estate agents and other dissemination channels, information about housing vacancies is an economic good; as such, it will continue to be disseminated in a manner designed to maximize economic return, not racial equality. Part of the incentive for biasing information flows can be removed by making vacancy information a public good. This requires: (1) development of an unbiased institutional structure for disseminating information; and (2) bringing vacancy information into the public domain. Several general policy recommendations may contribute to achieving these goals.

First, a basic policy initiative is required to develop an institutional structure devoted to disseminating market information in a nondiscriminatory manner. As one possible step towards this objective, HUD should encourage formation of a broad network of nonprofit fair housing councils at the county level in metropolitan areas. Local nonprofit fair housing groups are already operating in several locations and are providing housing counseling services, information about taxes, schools, and municipal services, and recommendations of nondiscriminatory brokers and mortgage lenders.[12] In recognition of the inadequacy of HUD's enforcement of Title VIII, fair housing groups increasingly have turned to providing advocacy services for victims of discrimination, focusing largely on testing and litigation. The existence of a widespread network of local fair housing councils would provide a nucleus for development of an alternative institutional structure for dissemination of housing information free from the discriminatory incentives besetting the real estate industry.

A second issue pertains to funding. Federal legislation is required to provide for direct HUD funding of local fair housing councils. Those currently in operation are typically supported with Community Development funds allocated by the local jurisdiction. Direct Federal funding is imperative to free fair housing councils from local political influence.

Third, fair housing councils should be able to play a direct role in disseminating housing market information. HUD should allocate sufficient funding for fair housing councils to establish housing information centers as one of their primary activities. Thus, in addition to the important role of advocacy and litigation, fair housing councils would become directly involved in information dissemination through operation of housing information centers. The function of housing information centers would be to collect, maintain, and disseminate information on housing availability within their counties of jurisdiction and to coordinate dissemination of such information with other centers within the metropolitan area. Through the auspices of the housing information center, housing information would be publicly available, thus eradicating the incentives for brokers to disseminate information in a discriminatory manner. Housing information centers, however, do not engage in brokerage activities and they are not seen as usurping the role of the broker in arranging for showing of units, advising prospects and clients, and serving as the intermediary between buyer and seller. The realtor's brokerage role is a crucial and enduring one; the proposals recommended here simply free the realtor from the inherently discriminatory role of social arbiter of community compatability. As John Yinger has pointed out, "... if no brokers can exclude blacks from white areas, then white customers cannot patronize brokers because of their exclusionary practices."[13]

Fourth, the remaining requirement is to bring market information into the public domain. The most direct approach to this objective would be to require owners or their agents to file a notification of intent to sell with county authorities (e.g., county clerk or county tax assessor) within a specified time period after entering into a listing agreement with a broker or publicly advertising the unit for sale. Disseminated through the local housing information center, this information would be publicly available. Black homebuyers would have access to the full set of available units and would no longer be dependent on "For Sale" signs or personal contacts to direct them to a broker for further information on particular units. For a black seller, information on the availability of the unit would be in the public domain and thus accessible to the broadest possible pool of potential buyers. While in both cases access to the unit would still be through the listing broker, unrestricted public knowledge of the unit's availability would greatly weaken the incentives for the broker to discriminate in showing the house. Enforcement of Title VIII would be facilitated through more effective targeting permitted by a reduction in the potential for discrimination.

These proposals would contribute to eliminating the incentives for housing market discrimination inherent in the present institutional structure of the market. As partial cures, they are necessary even if not sufficient to bring an end to housing discrimination. Public policy can neither legislate preferences nor determine one's neighbors; it can, however, move affirmatively to diminish barriers to equal opportunity. The basic objective is to develop an alternative structure designed to bring market information into the public domain. As with all civil rights legislation, these proposals affirm the prior claim of equal access over individual property rights. Only with such a direct affirmative approach will Federal policy begin to establish the conditions necessary for equal access to suburban homeownership.

NOTES

1. Pub. L. 90-284, Sec. 804(a),(b). Civil Rights Act of 1968, Title VIII—Fair Housing, 82 Stat. 81-90.
2. The statute also explicitly prohibits panic peddling [Sec. 804 (e)] and mortgage discrimination (Sec. 805).
3. When initially introduced as a floor amendment to the Civil Rights Act of 1968, Title VIII assigned administrative enforcement powers to HUD. Replacing administrative enforcement with the far weaker conciliation procedures was evidently the price of support from the Republican leadership in the Senate. See George W. Grayson, Jr. and Cindy Long Wedel, "Open Housing: How to Get Around the Law," *The New Republic*, June 22, 1968, pp. 15-16.
4. The provision for prior state jurisdiction was also a condition for Republican support. This requirement clearly weakens the measure by fragmenting enforcement and making coordination difficult. A GAO report found that the local enforcement provision adds substantially to the time required to investigate and conciliate complaints. HUD has found that because of staff and funding shortages, state agencies process first those complaints made directly to the agency and only then act on complaints referred from HUD. Comptroller General of the United States, *Stronger Federal Enforcements Needed to Uphold Fair Housing Laws* (Washington, D.C.: U.S. General Accounting Office, 1978).
5. See, for instance, Ronald E. Wienk, et al., *Measuring Racial Discrimination in American Housing Markets: The Housing Market Practices Survey,* (Washington, D.C.: U.S. Department of Housing and Urban Development, 1979).
6. Representative Don Edwards, "Some Questions and Answers on the Bill to Strengthen Federal Fair Housing Enforcement," mimeographed (Washington, D.C.: U.S. Congress, September 1979).
7. Regional Plan Association, "Segregation and Opportunity in the Region's Housing," *Regional Plan News,* No. 104 (July 1979).

8. U.S. Commission on Civil Rights, *The Federal Civil Rights Enforcement Effort* (Washington, D.C.: U.S. Government Printing Office, 1979).

9. Comptroller General of the United States, *Stronger Federal Enforcements Needed*, p. 28. See also, David Falk and Herbert M. Franklin, *Equal Housing Opportunity: The Unfinished Federal Agenda* (Washington, D.C.: The Potomac Institute, 1976); and Robert E. Mitchell and Richard A. Smith, "Race and Housing: A Review and Comments on the Content and Effects of Federal Policy," *Annals of the American Academy of Political and Social Science* 441 (January 1979): 168-85.

10. The House version of the Fair Housing Amendments Act of 1980 (H.R. 5200) was approved by the House on June 12, 1980. The Senate version (S.506) was approved by the Senate Judiciary Committee on July 30, 1980 but succumbed to a Republican filibuster in the final week of the 1980 session. As with the initial legislation twelve years ago, the amendment was subjected to intensive lobbying opposition by the real estate, appraisal, and insurance industries and came under severe partisan attack by Republican members of Congress. Amendments to the Bill that were rejected in Congressional debate include proposals by Rep. Ashbrook (R-Ohio) to delete provisions banning discrimination in insurance, by Rep. Hyde (R-Ill.) to exempt appraisers from antidiscrimination provisions, by Sen. Thurmond (R-S.C.) to limit punitive damages to $1,000, and by Rep. Sensenbrenner (R-Wis.) to delete administrative remedies entirely. The Senate filibuster responsible for the ultimate defeat of the Bill in the 96th Congress was led by Sen. Hatch (R-Utah). Republican conditions for ending the filibuster included provisions that discrimination cases be given jury trials in Federal courts and that conviction required proof of a defendant's intent to discriminate. Both provisions clearly contravene the aim of the amendment in facilitating redress for victims of discrimination.

11. National Academy of Sciences, *Freedom of Choice in Housing: Opportunities and Constraints* (Washington, D.C.: National Academy of Sciences, 1972).

12. For a description of the development of fair housing centers in several locations nationwide, see Juliet Saltman, *Open Housing: Dynamics of a Social Movement* (New York: Praeger, 1978).

13. John Yinger, *An Analysis of Discrimination by Real Estate Brokers,* Discussion Paper 252-75 (Madison, Wisc.: Institute for Research on Poverty, University of Wisconsin, 1975), pp. 35-36.

Appendix A.

CUPR
Recent Buyers Survey Questionnaire

— I.D.— —   /1-4

RUTGERS UNIVERSITY

CENTER FOR URBAN POLICY RESEARCH

SUBURBAN HOME OWNERSHIP SURVEY

NAME _____

ADDRESS _____

_____ TELEPHONE:(__ __ __) __ __ __ - __ __ __ __   /5-14
                                Area
                                Code

CALL-BACK RECORD

Date	Time	Result

Sales Price	__ __ __,__ __ __	/16-21
Total Assessed Value	__ __ __,__ __ __	/22-27
Land Assessed Value	__ __ __,__ __ __	/28-33
Assess/Sales Ratio	__ __.__ __ __ __	/34-39
Month Deed Executed	__ __	/40-41
Year Deed Executed	__ __	/42-43
Block Number	__ __ __ __ __	/44-48
Lot Number	__ __ __ __ __	/49-53

/ / / / /
-2-   ‾‾‾‾‾‾‾‾
                                                              I.D. #

TIME INTERVIEW BEGAN _____

Hello! [ASK TO SPEAK TO PERSON(s) NAMED ON COVER SHEET.] This is _____
(first and last name)   from the Rutgers University Center for Urban Policy
Research. We're doing a research study of people who have bought homes in New
Jersey in the last few years. We'd like to ask you a few questions about your
experiences in buying a house.

IF RESPONDENT REQUESTS MORE INFORMATION:

Your name has been selected at random from records of new home buyers. All
of your responses are absolutely confidential and your privacy will be protected
completely.

1. To begin with, how long have you lived in your current home?

                        / / / code number of months   /54-

2. Where was your previous residence?

        ENTER HERE AND──▶
        CODE BELOW   ───
                        (Town)   (County)   (State)

        2a. IF SAME TOWN AS STUDY AREA:

             Did you move within the same neighborhood or to a
             different neighborhood?

             1. SAME NEIGHBORHOOD
              2. DIFFERENT NEIGHBORHOOD, SAME TOWN
               3. DIFFERENT TOWN, SAME COUNTY
                4. DIFFERENT COUNTY   /56
                 5. OUT OF STATE
                  6. FOREIGN
                   7. OTHER _____
                    9. NA/DK

        2b. TO BE CODED LATER:

             1. CENTRAL CITY
              2. SUBURB
               3. NON-METRO   /57
                4. FOREIGN
                 9. NA/DK

-3-

. Have you ever owned a home before this one?

```
  / 1. YES  /
 /  2. NO      /          /SKIP TO Q. 4/              / 58
 / 9. DK/NA    /
```

(IF "YES" TO Q. 3, ASK:)
3a. How many other homes have you owned?

/____/____/   code number   / 59-60

. Besides being an American, what race or nationality background do you think of yourself as having: black, white, or other?

```
     1.  BLACK
     2.  WHITE
     3.  OTHER _____    / 61
     9.  NA/DK
```

IF RACIAL SAMPLE SIZE ATTAINED:
That's all the questions we have for you at this time.
Thank you very much.

OTHERWISE, GO TO QUESTION 5

CARD NUMBER: 1   / 80

-4-

/ / / / / /x
I.D. #

5. We're interested in some of the characteristics of your home.
   Is your house a single-family dwelling, a two-family house,
   a townhouse, or something else?

        1. SINGLE-FAMILY   /s
        2. TWO-FAMILY HOUSE
         3. TOWNHOUSE (rowhouse)
          4. SOMETHING ELSE (_____)
           9. NA/DK

6. How many rooms do you have in your house? (not counting bathrooms,
   entryways, or closets)

             /   /   /   /

7. How many bedrooms? (rooms used mainly for sleeping)

             /   /   /   /

8. And how many bathrooms?

        1. 1
        2. $1\frac{1}{2}$
         3. 2   /
          4. MORE THAN 2
           9. NA/DK

9. How old is your house? (years)

             /   /   /   /

10. Do you have a garage?

        1. YES
        2. NO   /
        9. NA/DK

11. Over the next five years or so, do you think the value of your house
    will increase a lot, increase some, stay about the same, or will it
    decrease?

        1. INCREASE LOT
        2. INCREASE SOME
         3. STAY THE SAME   /
          4. DECREASE
           9. NA/DK

-5-

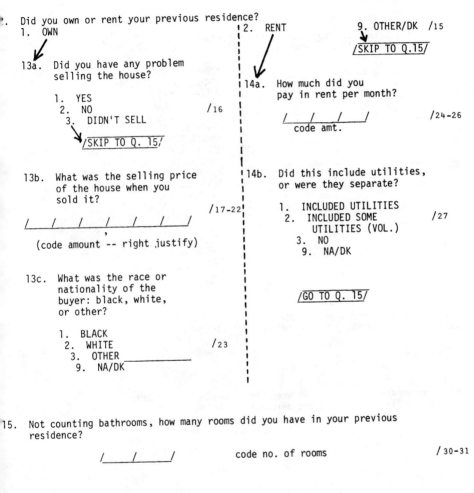

Did you own or rent your previous residence?
1. OWN   2. RENT   9. OTHER/DK /15

/SKIP TO Q.15/

13a. Did you have any problem
selling the house?

     1. YES
     2. NO   /16
       3. DIDN'T SELL

      /SKIP TO Q. 15/

14a. How much did you
pay in rent per month?

/___/___/___/___/   /24-26
    code amt.

13b. What was the selling price
of the house when you
sold it?

/___/___/___/___/___/___/ /17-22

(code amount -- right justify)

14b. Did this include utilities,
or were they separate?

    1. INCLUDED UTILITIES
    2. INCLUDED SOME   /27
       UTILITIES (VOL.)
     3. NO
     9. NA/DK

13c. What was the race or
nationality of the
buyer: black, white,
or other?

/GO TO Q. 15/

    1. BLACK
    2. WHITE   /23
     3. OTHER _____
      9. NA/DK

15. Not counting bathrooms, how many rooms did you have in your previous
residence?

         /___/___/   code no. of rooms   /30-31

16. Considering only the house itself, how does your present home
compare with your previous residence? Is it a big improvement,
some improvement, was your previous residence better, or are
they about the same?

         1. BIG IMPROVEMENT
          2. SOME IMPROVEMENT
           3. SAME   /32
            4. PREVIOUS BETTER
           9. NA/DK

-6-

17. Why did you move away from your previous residence?
    /WRITE RESPONSE--will be coded later/

    _____   01. JOB CHANGE/TRANSFER
                                   02. COMMUTING/ACCESSIBILITY
    _____   (same job)
                                   03. UNIT TOO SMALL
    _____   04. UNIT TOO BIG
                                   05. OTHER HOUSING UNIT REASON
    _____   06. WANTED TO OWN
                                   07. NEWLY MARRIED/TO START OWN   /33-34
    _____   HOUSEHOLD
                                   08. WIDOWED/SEPARATED/DIVORCED
    _____   10. DISSATISFIED WITH NEIGHBOR-
                                       HOOD
    _____   11. DISSATISFIED WITH SCHOOLS
                                   12. URBAN RENEWAL, ETC. (public
                                       displacement
                                   13. EVICTION, ETC. (private
                                       displacement)
                                   14. OTHER _____

                                   99. NA/DK

18. How many months were there between the time you began thinking of
    moving and you actually began looking for a house?

              /___/___/   code number   /35-36

19. How many months did it take between the time you first started
    looking and the signing of the purchase agreement?

              /___/___/   code number   /37-38

-7-

0. Now, I'm going to read a list of things that people sometimes do to look for a house. For each one I read, please tell me if you did this when you were looking, and if so, whether it was very helpful, somewhat helpful, or not at all helpful in looking for a house.

DID YOU:	No	YES				NA/DK	
		None	DK(Vol)	Some	Very		
A. Talk to friends	1	2	3	4	5	9	/ 39
B. Talk to relatives	1	2	3	4	5	9	/ 40
C. Talk to fellow employees	1	2	3	4	5	9	/ 41
D. Check newspaper listings	1	2	3	4	5	9	/ 42
E. Walk around	1	2	3	4	5	9	/ 43
F. Drive around	1	2	3	4	5	9	/ 44
G. Look for "For Sale" signs	1	2	3	4	5	9	/ 45
H. Go to a real estate agency	1	2	3	4	5	9	/ 46
I. Go to a community group	1	2	3	4	5	9	/ 47
J. Consult bank personnel	1	2	3	4	5	9	/ 48
K. Go to a builder or contractor	1	2	3	4	5	9	/ 49

L. Did you do anything else I haven't mentioned?

     IF YES: "What was that"?

	1	2	3	4	5	9	/ 50

(SPECIFY) _____

-8-

21. Which source was the most helpful to you in locating a house?
     /IF MORE THAN ONE GIVEN, PROBE: Which would you say was the
     most important source?/

                    01. TALKED TO FRIENDS
                    02. TALKED TO RELATIVES
                    03. TALKED TO FELLOW EMPLOYEES
                    04. CHECKED NEWSPAPER LISTINGS
                    05. WALKING AROUND THE AREA
                    06. DRIVING AROUND THE AREA
                    07. LOOKED FOR "FOR SALE" SIGNS
                    08. WENT TO REAL ESTATE AGENCY   /55-56
                    10. WENT TO COMMUNITY GROUPS
                    11. CONSULTED BANK PERSONNEL
                    12. WENT TO BUILDER OR CONTRACTOR
                    13. OTHER _____

                        99. NA/DK

IF NO REAL ESTATE AGENCY USED IN Q. 20, SKIP TO Q. 26, P. 9.
IF "YES" TO REAL ESTATE AGENCY IN Q. 20, ASK:

22. How many real estate agencies or brokers did you contact for a
     house?
                    /___/___/___/   code number   /57-58

23. Did any of the realtors you contacted refuse to help you in
     looking for a house?

              / 1. YES /
             // 2. NO _____
            /   /9. DON'T KNOW/ ———> /SKIP TO Q. 24/   /59
           V
     (IF "YES" TO Q. 23, ASK:)

     23a. Why do you think they wouldn't help you?
              (PROBE for most important reason)

                    01. RACE
                    02. SEX
                    03. AGE
                    04. FAMILY SIZE
                    05. FINANCIAL   /60-61
                    06. HOUSING NEEDS
                    07. AREA COVERAGE
                    08. OTHER _____

                        99. NA/DK

- 8A -

A1. Did any real estate agent refuse to show you a house in a neighborhood you were interested in?

       1. YES
       2. NO   /61
        9. NA/DK

A2. Do you recall the name of the broker and the agency that you
finally used?

   IF YES: What was the name and location of the broker?

       BROKER:_____

       LOCATION:_____

   And what agency was that?

       AGENCY:_____

A3. What was the race or nationality background of the real estate
agent: black, white, or something else?

       1. BLACK
       2. WHITE   /62
        3. OTHER_____
        9. NA/DK

Go to Q. 24, p. 9.

                             Card Number: 6   /80

-9-

24. What was the main reason why you selected the agency or broker
    that you did? /IF NOT CLEAR: "The final broker that you used."/

                01. PROFESSIONAL REPUTATION
                02. PERSONAL RECOMMENDATION
                03. RACIAL IDENTITY
                04. "FOR SALE" SIGN
                 05. NEWSPAPER LISTING   /62-63
                  06. ADVERTISING BY REALTOR
                  07. PHONE BOOK LISTING
                  08. OTHER
                        _____

                   99. NA/DK

25. Were you satisfied or dissatisfied with the service provided by
    the broker? PROBE: Would you say very or only somewhat
    satisfied/dissatisfied?

                 1. VERY SATISFIED
                 2. SOMEWHAT SATISFIED
                  3. SOMEWHAT DISSATISFIED
                   4. VERY DISSATISFIED
                    9. DON'T KNOW   /64

26. When you started looking for a new home, which was the more
    important factor--the house itself or the neighborhood the
    house was in? IF RESPONDENT SAYS "BOTH," PROBE: If you had
    to choose, which one would you say was more important?

                 1. HOUSE
                  2. NEIGHBORHOOD AND HOUSE (VOL. ONLY)   /65
                   3. NEIGHBORHOOD
                    9. NA/DK

-10-

27. In looking for a home, did you feel you were discriminated against in any way?

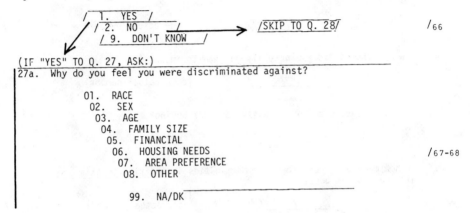

/ 1. YES /
/ 2. NO / ⟶ /SKIP TO Q. 28/   /66
/ 9. DON'T KNOW /

(IF "YES" TO Q. 27, ASK:)
27a. Why do you feel you were discriminated against?

01. RACE
02. SEX
03. AGE
04. FAMILY SIZE
05. FINANCIAL
06. HOUSING NEEDS   /67-68
07. AREA PREFERENCE
08. OTHER _____

99. NA/DK

28. What was the race or nationality background of the family from whom you bought your house: black, white, or other?

1. BLACK
2. WHITE
3. OTHER _____   /69
4. NOT PRIVATE PARTY
9. NA/DK

-11-

/ / / / / / 1-4
I.D. #

29. How many homes did you look at when you were looking
    for a new house?

            /____/____/   (code actual number)   / 5-6

30. How many homes did you actually go into to inspect?

            /____/____/   (code actual number)   / 7-8

31. How many homes did you seriously consider buying?

            /____/____/   (code actual number)   / 9-10

32. In how many different towns or communities in addition to this one
    did you look at houses?

            /____/____/   (code actual number)   / 11-12

32a. IF ONE OTHER: Which was that?

      IF SEVERAL: Which other communities?   / 13-53

        _____

        _____

        _____

        _____

        _____

        _____

        _____

        _____

-12-

33. What was the most important reason why you chose the community
you did? (PROBE for most important) WRITE RESPONSE--WILL
BE CODED LATER:

_____

_____

_____

_____

_____

01.	HOUSING PRICES
02.	HOUSING CHARACTERISTICS
03.	ATTRACTIVENESS/ATMOSPHERE
04.	FRIENDS/RELATIVES NEARBY
05.	SOCIABILITY OF NEIGHBORS
06.	RACIAL CHARACTERISTICS
07.	RELIGIOUS REASONS
08.	DISTANCE TO WORK/LOCATION
10.	SCHOOLS
11.	QUALITY OF SERVICES
12.	TAX RATE
13.	PUBLIC TRANSPORTATION
14.	INVESTMENT REASONS
15.	FAMILIARITY WITH AREA
16.	PLACE TO RAISE CHILDREN
17.	SENSE OF COMMUNITY
18.	OTHER _____
99.	NA/DK

/ 54-55

34. Did you know anything about this community before you started to
look for a house? IF YES, PROBE: How well did you know
the community--very well, somewhat, or only a little?

/ 1. YES, VERY WELL/
   2. YES, SOME   /
   3. YES, LITTLE /
/ 4. NO   / ➝ /SKIP TO Q. 35, P. 13 /
/ 9. DON'T KNOW   /

/ 56

(IF "YES" TO Q. 34, ASK:)

34a. How did you find out about it?

01. LIVED THERE
02. WORKED THERE
03. WALKING AROUND
04. DRIVING AROUND
05. FRIENDS
06. RELATIVES
07. FELLOW EMPLOYEES
08. NEWSPAPER
10. OTHER MEDIA
11. REAL ESTATE AGENCY
12. COMMUNITY GROUP
13. CHURCH GROUP
14. BANK
15. BUILDER OR CONTRACTOR
16. OTHER _____
99. NA/DK

/ 57-58

-13-

35. Did you finance your purchase with a mortgage?

/ 1. YES /──────────────────────→
/ 2. NO   /   /SKIP TO Q. 36/   / 59
  / 9. NA/DK   /

IF "NO" OR NA/DK TO Q. 35, ASK:

35a. What payment arrangement did you use?

    1. PAID CASH IN FULL
    2. DEED OF TRUST
     3. LAND CONTRACT   /SKIP TO Q. 49, P.17/   / 60
      4. PURCHASE MONEY MORTGAGE
        (i.e., from owner)
      5. OTHER_____
      9. NA/DK

---

36. What kind of mortgage loan do you have: conventional, FHA,
    VA, or something else?

      1. CONVENTIONAL
      2. FHA
       3. VA   / 61
        4. OTHER_____
        9. NA/DK

37. What was the source of your downpayment: sale of a previous
    house, personal savings, relatives or friends, bank loan,
    or something else?

      1. SALE OF PREVIOUS HOUSE
      2. PERSONAL SAVINGS
       3. RELATIVES/FRIENDS   / 62
        4. BANK LOAN
        5. OTHER_____
        9. NA/DK

38. What is the length of the mortgage in years?

      /_____/_____/   (code # of years)   / 63-64

-14-

39. What is the interest rate?

      1. LESS THAN 7%
      2. 7.0 - 7.4
      3. 7.5 - 7.9
      4. 8.0 - 8.4   / 65
      5. 8.5 - 8.9
      6. 9.0 - 9.4
      7. 9.5 - 9.9
      8. 10% or more
      9. NA/DK

40. What is the total amount of your mortgage?

/   /   / ,/   /   /   /   (code amt.--right justify)   /66-71

40a. IF REFUSED: Let me read you a list of categories, and you can just tell me the category of the amount of your mortgage.

      1. LESS THAN $5,000
      2. 5 to 9
      3. 10 to 14
      4. 15 to 19   / 72
      5. 20 to 24
      6. 25 to 29
      7. 30 to 49
      8. $50,000 or more
      9. NA/DK

CARD NUMBER: <u>3</u> / 80

-15-

/ / / / /
I.D. #

41. Did you arrange the mortgage loan or did someone else?
    (IF OTHER, PROBE: "Who was that?")

       1. SELF
       2. REALTOR
        3. ATTORNEY
         4. MORTGAGE BROKER
        5. OTHER _____

         9. NA/DK

42. How many institutions or agencies did you contact to
    arrange a mortgage loan?

      /   /   /   (code number)

          /IF ONLY ONE, SKIP TO Q. 44/

43. Do you recall the names of the places you contacted?
    IF YES: What were their names and where were they
    located?

      LIST NAME AND LOCATION OF EACH:

      1. _____

      2. _____

      3. _____

      4. _____

      5. _____

44. Which did you finally select?_____
                                   (Name)   (Location)

ASK IF NOT OBVIOUS:

     44a. What type of bank or institution is that?

           1. SAVINGS AND LOAN
           2. MUTUAL SAVINGS BANK
            3. COMMERCIAL BANK
             4. MORTGAGE COMPANY
            5. OTHER _____
             9. NA/DK

-16-

5. Why did you select this one?
(WRITE RESPONSE--Will be
coded later)

_____
_____
_____
_____
_____
_____

01. INTEREST RATE
02. DOWNPAYMENT REQUIREMENT
03. MONTHLY PAYMENT
04. TERM FOR REPAYMENT
05. PRE-PAYMENT PENALTY
06. FHA/VA GUARANTEE
07. GENERAL TERMS   /16-17
08. CONVENIENCE
10. REPUTATION OF LENDER
11. RECOMMENDATION BY
      BROKER/ATTORNEY
12. PERSONAL RECOMMENDATION
13. ONLY ONE WHICH WOULD
      GRANT LOAN
14. RACIAL REASONS
15. PREVIOUS ACCOUNT
16. OTHER (_____)
99. NA/DK

6. Was your mortgage application rejected by any banks
or lending institutions?

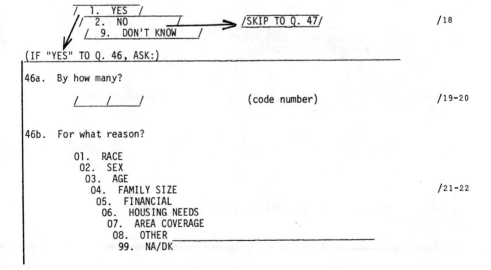

/ 1. YES /
/ 2. NO / ⟶ /SKIP TO Q. 47/   /18
/ 9. DON'T KNOW /

(IF "YES" TO Q. 46, ASK:)

46a. By how many?

/ / /   (code number)   /19-20

46b. For what reason?

01. RACE
02. SEX
03. AGE
04. FAMILY SIZE   /21-22
05. FINANCIAL
06. HOUSING NEEDS
07. AREA COVERAGE
08. OTHER _____
99. NA/DK

-17-

47. Did you feel you were discriminated against in any way in
    obtaining a mortgage?

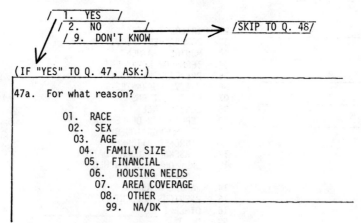

/ 1. YES /
/ 2. NO   /   ────────►   /SKIP TO Q. 48/   / 23
/ 9. DON'T KNOW /

(IF "YES" TO Q. 47, ASK:)

47a. For what reason?

            01. RACE
            02. SEX
             03. AGE
              04. FAMILY SIZE
               05. FINANCIAL   / 24 ─
                06. HOUSING NEEDS
                 07. AREA COVERAGE
                  08. OTHER _____
                   99. NA/DK

48. Overall would you say you were satisfied or dissatisfied with
    the service provided by the lending institution in arranging
    your loan? PROBE: Would you say very or somewhat
    (satisfied/dissatisfied)?

            1. VERY SATISFIED
             2. SOMEWHAT SATISFIED
              3. SOMEWHAT DISSATISFIED   /26
               4. VERY DISSATISFIED
                9. DON'T KNOW

49. All in all, how would you rate this community as a place to live--
    excellent, pretty good, fair, or poor?

            4. EXCELLENT
             3. GOOD
              2. FAIR   / 27
               1. POOR
                9. NA/DK

50. And how about your housing unit--excellent, pretty good, fair,
    or poor?

            4. EXCELLENT
             3. GOOD
              2. FAIR   / 28
               1. POOR
                9. NA/DK

-18-

1. Now, I'm going to read off a list of characteristics of some communities, such as the school system or the crime rate. For each one, I'd like you to tell me how important it was to you in looking for a place to live--very important, somewhat important, or not important at all. (DESIGNATED POINT)

et's start with:	Very Import.	Some-what Import.	Can't Say	Not Import.	NA/ DK	
. Facilities for the elderly	4	3	2	1	9	/29
. Teenage recreation facilities	4	3	2	1	9	/30
. Police protection	4	3	2	1	9	/31
. Quality of public education	4	3	2	1	9	/32
. Neighborhood shopping	4	3	2	1	9	/33
. Heavy street traffic	4	3	2	1	9	/34
. Racial composition	4	3	2	1	9	/35
. Day care facilities	4	3	2	1	9	/36

2. Now, a few questions on housing costs. On the average, how much do you pay per month for utilities--electric, gas, water--not including heating costs?

/___/___/___/___/
(code amt--right justify)   /37-40

3. And what are your average heating costs per month?

/___/___/___/___/
(code amt--right justify)   /41-44

4. How about general upkeep and maintenance per year, on average?

/___/___/___/___/
(code amt--right justify)   /45-48

55. How much do you pay in homeowners insurance a year?

/_____/_____/_____/_____/
(code amt--right justify)

56. Property taxes a year?

/_____/_____/_____/_____/
(code amt--right justify)

57. What are your monthly mortgage payments, not including taxes?

/_____/_____/_____/_____/
(code amt--right justify)

	1.	INCLUDES TAXES
57a. CODE BUT DO NOT ASK	2.	NOT INCLUDING TAXES
	9.	NA/DK

58. Now let me read you a few more characteristics of some communities
     and have you tell me if these were very, somewhat, or not at all
     important in looking for a place to live? (DESIGNATED POINT)

		Very Import.	Some-what Import.	Can't Say	Not Import.	NA/ DK
a.	Street crime	4	3	2	1	9
b.	Rundown houses	4	3	2	1	9
c.	Welfare families in the area	4	3	2	1	9
d.	Tax rate	4	3	2	1	9
e.	Burglary of homes or apts.	4	3	2	1	9
f.	Noise	4	3	2	1	9
g.	Public transportation	4	3	2	1	9
h.	Discipline in the schools	4	3	2	1	9

CARD NUMBER: 4 /

-20-

/ / / / /   /1-4
        I.D. #

59. Now I'm going to read a list of aspects of some communities.
     For each one, I'd like to know how you evaluate these in your
     community--excellent, good, fair, or poor? (DESIGNATED POINT)

Let's start with:	Excel-lent	Good	Fair	Poor	Not Found Here	NA/DK	
a. Facilities for the elderly	4	3	2	1	8	9	/5
b. Teenage recreation facilities	4	3	2	1	8	9	/6
c. Police protection	4	3	2	1	8	9	/7
d. Quality of public education	4	3	2	1	8	9	/8
e. Neighborhood shopping	4	3	2	1	8	9	/9
f. Day care facilities	4	3	2	1	8	9	/10
g. Racial composition	4	3	2	1	8	9	/11
h. Public transportation	4	3	2	1	8	9	/12

60. Finally, here is a list of conditions that some people say exist
     in their communities. For your community, tell me if this is
     a very serious problem, fairly serious, not too serious, or no
     problem at all. (DESIGNATED POINT)

Let's start with:	Very Serious	Fairly Serious	Not too Serious	No Problem	NA/DK	
a. Heavy street traffic	4	3	2	1	9	/13
b. Street crime	4	3	2	1	9	/14
c. Welfare families in the area	4	3	2	1	9	/15
d. Rundown houses	4	3	2	1	9	/16
e. Tax rate	4	3	2	1	9	/17
f. Burglary of homes or apts.	4	3	2	1	9	/18
g. Noise	4	3	2	1	9	/19
h. Discipline in the schools	4	3	2	1	9	/20

-21-

61. How do you think most of your neighbors rate your community as a place to live: excellent, good, fair, or poor?

    4. EXCELLENT
    3. GOOD
    2. FAIR
    1. POOR   / 21
    9. NA/DK

62. How about your friends? (Repeat options as necessary)

    4. EXCELLENT
    3. GOOD
    2. FAIR
    1. POOR   / 22
    9. NA/DK

63. And how about your relatives? (Repeat options as necessary)

    4. EXCELLENT
    3. GOOD
    2. FAIR
    1. POOR   / 23
    9. NA/DK

64. Would you describe this community as mainly white, mainly black or a mix of black and white?

    1. MAINLY WHITE
    2. INTEGRATED
    3. MAINLY BLACK
    4. OTHER_____   / 24
    9. NA/DK

65. What percent of the overall community would you say is black?

    /___/___/___/   (999=Don't know)   / 25

66. How would you describe your immediate neighborhood--the block on either side of your house: mainly white, mainly black, or a mixture?

    1. MAINLY WHITE
    2. INTEGRATED
    3. MAINLY BLACK   / 28
    4. OTHER (_____)
    9. NA/DK

-22-

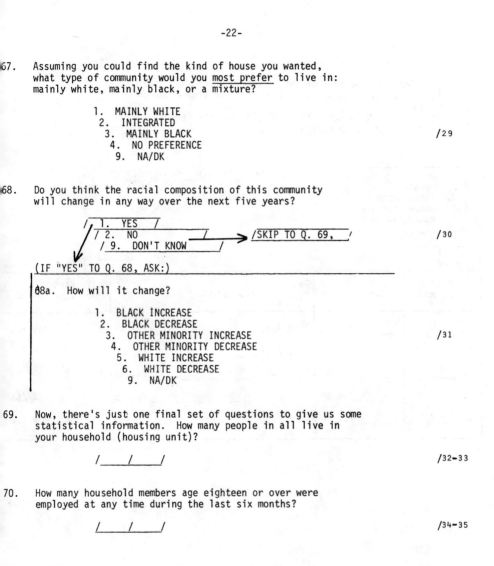

67. Assuming you could find the kind of house you wanted,
what type of community would you <u>most prefer</u> to live in:
mainly white, mainly black, or a mixture?

      1. MAINLY WHITE
      2. INTEGRATED
       3. MAINLY BLACK   /29
        4. NO PREFERENCE
         9. NA/DK

68. Do you think the racial composition of this community
will change in any way over the next five years?

    / 1. YES /
    / 2. NO   /   → /SKIP TO Q. 69, /   /30
    / 9. DON'T KNOW   /

(IF "YES" TO Q. 68, ASK:)

68a. How will it change?

      1. BLACK INCREASE
      2. BLACK DECREASE
       3. OTHER MINORITY INCREASE   /31
        4. OTHER MINORITY DECREASE
         5. WHITE INCREASE
         6. WHITE DECREASE
         9. NA/DK

69. Now, there's just one final set of questions to give us some
statistical information. How many people in all live in
your household (housing unit)?

      /   /   /   /32-33

70. How many household members age eighteen or over were
employed at any time during the last six months?

      /   /   /   /34-35

-23-

71.   Starting with the head of the household, could you give me
      the age and main job or occupation for everyone eighteen
      or over?
      (CODE RELATION TO HEAD, AGE, AND SEX FOR EACH PERSON.
      PROBE FOR FULL INFORMATION)

```
 1.  Head
 2.  Spouse
 3.  Son/daughter
 4.  Other relative
 5.  Non-relative
```
ENTER CODE: _____

71a. FOR EACH EMPLOYED PERSON:
      Is that usually full-time or
      part-time?

Relation to Head	Age	Sex M F	Occupation	Full time	Part time	NA/DK
1. ___ /36	___ ___ /37-38	1 2 /39	_____ /40-41	1	2	9 /42
2. ___ /43	___ ___ /44-45	1 2 /46	_____ /47-48	1	2	9 /49
3. ___ /50	___ ___ /51-52	1 2 /53	_____ /54-55	1	2	9 /56
4. ___ /57	___ ___ /58-59	1 2 /60	_____ /61-62	1	2	9 /63
5. ___ /64	___ ___ /65-66	1 2 /67	_____ /68-69	1	2	9 /70

CARD NUMBER: 5 /80

-24-

/ / / / /   / 1-4
I.D. #

72. For each person under eighteen, could you give me their age, if they're in school, and what grade they completed last year? (CODE AGE, SEX, AND SCHOOL INFO.)

    72a. IF IN SCHOOL: Is that a public private, or parochial school?

	Age	Sex M F	In School Yes No NA/DK	Grade	Type of School Pub. Priv. Par. NA/DK
1.	__ __ / 5-6	1 2 /7	1 2 9 / 8	__ __ /9-10	1 2 3 9 /11
2.	__ __ /12-13	1 2 /14	1 2 9 /15	__ __ /16-17	1 2 3 9 /18
3.	__ __ /19-20	1 2 /21	1 2 9 /22	__ __ /23-24	1 2 3 9 /25
4.	__ __ /26-27	1 2 /28	1 2 9 /29	__ __ /30-31	1 2 3 9 /32
5.	__ __ /33-34	1 2 /35	1 2 9 /36	__ __ /37-38	1 2 3 9 /39
6.	__ __ /40-41	1 2 /42	1 2 9 /43	__ __ /44-45	1 2 3 9 /46

ASK Q. 73 TO 76 FOR HEAD OF HOUSEHOLD:

---

73. How long does it take (you/the head of the household) to get to work?

        01. NO FIXED PLACE OF WORK
        02. WORKS AT HOME
        03. LESS THAN 5 MINUTES   /47-48
        04. 5-9 MINUTES
        05. 10-14 MINUTES
        06. 15-19 MINUTES
        07. 20-29 MINUTES
        08. 30-44 MINUTES
        10. 45-59 MINUTES
        11. AN HOUR OR MORE
        99. NA/DK

-25-

74. How long did it take (you/the head of the household) to get to
    work at your previous residence?

                    01. NO FIXED PLACE OF WORK
                    02. WORKS AT HOME
                    03. LESS THAN 5 MINUTES
                    04. 5-9 MINUTES
                    05. 10-14 MINUTES   /49-50
                    06. 15-19 MINUTES
                    07. 20-29 MINUTES
                    08. 30-44 MINUTES
                    10. 45-59 MINUTES
                    11. AN HOUR OR MORE
                    99. NA/DK

75. How (do you, does he/she) travel to work?

                    1. PRIVATE CAR ALONE
                    2. CARPOOL
                    3. TRAIN
                    4. BUS
                    5. WALK   /51
                    6. BICYCLE
                    7. OTHER
                    9. NA/DK

76. What was the highest grade of school (you/the head of
    household) completed?

                    1. EIGHT OR LESS
                    2. SOME HIGH SCHOOL
                    3. HIGH SCHOOL GRAD
                    4. SOME COLLEGE
                    5. COLLEGE GRAD   /52
                    6. VOCATIONAL TRAINING
                    7. PROFESSIONAL/GRADUATE SCHOOL
                    8. OTHER_____
                    9. NA/DK

-26-

. Finally, for statistical purposes, what was your total family
  income from all sources last year?
  (all sources means wages, salary, interest, dividends,
  pensions, social security, etc.....)

                    / / / . / / /
                    (enter amount--right justify)   /53-58

77a. IF REFUSED: Let me read you a list of categories, and
      you can just tell me the category of your total
      family income last year.

              1. LESS THAN $5,000
              2. 5 to 9
              3. 10 to 14   /59
              4. 15 to 19
              5. 20 to 24
              6. 25 to 29
              7. 30 to 49
              8. $50,000 OR MORE
              9. NA/DK

ank you. That completes the interview.

're planning to do a follow-up study in a year or two and we'd
ke to contact you again then. In case we have trouble getting in
uch with you, can you give us the name and address of someone
o would always know how to reach you?

    Name_____

    Address_____

    Telephone:_____

ank you very much.

you have any comments or questions about the interview or
y of the questions?

-27

THANK RESPONDENT AND HANG UP

78. Respondent's sex

            1. MALE
            2. FEMALE   /60

TIME INTERVIEW ENDED_____   LENGTH OF INTERVIEW

                                              /____/____/

INTERVIEWER'S NUMBER
                        /____/____/____/

      BOOTH NUMBER   /____/____/

                                                      CARD NUMBER: 6   /80

Appendix B.

RUTGERS UNIVERSITY
CENTER FOR URBAN POLICY RESEARCH

SUBURBAN REAL ESTATE SURVEY

FIELD PROTOCOL
August-September 1979

A. *LOCAL HOUSING MARKET CONDITIONS*

(1) Supply/demand: buyer's vs. seller's market

(2) Sub-market areas within town
    - by housing value (price/quality)
    - by racial composition

(3) Demand levels by sub-area

(4) Turnover rates by sub-area

(5) Price inflation/resale value by sub-area

(6) Municipal services/amenities/schools by sub-area

(7) Neighborhood attitudes, problems, satisfaction
    by sub-area

B. *HOME PURCHASE CRITERIA*

(1) Who can buy a house in _____?
    Description of average buyer

(2) Minimum income requirements; equity; previous
    ownership; assets

(3) Treatment of second income; part-time income; overtime

(4) Downpayment/credit requirements

(5) Maximum value-to-income ratio

(6) Maximum housing cost-to-income ratio

C. OBTAINING BUYERS

(1) Origin of buyers/previous residence: where do
    they come from?

(2) Other characteristics:
    - first-time vs. previous owners
    - female-headed families
      - minority families

(3) How obtain/attract buyers?
    - advertising
    - repeat customers
    - word-of-mouth referrals
    - other brokers

(4) How/why do buyers select this agency?

(5) The ideal buyer: what do you look for?

(6) Selecting/screening buyers
    - finding out the buyers requirements
    - obtaining financial info
    - compatability/subjective elements

(7) Protecting the seller vs. serving the buyer

D. SHOWING HOMES

(1) Matching buyers with listings: how do you decide on
    what to show/recommend?

(2) Use of the listing book: buyer access to listings:
    - go through listing book together?
    - let buyer look through listings?
    - recommend specific units?

(3) Showing specific houses - how many?

(4) Services provided to buyers:
    - moving vans/arrangements with moving company
    - home inspection service
    - terminte inspection
    - tax specialists/accountants

E. FINANCING

(1) Do you help buyers arrange a mortgage?
    - What proportion of buyers?
    - Characteristics: Which ones?

   (2) Important to maintain good ties with a particular
       financial institution?

   (3) Deal mostly with same bank or with different banks
       for different customers?

   (4) Does the bank expect that you will screen customers
       before you send them over.

F. *OBTAINING LISTINGS*

   (1) Belong to Multiple Listing Service(s)?
       - which one(s)?
       - voluntary or mandatory?

   (2) Use of exclusive listings:
       - time period of exclusive
       - all units or some?

   (3) What proportion of listings given to MLS?

   (4) How do you get listings?
       - repeat sales
       - referrals (from what sources?)
       - canvassing/direct solicitation (mail, door-
          to-door, telephone)
       - advertising, phone book listing, For Sale signs

   (5) Importance of community reputation; good-will;
       catering to community preferences

   (6) Importance of working an area to get the listings -
       control over particular area, part of the community

G. *RELATIONSHIPS WITH OTHER BROKERS*

   (1) Compete for listings?

   (2) General characterization: competition or cooperation?
       How are these manifested?

   (3) Belong to local board(s)?
       - cooperation among members?
       - if not, why not?
       - good for business?

   (4) Commission rate/discounting?

BIBLIOGRAPHY

Abrams, Charles. *Forbidden Neighbors—A Study of Prejudice in Housing.* New York: Harper, 1955.

Aleinikoff, T. Alexander. "Racial Steering: The Real Estate Broker and Title VIII." *Yale Law Journal* 85 (May 1976): 808-25.

Alexis, Marcus. "The Economic Status of Blacks and Whites." *American Economic Review* 68 (May 1978): 179-85.

Alonso, William. "A Theory of the Urban Land Market." *Papers and Proceedings of the Regional Science Association* 6 (1960): 149-57.

Bailey, Martin J. "Effects of Race and Other Demographic Factors on the Value of Single-Family Homes." *Land Economics* 42 (May 1966): 215-20.

———. "A Note on the Economics of Residential Zoning and Urban Renewal." *Land Economics* 35 (August 1959): 288-92.

Barnett, C. Lance. *Using Hedonic Indexes to Measure Housing Quantity.* Santa Monica, Calif.: Rand Corporation, 1979.

Barresi, Charles M. "The Role of the Real Estate Agent in Residential Location." *Sociological Focus* 1 (Summer 1968): 59-71.

Becker, Gary. *The Economics of Discrimination.* Chicago: University of Chicago Press, 1957.

Berry, Brian J. L. "Ghetto Expansion and Single-Family Housing Prices: Chicago, 1968-1972," *Journal of Urban Economics* 3 (October 1976): 397-423.

———. *The Open Housing Question: Race and Housing in Chicago, 1966-1976.* Cambridge, Mass.: Ballinger, 1979.

Berry, Brian J. L., and Dahmann, Donald C. *Population Distribution in the United States in the 1970s.* Washington, D.C.: National Academy of Sciences, 1977.

Berry, Brian J. L., Goodwin, Carole A.; Lake, Robert W.; and Smith, Katherine B.; "Attitudes Toward Integration: The Role of Status in Community Response to Racial Change." In *The Changing Face of the Suburbs,* edited by Barry Schwartz, pp. 221-64. Chicago: University of Chicago Press, 1976.

Blumberg, Leonard, and Lalli, Michael. "Little Ghettoes: A Study of Negroes in the Suburbs." *Phylon* 27 (September 1966): 117-31.

Boichel, Margery R.; Aurbach, Herbert A.; Bakerman, Theodore; and Elliott, David H. "Exposure, Experience and Attitudes: Realtors and Open Occupancy." *Phylon* 30 (Winter 1969): 325-37.

Bradburn, Norman M.; Sudman, Seymour; and Gockel, Galen L. *Racial Integration in American Neighborhoods: A Comparative Study.* Chicago: National Opinion Research Center, 1970.

Brown, Lawrence A., and Moore, Eric G. The Intra-Urban Migration Process: A Perspective." In *Internal Structure of the City,* edited by Larry S. Bourne, pp. 200-209, New York: Oxford University Press, 1971.

Brown, William H. "Access to Housing: The Role of the Real Estate Industry." *Economic Geography* 48 (January 1972): 66-78.

Calef, Wesley, and Nelson, Howard J. "Distribution of the Negro Population in the United States." *Geographical Review* 46 (January 1956): 82-97.

Campbell, Angus. *White Attitudes Toward Black People,* Ann Arbor, Mich.: Institute for Social Research, The University of Michigan, 1971.

Casey, Stephen C. "The Effect of Race on Opinions of Housing and Neighborhood Quality." In *America's Housing: Prospects and Problems,* edited by George Sternlieb and James W. Hughes, pp. 485-542. New Brunswick, N.J.: Center for Urban Policy Research, 1980.

Chicago Commission on Race Relations. *The Negro in Chicago: A Study of Race Relations and a Race Riot in 1919.* 1922. Reprint. New York: Arno Press and the New York Times, 1968.

Clark, Thomas A. *Blacks in Suburbs: A National Perspective.* New Brunswick, N.J.: Center for Urban Policy Research, 1979.

———. "Race, Class, and Suburbanization: Prior Trends and Policy Perspectives." Unpublished paper. New Brunswick, N.J.: Rutgers University, Department of Urban Planning and Policy Development.

Clark, W.A.V., and Smith, T. R. "Modelling Information Use in a Spatial Context." *Annals of the Association of American Geographers* 69 (December 1979): 575-88.

Clay, Phillip L. "The Process of Black Suburbanization." *Urban Affairs Quarterly* 14 (June 1979): 405-24.

Comptroller General of the United States. *Stronger Federal Enforcements Needed to Uphold Fair Housing Laws.* Washington, D.C.: General Accounting Office, 1978.

Connolly, Harold X. "Black Movement into the Suburbs: Suburbs Doubling Their Black Population During The Sixties." *Urban Affairs Quarterly* 9 (September 1973): 91-111.

Cottingham, Phoebe H. "Black Income and Metropolitan Residential Dispersion." *Urban Affairs Quarterly* 10 (March 1975): 273-96.

Damerell, Reginald G. *Triumph in a White Suburb.* New York: William Morrow, 1968.

Danielson, Michael N. *The Politics of Exclusion.* New York: Columbia University Press, 1976.

Delaney, Paul. "Black Middle Class Joining the Exodus to White Suburbia." *New York Times,* January 4, 1976.

Denton, John H. *Apartheid American Style.* Berkeley, Calif.: Diablo Press, 1967.

Downs, Anthony. *Opening up the Suburbs: An Urban Strategy for America.* New Haven, Conn.: Yale University Press, 1973.

Erickson, Rodney A., and Miller, Theodore K. "Race and Resources in Large American Cities: An Examination of Intraurban and Interregional Variations." *Urban Affairs Quarterly* 13 (July 1978): 401-20.

Fainstein, Norman, and Fainstein, Susan, *Urban Political Movements: The Search for Power by Minority Groups in American Cities.* Englewood Cliffs, N.J.: Prentice-Hall, 1974.

Falk, David, and Franklin, Herbert M. *Equal Housing Opportunity: The Unfinished Federal Agenda.* Washington, D.C.: The Potomac Institute, 1976.

Farley, Reynolds. "The Changing Distribution of Negroes Within Metropolitan Areas: The Emergence of Black Suburbs." *American Journal of Sociology* 75 (January 1970): 512-29.

――. "Components of Suburban Population Growth." In *The Changing Face of the Suburbs,* edited by Barry Schwartz, pp. 3-38. Chicago: University of Chicago Press, 1976.

――. "Trends in Racial Inequalities: Have the Gains of the 1960s Disappeared in the 1970s?" *American Sociological Review* 42 (April 1977): 189-208.

Farley, Reynolds, and Hermalin, Albert I. "The 1960s: A Decade of Progress for Blacks?" *Demography* 9 (August 1972): 353-70.

Farley, Reynolds; Schuman, Howard; Bianchi, Suzanne; Colasanto, Diane; and Hatchett, Shirley. " 'Chocolate City, Vanilla Suburbs': Will the Trend Toward Racially Separate Communities Continue?" *Social Science Research* 7 (December 1978): 319-44.

Foley, Donald L. "Institutional and Contextual Factors Affecting the Housing Choices of Minority Residents." In *Segregation in Residential Areas,* edited by Amos H. Hawley and Vincent P. Rock, pp. 85-147. Washington, D.C.: National Academy of Sciences, 1973.

Follain, James R., Jr., and Malpezzi, Stephen. *Dissecting Housing Value and Rent: Estimates of Hedonic Indexes for Thirty-Nine Large SMSAs.* Washington, D.C.: The Urban Institute, 1980.

Freeman, Richard. "Black Economic Progress Since 1964." *The Public Interest* 52 (Summer 1978): 52-69.

Frey, William H. "Black Movement to the Suburbs: Potentials and Prospects for Metropolitan-Wide Integration." In *The Demography of Racial and Ethnic Groups,* edited by Frank D. Bean and W. Parker Frisbie, pp. 79-118. New York: Academic Press, 1978.

Frieden, Bernard J. "Blacks in Suburbia: The Myth of Better Opportunities." In *Minority Perspectives,* pp. 31-50. Washington, D.C.: Resources for the Future, Inc., 1972.

Friesema, H. Paul. "Black Control of Central Cities: The Hollow Prize." *Journal of the American Institute of Planners* 35 (March 1969): 75-79.

Galster, George C. *Preferences for Neighborhood Racial Composition.* Unpublished report prepared for the U.S. Department of Housing and Urban Development, 1978, Washington, D.C. Distributed by National Technical Information Service.

Gappert, Gary, and Rose, Harold M. *The Social Economy of Cities.* Beverly Hills, Calif.: Sage Publications, 1975.

Glazer, Nathan. "On 'Opening Up' the Suburbs." *The Public Interest* 37 (Fall 1974): 89-111.

Grant, R. B. *The Black Man Comes to the City.* Chicago: Nelson-Hall, 1972.

Grayson, George W., and Wedel, Cindy L. "Open Housing: How to Get Around the Law." *The New Republic*, June 22, 1968, pp. 15-16.

Grier, Eunice, and Grier, George. *Black Suburbanization at the Mid-1970s.* Washington, D.C.: The Washington Center for Metropolitan Studies, 1978.

Grodzins, Morton. *The Metropolitan Area as a Racial Problem.* Pittsburgh, Penn.: University of Pittsburgh Press, 1958.

Guest, Avery M. "The Changing Racial Composition of Suburbs, 1950-1970." *Urban Affairs Quarterly*, 14 (December 1978): 195-206.

Harrison, Bennett. *Urban Economic Development: Suburbanization, Minority Opportunity, and the Condition of the Central City.* Washington, D.C.: The Urban Institute, 1974.

Hart, John Fraser. "The Changing Distribution of the American Negro." *Annals of the Association of American Geographers* 50 (September 1960): 242-66.

Helper, Rose. *Racial Policies and Practices of Real Estate Brokers.* Minneapolis, Minn.: University of Minnesota Press, 1969.

Hempel, Donald J. *The Role of the Real Estate Broker in the Home Buying Process.* Storrs, Conn.: Center for Real Estate and Urban Economic Studies, University of Connecticut, 1969.

———.*Search Behavior and Information Utilization in the Home Buying Process.* Storrs, Conn.: Center for Real Estate and Urban Economic Studies, University of Connecticut, 1969.

Henri, F. *Black Migration: Movement North 1900-1920.* Garden City, N.Y.: Doubleday, 1975.

Hermalin, Albert I., and Farley, Reynolds. "The Potential for Residential Integration in Cities and Suburbs: Implications for the Busing Controversy." *American Sociological Review* 38 (October 1973): 595-610.

House, J. Douglas. *Contemporary Entrepreneurs: The Sociology of Residential Real Estate Agents.* Westport, Conn.: Greenwood Press, 1977.

———. "Middlemen in Housing Exchanges: The Social Role of the Real Estate Agent." *Western Canadian Journal of Anthropology* 4 (1975): 37-52.

Kain, John F. "Theories of Residential Location and Realities of Race." In *Essays in Urban Spatial Structure*, pp. 133-59. Cambridge, Mass.: Ballinger, 1975.

Kain, John F., and Quigley, John M. *Housing Markets and Racial Discrimination.* New York: National Bureau of Economic Research, 1975.

———. "Measuring the Value of Housing Quality." *Journal of the American Statistical Association* 5 (June 1970): 532-48.

Kaplan, Samuel. " 'Them' Blacks in Suburbia." *New York Affairs* 3 (Winter 1976): 20-41.

King, A. Thomas, and Mieszkowski, Peter. "Racial Discrimination, Segregation, and the Price of Housing." *Journal of Political Economy* 81 (May/June 1973): 590-606.

Laurenti, Luigi. *Property Values and Race.* Berkeley, Calif.: University of California Press, 1960.

Lieberson, Stanley. *Ethnic Patterns in American Cities.* Glencoe, Ill.: Free Press, 1963.

Lieberson, Stanley. "The Impact of Residential Segregation on Ethnic Assimilation."*Social Forces* 40 (October 1961): 52-57.

Long, Larry H., and Spain, Daphne. *Racial Succession in Individual Housing Units.* U.S. Bureau of the Census, Current Population Reports, Special Studies, Series P-23, No. 71. Washington, D.C.: U.S. Government Printing Office, 1978.

Mandelbaum, Joel. "Race Discrimination in Home Buying Resists Tough Laws." *New York Times,* December 3, 1972.

Marshall, Harvey H., and Stahura, John M. "Black and White Population Growth in American Suburbs: Transition or Parallel Development?" *Social Forces* 58 (September 1979): 305-27.

————. "Determinants of Black Suburbanization: Regional and Suburban Size Category Patterns." *The Sociological Quarterly* 20 (Spring 1979): 237-53.

Masters, Stanley H. *Black-White Income Differentials.* New York: Academic Press, 1975.

Maxwell, Neil. "Black Flight: Much Like Whites, Many Blacks Move Out to the Suburbs." *Wall Street Journal,* August 20, 1979.

McCarthy, Kevin F. *Housing Search and Consumption Adjustment.* Santa Monica, Calif.: Rand Corporation, 1980.

————. *Housing Search and Mobility.* Santa Monica, Calif.: Rand Corporation, 1979.

Michelson, William. *Environmental Choice, Human Behavior, and Residential Satisfaction.* New York: Oxford University Press, 1977.

————. *Man and His Urban Environment.* Rev. ed. Reading, Mass.: Addison-Wesley, 1976.

Mieszkowski, Peter. *Studies of Prejudice and Discrimination in Urban Housing Markets.* Boston: Federal Reserve Bank of Boston, 1979.

Mitchell, Robert E., and Smith, Richard A. "Race and Housing: A Review and Comments on the Context and Effects of Federal Policy." *Annals of the American Academy of Political and Social Science* 441 (January 1979): 168-85.

Moore, Eric G. *Residential Mobility in the City.* Commission on College Geography Resource Paper No. 13. Washington, D.C.: Association of American Geographers, 1972.

Muth, Richard F. *Cities and Housing.* Chicago: University of Chicago Press, 1969.

National Academy of Sciences. *Freedom of Choice in Housing: Opportunities and Constraints.* Washington, D.C.: National Academy of Sciences, 1972.

National Association of Realtors. *Affirmative Marketing Handbook.* Chicago: National Association of Realtors, 1975.

————. *Realtors Guide to Practice Equal Opportunity in Housing.* Chicago: National Association of Realtors, 1976.

National Committee Against Discrimination in Housing. *Guide to Fair Housing Law Enforcement.* Washington, D.C.: U.S. Department of Housing and

Urban Development, 1979.

———.*Jobs and Housing: A Study of Employment and Housing Opportunities for Racial Minorities in Suburban Areas of the New York Metropolitan Area.* Interim Report. New York: NCDH, 1970.

Nelson, Kathryn P. *Recent Suburbanization of Blacks: How Much, Who, and Where.* Washington, D.C.: Office of Policy Development and Research, U.S. Department of Housing and Urban Development, 1979.

New Jersey Department of Community Affairs. *U.S. Census Data for New Jersey Townships, 1970.* Trenton: New Jersey Department of Community Affairs, 1975.

Northwood, L. K., and Barth, Ernest A.T. *Urban Desegregation: Negro Pioneers and Their White Neighbors.* Seattle, Wash.: University of Washington Press, 1965.

Olsson, Gunnar. *Distance and Human Interaction.* Philadelphia, Penn.: Regional Science Research Institute, 1965.

Osofsky, Gilbert. *Harlem: The Making of a Ghetto, Negro New York, 1890-1930.* New York: Harper, 1963.

Ozanne, Larry; Andrews, Marcellus; and Malpezzi, Stephen. *An Assessment of Annual Housing Survey Hedonic Indexes Using Demand Experiment Data.* Washington, D.C.: The Urban Institute, 1979.

Palm, Risa. "Financial and Real Estate Institutions in the Housing Market: A Study of Recent House Price Changes in the San Francisco Bay Area." In *Geography and the Urban Environment: Progress in Research and Applications, Volume II,* edited by D. T. Herbert and R. J. Johnston, pp. 83-123. New York: John Wiley and Sons, 1979.

———. "Real Estate Agents and Geographical Information." *Geographical Review* 66 (July 1976): 266-80.

———.*Urban Social Geography from the Perspective of the Real Estate Salesman.* Berkeley, Calif.: Center for Real Estate and Urban Economics, University of California, 1976.

Parker, Frank J., and Schoenfeld, Norman P. *Modern Real Estate: Principles and Practices.* Lexington, Mass.: D. C. Heath, 1979.

Pearce, Diana M. "Black, White, and Many Shades of Gray: Real Estate Brokers and Their Racial Practices." Ph.D. dissertation, University of Michigan, 1976.

———."Gatekeepers and Homeseekers: Institutional Patterns in Racial Steering." *Social Problems* 26 (February 1979): 325-42.

Pendleton, William W. "Blacks in Suburbs." In *The Urbanization of the Suburbs,* edited by Louis H. Masotti and Jeffrey K. Hadden, pp. 171-84. Beverly Hills, Calif.: Sage Publications, 1973.

Pettigrew, Thomas F. "Attitudes on Race and Housing: A Social-Psychological View." In *Segregation in Residential Areas,* edited by Amos H. Hawley and Vincent P. Rock, pp. 21-84. Washington D.C.: National Academy of Sciences, 1973.

——."Racial Change and Social Policy." *Annals of the American Academy of Political and Social Science* 441 (January 1979): 114-31.

Piven, Frances Fox, and Cloward, Richard A. "Black Control of Cities." *The New Republic*, September 30 and October 7, 1967.

Rabinovitz, Francine F., and Siembieda, William J. *Minorities in Suburbs: The Los Angeles Experience*. Lexington, Mass.: D.C. Heath, 1977.

Raines, Howell. "Whites Grow Reluctant to Back Integration Steps." *New York Times*, December 12, 1979.

Rapkin, Chester. "Price Discrimination Against Negroes in the Rental Housing Market." In *Essays in Urban Land Economics*, pp. 333-45. Los Angeles: Real Estate Research Program, University of California, 1966.

Rapkin, Chester, and Grigsby, William. *The Demand for Housing in Racially Mixed Areas*. Los Angeles: University of California Press, 1960.

Regional Plan Association. "Segregation and Opportunity in the Region's Housing." *Regional Plan News*, No. 104 (July 1979).

Report of the National Advisory Commission on Civil Disorders. New York: Bantam, 1968.

Ridker, Ronald, and Henning, John A. "The Determinants of Residential Property Values with Special Reference to Air Pollution." *Review of Economics and Statistics* 44 (May 1967): 246-55.

Roof, Wade Clark, and Spain, Daphne. "A Research Note on City-Suburban Socio-Economic Differences Among American Blacks." *Social Forces* 56 (September 1977): 15-20.

Rose, Harold M. "The All-Black Town: Suburban Prototype or Rural Slum?" In *People and Politics in Urban Society*, edited by Harlan Hahn, pp. 397-431. Beverly Hills, Calif.: Sage Publications, 1972.

——. "The All-Negro Town: Its Evolution and Function." *Geographical Review* 55 (July 1965): 362-81.

——. *Black Suburbanization: Access to Improved Quality of Life or Maintenace of the Status Quo?* Cambridge, Mass.: Ballinger, 1976.

Saltman, Juliet. "Housing Discrimination: Policy Research, Methods and Results." *Annals of the American Academy of Political and Social Science* 441 (January 1979): 186-96.

——. *Open Housing: Dynamics of a Social Movement*. New York: Praeger, 1978.

Schafer, Robert. "Racial Discrimination in the Boston Housing Market." *Journal of Urban Economics* 6 (April 1979): 176-96.

Schechter, Alan H. "Impact of Open Housing Laws on Suburban Realtors." *Urban Affairs Quarterly* 8 (June 1973): 439-63.

Schnare, Ann B. *Externalities, Segregation and Housing Prices*. Washington, D.C.: The Urban Institute, 1974.

——. *The Persistence of Racial Segregation in Housing*. Washington, D.C.: The Urban Institute, 1978.

——. "Racial and Ethnic Price Differentials in an Urban Housing Market." *Urban Studies* 13 (June 1976): 107-20.

—— . *Residential Segregation by Race in U.S. Metropolitan Areas: An Analysis Across Cities and Over Time.* Washington, D.C.: The Urban Institute, 1977.

—— "Trends in Residential Segregation by Race." *Journal of Urban Economics* 7 (May 1980): 293-301.

Schnare, Ann B., and Struyk, Raymond J. "An Analysis of Ghetto Housing Prices Over Time." In *Residential Location and Urban Housing Markets,* edited by Gregory K. Ingram, pp. 95-133. New York: National Bureau of Economic Research, 1977.

Schnore, Leo F.; Andre, Carolyn D.; and Sharp, Harry. "Black Suburbanization, 1930-1970." *In The Changing Face of the Suburbs,* edited by Barry Schwartz, pp. 69-94. Chicago: University of Chicago Press, 1976.

Sharp, Harry, and Schnore, Leo F. "The Changing Color Composition of Metropolitan Areas." *Land Economics* 38 (May 1962): 169-85.

Simmons, James W. "Changing Residence in the City, A Review of Intra-Urban Mobility." *Geographical Review* 58 (October 1968): 622-51.

Smith, James P. "The Improving Economic Status of Black Americans." *American Economic Review* 68 (May 1978): 171-78.

Sorenson, Annemette; Taeuber, Karl E.; and Hollingsworth, Leslie J., Jr. "Indexes of Racial Residential Segregation for 109 Cities in the United States, 1940 to 1970." *Sociological Focus* 8 (April 1975): 125-42.

Spain, Daphne; Reid, John; and Long, Larry. *Housing Successions Among Blacks and Whites in Cities and Suburbs.* U.S. Bureau of the Census, Current Population Reports, Special Studies, Series P-23, No. 101. Washington, D.C.: U.S. Government Printing Office, 1980.

Spear, Allan H. *Black Chicago: The Making of a Ghetto, 1890-1920.* Chicago: University of Chicago Press, 1967.

Sternlieb, George, and Hughes, James W. "New Regional and Metropolitan Realities of America." *Journal of the American Institute of Planners* 43 (July 1977): 227-41.

Sternlieb, George, and Lake, Robert W. "Aging Suburbs and Black Homeownership." *Annals of the American Academy of Political and Social Science* 422 (November 1975): 105-17.

Taeuber, Karl E. "Racial Segregation: The Persisting Dilemma." *Annals of the American Academy of Political and Social Science* 422 (November 1975): 87-96.

Taeuber, Karl E., and Taeuber, Alma F. *Negroes in Cities: Residential Segregation and Neighborhood Change.* New York: Atheneum, 1969.

Taylor, D. Garth. "Housing, Neighborhoods, and Race Relations: Recent Survey Evidence." *Annals of the American Academy of Political and Social Science* 441 (January 1979): 26-40.

U.S. Bureau of the Census. Census of Population: 1970. *General Population Characteristics.* Final Report PC(1)-B32 New Jersey. Washington, D.C.: U.S. Government Printing Office, 1971.

——. Census of Population: 1970. *General Population Characteristics.* Final

Report PC(1)-B1 United States Summary. Washington, D.C.: U.S. Government Printing Office, 1971.

——. *Financial Characteristics of the Housing Inventory for the United States and Regions.* Current Housing Reports, Series H-150-77, Annual Housing Survey: 1977, Part C. Washington, D.C.: U.S. Government Printing Office, 1979.

——. *General Housing Characteristics for the United States and Regions: 1976.* Current Housing Reports, Series H-150-76, Annual Housing Survey: 1976, Part A. Washington, D.C.: U.S. Government Printing Office, 1978.

——. *1977 Per Capita Income Estimates for States, Counties, Incorporated Places, and Selected Minor Civil Divisions in the Northeast Region of the United States.* Current Population Reports, Population Estimates and Projections, Series P-25, No. 882. Washington, D.C.: U.S. Government Printing Office, 1980.

——. *1977 Population Estimates for Counties, Incorporated Places, and Minor Civil Divisions in New Jersey.* Current Population Reports, Population Estimates and Projections, Series P-25, No. 843. Washington, D.C.: U.S. Government Printing Office, 1979.

——. *Social and Economic Characteristics of the Metropolitan and Nonmetropolitan Population, 1977 and 1970.* Current Population Reports, Special Studies, Series P-23, No. 75. Washington, D.C.: U.S. Government Printing Office, 1978.

——. *The Social and Economic Status of the Black Population in the United States, 1790-1978.* Current Population Reports, Special Studies, Series P-23, No. 80. Washington, D.C.: U.S. Government Printing Office, 1979.

——. *Statistical Abstract of the United States: 1978.* Washington, D.C.: U.S. Government Printing Office, 1978.

U.S. Commission on Civil Rights. *Equal Opportunity in Suburbia.* Washington, D.C.: U.S. Commission on Civil Rights, 1974.

——. *The Federal Fair Housing Enforcement Effort.* Washington, D.C.: U.S. Government Printing Office, 1979.

U.S. Department of Housing and Urban Development. *The Role of the Real Estate Sector in Neighborhood Change.* Washington, D.C.: Office of Policy Development and Research, U.S. Department of Housing and Urban Development, 1979.

Walker, Richard A. "The Transformation of Urban Structure in the Nineteenth Century and the Beginnings of Suburbanization.'" In *Urbanization and Conflict in Market Societies,* edited by Keving A. Cox, pp. 165-212. Chicago: Maaroufa Press, 1978.

Webber, Melvin. "Culture, Territoriality, and the Elastic Mile." *Papers and Proceedings of the Regional Science Association* 13 (1964): 59-69.

Wienk, Ronald E.; Reid, Clifford E.; Simonson, John C.; and Eggers, Frederick J. *Measuring Racial Discrimination in American Housing Markets: The Hous-*

ing Market Practices Survey. Washington, D.C.: U.S. Department of Housing and Urban Development, 1979.

Wilson, Franklin D., and Taeuber, Karl E. "Residential and School Segregation: Some Tests of Their Association." In *The Demography of Racial and Ethnic Groups*, edited by Franklin D. Bean and W. Parker Frisbie, pp. 51-78. New York: Academic Press, 1978.

Wilson, William J. *The Declining Significance of Race: Blacks and Changing American Institutions*. Chicago: University of Chicago Press, 1978.

Wolpert, Julian. "Behavioral Aspects of the Decision to Migrate." *Papers of the Regional Science Association* 15 (1965): 159-72.

———."Migration as an Adjustment to Environmental Stress." *Journal of Social Issues*, 22 (October 1966): 92-102.

Yinger, John. *An Analysis of Discrimination by Real Estate Brokers*. Discussion Paper 252-75. Madison, Wis.: Institute for Research on Poverty, University of Wisconsin, 1975.

———."The Black-White Price Differential in Housing: Some Further Evidence." *Land Economics* 54 (May 1978): 187-206.

———."Prejudice and Discrimination in the Urban Housing Market." In *Current Issues in Urban Economics*, edited by Peter Mieszkowski and Mahlon Straszheim, pp. 430-68. Baltimore, Md.: Johns Hopkins University Press, 1979.

———."Racial Prejudice and Racial Residential Segregation in an Urban Model." *Journal of Urban Economics* 3 (October 1976): 383-96.

Index